GREAT
FIGHTING
PLANES

GREAT FIGHTING PLANES

ALAN AUSTIN
ANTHONY DICKS

WORLD WAR I TO THE PRESENT DAY

OCTOPUS BOOKS

AUTHORS' NOTE

To anyone with an interest in aircraft a time of war provides the most intriguing planes as well as the most exciting flying stories. The ingredients are all there: variety of design, technical development, competition, acts of courage and heroism, patriotism and a sense of purpose. Regrettably there is suffering too. But to those who fly, or are interested in flying, it is still possible to appreciate the beauty of the machinery and the thrill of air combat.

The progress made by the aircraft industry from the beginning of World War I to the present day has been phenomenal. It was only ten years before the 1914-18 war broke out that man first left the ground in a heavier-than-air machine. Every enthusiast has his own view of which aspect of flying is the most interesting or significant. And there is no doubt that there is an abundance of excellent literature available to satisfy the most ardent fact-finder.

However, one aspect, often missing from these treatments, is the ability to communicate the unique 'feel' of an aircraft, its particular character and behaviour. We hope that the novel content and layout of the illustrations in this book achieve just that. For this reason also we have avoided giving metric and imperial equivalents for weights and measures in the main text and captions and adopted the 'convention of the day', in order not to interrupt the flow of the story. The specification panels provide a wealth of technical data and together with the three-view profiles draw attention to the different types of each model. Where a specification and profile differ from the main type described it is noted in the heading.

Finally, our book walks you round 50 outstanding fighting planes, all of which have played — or are playing — a significant role in the defence of their countries and shows them in an appealing and dramatic way that has never been attempted before.

A Ridgmount book

First published 1985 by Octopus Books Ltd
59 Grosvenor Street, London W1

Devised by Savitri Books Ltd

© 1985 This edition Savitri Books Ltd
© 1985 Illustrations Alan Austin
© 1985 Text Anthony Dicks

ISBN 0 7064 2554 5

Produced by Mandarin Publishers Ltd
22a Westlands Road
Quarry Bay, Hong Kong

Printed in Hong Kong

CONTENTS

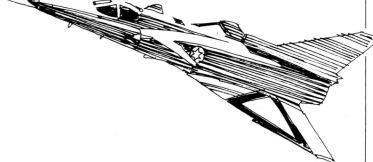

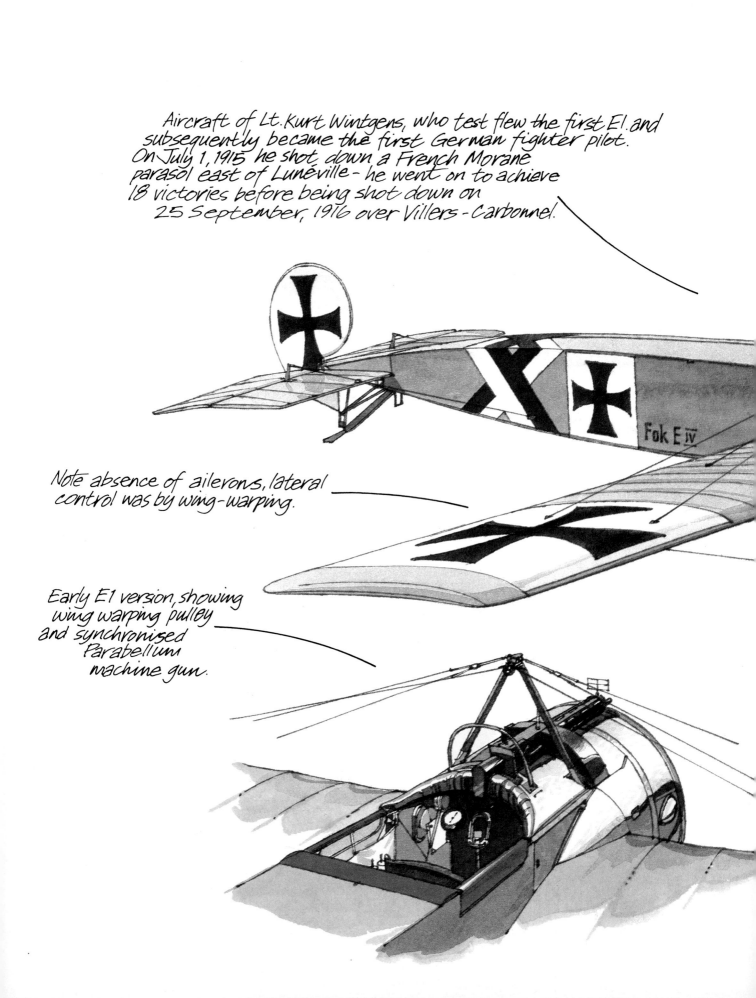

Aircraft of Lt. Kurt Wintgens, who test flew the first E.I. and subsequently became the first German fighter pilot. On July 1, 1915 he shot down a French Morane parasol east of Lunéville – he went on to achieve 18 victories before being shot down on 25 September, 1916 over Villers-Carbonnel.

Note absence of ailerons, lateral control was by wing-warping.

Early E1 version, showing wing warping pulley and synchronised Parabellum machine gun.

FOKKER EINDECKER

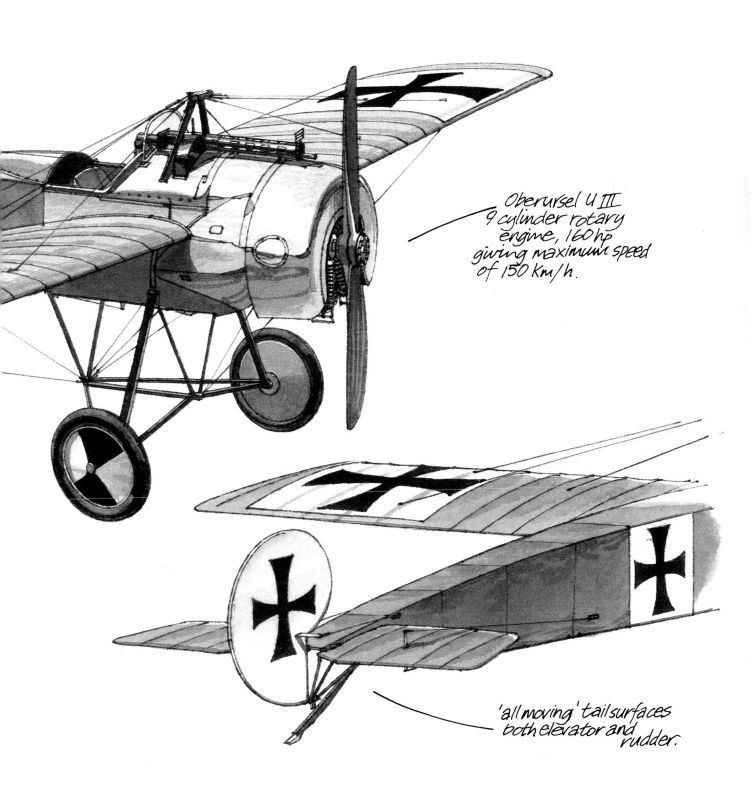

Oberursel U III
9 cylinder rotary
engine, 160 hp
giving maximum speed
of 150 Km/h.

'all moving' tail surfaces
both elevator and
rudder.

FOKKER EINDECKER

In June 1915, during World War I, a relatively innocent little German monoplane began to see service on the Western Front. However, it soon made a significant impact because it had a fighting capability that made it unique. And this gave rise to the legend known as the 'Fokker Scourge'.

There was almost nothing remarkable about the Fokker E.I – E standing for Eindecker (monoplane). It had a maximum speed of less than 145km/h. It could only climb to around 3050m. It certainly wasn't very manoeuvrable, and its single Parabellum machine gun was hardly original. But this weapon was extremely deadly, nevertheless. It was fitted with an interrupter gear which allowed it to fire forwards, without shooting the propeller to pieces. Imagine the feelings of the pilot and observer of a B.E.2c from No 13 Squadron, Royal Flying Corps, on 5 December when they saw a German aircraft flying towards them in a long, shallow dive. No problem. It was a single-seater. There was no way it could do any damage, flying straight at them.

We can only imagine their feelings when, seconds later, they plunged straight into the ground. Leutnant Gustav Leffers was part of the Fokker Scourge. The choice of the Eindecker to be the platform for the first machine gun to fire through the propeller with any degree of success was hardly coincidental. In April 1915 the French pioneer pilot Roland Garros had fitted steel deflector plates to the prop blades of his Morane-Saulnier. The idea worked: in a couple of weeks he shot down five German aircraft. Almost immediately afterwards he was forced to land himself behind enemy lines. His Morane was only slightly damaged, and the rudimentary gear certainly made the German authorities think twice. Oddly enough, they already held patents from two years earlier for a mechanical interrupter designed by Franz Schneider of the LVG aircraft factory. So Anthony Fokker was given the task of copying the Frenchman's idea, but Fokker went

one better and invented a practical machine gun synchronized to fire past the propeller blades.

In fact, the Eindecker bears a more than passing resemblance to the Morane-Saulnier. If it weren't for the distinctive Fokker rudder and the German crosses, you would hardly be able to tell them apart. In any case it was the obvious choice to carry Fokker's interrupter gear.

The unarmed Eindecker E.I had been rushed into service in the summer of 1915. It was a relatively simple aircraft to fly, once pilots got used to the old-fashioned wing-warping method of lateral control. Only 30 or so were made before its 80hp seven-cylinder Oberursel UO rotary engine was replaced by a more powerful 100hp version, the UI. This updated model, the E.II, first saw service in September 1915, but again very few – only 23 – were built before further modifications were made, including the installing of a much larger wing.

Seen from our sophisticated world in which fighter engines develop more than 1000 times as much as the sputtering rotary of the E-series these pioneer fighters may appear quaint rather than deadly. We find it hard to comprehend the situation in which a machine's air-combat performance was significantly affected by the size and weight of the pilot! Even an extra machine gun had a noticeable effect on rate of climb and all-round agility. Thus, though at least two pilots experimented with fitting three guns on the E.III – which was by far the most numerous model with about 260 being delivered – the standard armament remained a single gun until, at the end of the line, Fokker built a few E.IVs. These were larger all-round, and fitted with the Oberursel U.III engine with 14 cylinders in two rows, giving 160 hp. This was enough to carry two machine guns as the standard fit, but instead of producing a superior fighter the result was judged less agile than the almost featherweight E.IIIs, and engine failures were more common.

It is curious that, throughout the E-series, Fokker – always go-ahead and eager to beat the competition – never fitted ailerons to these monoplanes. By 1915 wing-warping was distinctly outdated.

Opinions vary as to how many Eindeckers were made, from as few as 300 to just over 350. Taking the most optimistic figure 350 is a remarkably small number of aircraft to create and sustain such a legend. But then they were flown by some remarkable pilots. Two must be mentioned. Oswald Boelcke was the father of all fighter aces. He invented the concept of large formations of aircraft fighting as a unit which led to the formation of the famous *Jagdstaffeln*. And there was Leutnant Max Immelmann who became immortal almost overnight and was

SPECIFICATION

Country of origin: Germany.

Manufacturer: Fokker Flugzeug-Werke GmbH.

Type: Single-seat fighter.

Year: 1915.

Engine: 100hp Oberursel UI nine-cylinder air-cooled rotary.

Wingspan: 9.52m (31ft 2in).

Length: 7.3m (23ft 11in).

Height: 2.8m (9ft 2in).

Weight: 610kg (1342lb).

Maximum speed: 140km/h (87.5mph) at sea level.

Ceiling: 3500m (11,500ft).

Range: 182km (113 miles).

Armament: One LMG 08/15, machine gun (occasionally two and with individual aircraft three machine guns were fitted).

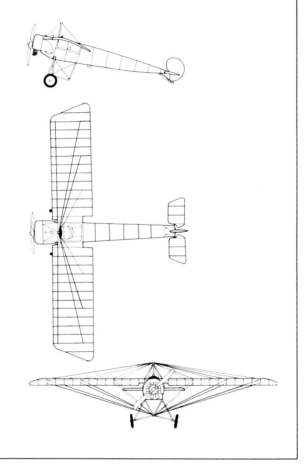

responsible for the famous Immelmann turn. Still used today as an exciting standard aerobatic manoeuvre, it was simply a half roll followed by a half loop or a half loop followed by a half roll. It was a very sleek way of changing direction by 180 degrees. Immelmann also perfected attack from below in the stall turn that allowed the Leutnant to attack his opponents from side to side without losing height and keeping them in his sights for the maximum amount of time.

Dive, open fire, pull back, stall, full rudder, dive, open fire. In the little Eindecker, against the ponderous B.E.2cs, it sounds almost child's play – or 'Fokker fodder'. But, of course, it wasn't. Max Immelmann, the first of the 'truly greats' from either side, was killed in June 1916 at the tragically early age of 26 in a dogfight with a British F.E.2b of No 25 Squadron, flown by Lieutenant H. McCubbin with his observer, Corporal J. H. Waller.

In 1916, faster, more manoeuvrable Allied aircraft, now fitted with Constantinesco interrupter gears, sent the Eindeckers off to the less demanding battle ground of Mesopotamia and to training duties, while the task of fighting Allied aircraft on the Western Front was left in the capable hands of the Albatros biplanes.

The Fokker Scourge subsided.

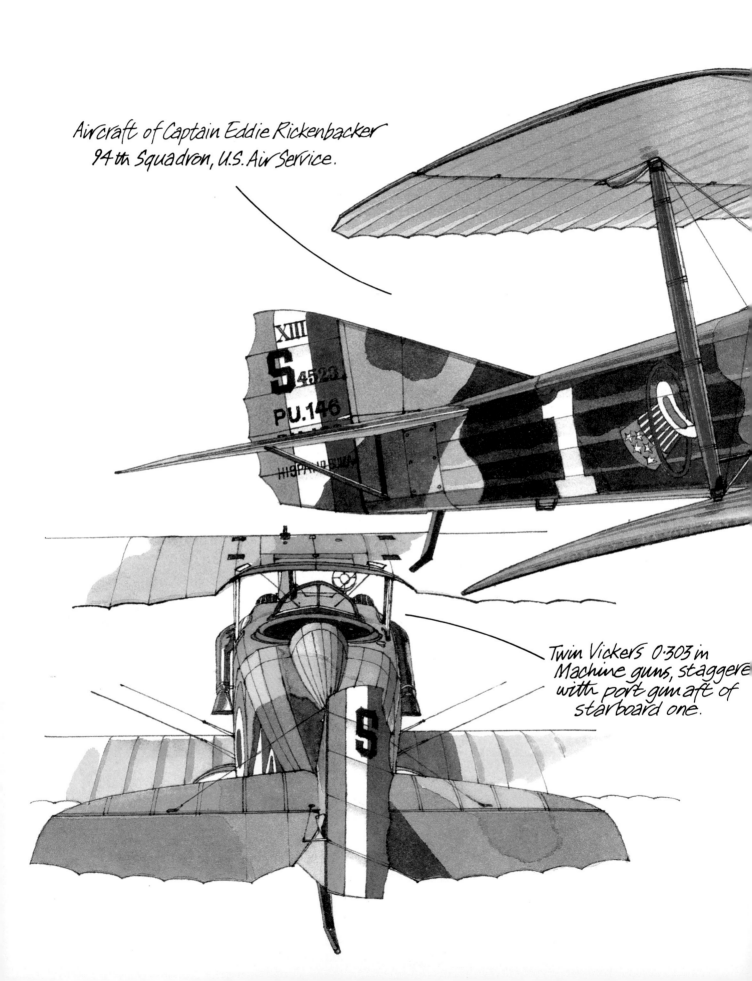

Aircraft of Captain Eddie Rickenbacker
94th Squadron, U.S. Air Service.

Twin Vickers 0·303 in
Machine guns, staggered
with port gun aft of
starboard one.

SPAD XIII

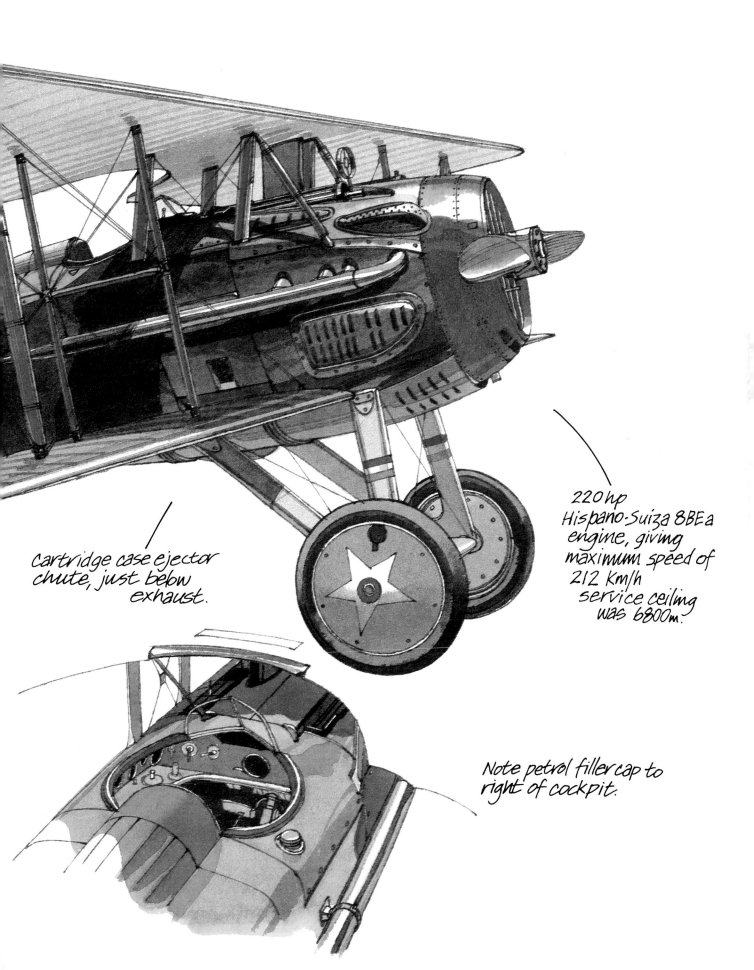

cartridge case ejector chute, just below exhaust.

220 hp Hispano-Suiza 8BEa engine, giving maximum speed of 212 Km/h service ceiling was 6800m.

Note petrol filler cap to right of cockpit.

SPAD VII & XIII

There can be no question that the SPAD scouts were the most successful French fighter aircraft of World War 1. Indeed, many would say (and not only Frenchmen) that the SPAD was the finest fighter produced by any nation at that time. Yet, like so many great aeroplanes, the SPAD twins, the VII and the XIII, had relatively humble beginnings.

Before the war the Deperdussin company's brilliant young designer, Louis Béchereau, designed a sleek, braced wing monoplane with an ultra-streamlined fuselage. Known as the Monocoque, because of its fuselage construction, the Deperdussin was planned from the outset to go fast. It did. In its first year, 1912, it won the Gordon Bennett Cup with a speed of 173.97km/h and the following year the Deperdussin racer captured the world air-speed record at 204km/h. Powering this stubby, but sleek little racer was a Gnome 14-cylinder rotary engine.

The full name of the original Deperdussin company was the Société des Productions Armand Deperdussin, hence the name SPAD. Later, the company name was changed, but in such a way that the acronym SPAD could be retained (see specifications).

However, the first aircraft to use the name hardly distinguished themselves. The A2 and A4 rejoiced in one of the most unconventional – and least successful – configurations in aviation history. They were tractor aircraft (i.e. the propeller was at the nose of the aeroplane and pulled it forward) but the observer/gunner was seated *in front of* the propeller. This arrangement was hardly popular with the crew but the idea was to get over the problem of firing through the propeller. It was a freakish design and it didn't last.

In April 1916, the SPAD VII arrived. Designed by Béchereau, it was a conventional biplane in appearance, but it was immediately apparent that it could outperform the Nieuports that were then supplying the main fighter strength for the French Aviation Militaire. It was also a much stronger aircraft all round. The first contract was awarded in the spring of 1916. Production started almost immediately and SPAD VIIs began to be delivered in September.

The SPAD VII was powered by Marc Birkigt's marvellous new Hispano-Suiza water-cooled V8 engine which developed 150hp. Armament was a single 7.65mm Vickers offset to the right, using Birkigt synchronizing gear (no need to sit in front of the propeller now!). Fuel was carried under the lower wing in a fuselage tank specially curved to conform with the sleek fuselage lines, and a notable first for the SPAD VII was the fact that this fuel could be jettisoned in an emergency.

One of the very first SPAD VIIs to enter service was

delivered to a 21-year-old lieutenant in the *Escadrille de Chasse N3*. His name was Georges Guynemer. The fact that he claimed a victim on his second flight with the SPAD was remarkable; what was more unusual was that he shot down another three on a sortie only a few days later. However, this sad-looking young lieutenant *was* unusual. By the end of January, his total aircraft kills had reached 30, and because of this he christened his beloved SPAD *La Mitrailleuse Volante*, the Flying Machine Gun.

Georges Guynemer flew in good company. His fellow pilots in *Escadrille N3* – the renamed SPA.3 but always known as *Les Cigognes*, or The Storks – included such aces as Capitaine Armand Pinsard (with 27 victories), Sous-Lieutenant René Dorme (with 23), Capitaine Alfred Hertaux (with 21) and Capitaine Albert Deullin (with 20).

The SPAD VII was so successful during this period that the other Allies all clamoured to use it. Many companies began to manufacture the VII under licence, including two British-based companies, the British Blériot and Spad Company at Brooklands and Mann Egerton in Norwich. Most of these British-built SPADs never found their way to the Western Front. Nevertheless, the SPAD served with great distinction in the Middle East, Belgium and Italy, where Maggiore (Major) Francesco Baracca of the *Gia Squadriglia* achieved 23 of his 34 victories in SPADs, before he was killed in action on 19 June 1918.

However back in the spring of 1917, a new SPAD was demonstrated to the *Escadrilles de Chasse*. The SPAD XIII was fitted with a more powerful Hispano-Suiza V8 engine which delivered 200hp. It also carried two Vickers 7.65mm guns mounted above the engine.

Georges Guynemer took delivery of one of these aircraft during the summer. His inevitable toll of victories seemed set to continue, but on 11 September 1917 he disappeared while on a patrol over Poelcapelle. The great French ace of the war had claimed his last victim, with an amazing total of 54 confirmed kills. But as always, someone was ready to take his place. René Fonck, who was by now also flying a SPAD XIII, had already shot down over 30 German aircraft. He went on to achieve a total score of 75 victories, making him the leading Allied ace. Eleven of his kills were gained with a SPAD fitted with a 37mm

SPECIFICATION

SPAD VII

Country of origin: France.

Manufacturer: SPAD (Société Anonyme pour l'Aviation et ses Dérivés).

Type: Single-seat fighter.

Year: 1916.

Engine: 150hp Hispano-Suiza 8Aa water-cooled V8.

Wingspan: 7.77m (25ft 6in).

Length: 6.13in (20ft 1in).

Height: 2.13m (7ft).

Weight: 703kg (1550lb).

Maximum speed: 192km/h (119mph) at 2000m (6560ft).

Ceiling: 5485m (18,000ft).

Range: 298km (185 miles).

Armament: One synchronized 7.65mm Vickers machine gun.

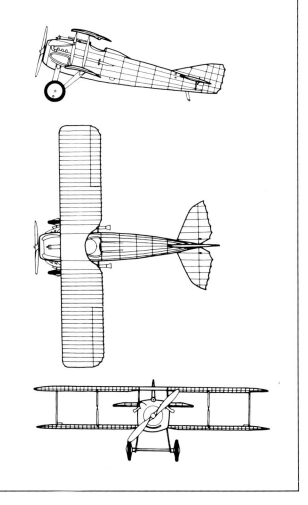

cannon, firing through the hub of the propeller. Guynemer gained four victories with a similar aircraft.

By March 1918, after Birkigt had made some hurried improvements to the new engine, which had proved somewhat unreliable, SPADs were being turned out at a remarkable rate and in fact, total French production of the aircraft reached 8472 by the time it stopped in 1919. Around 14,700 were manufactured in total, outnumbering all other World War I fighters. American interest in the SPAD was spearheaded by the successes of their two great aces, Eddie Rickenbacker and Frank Luke. Rickenbacker scored the majority of his 26 victories in the SPAD XIII, and the good reports he and his fellow Americans sent back resulted in the ambitious decision to build no less than 6000 SPADs in the United States.

The Armistice, of course, intervened in 1918. Notwithstanding, the two SPAD's overall contribution to the Allies' fortunes cannot be overstated. They rank, along with the S.E.5 and the Camel, as the greatest Allied fighters of the entire war.

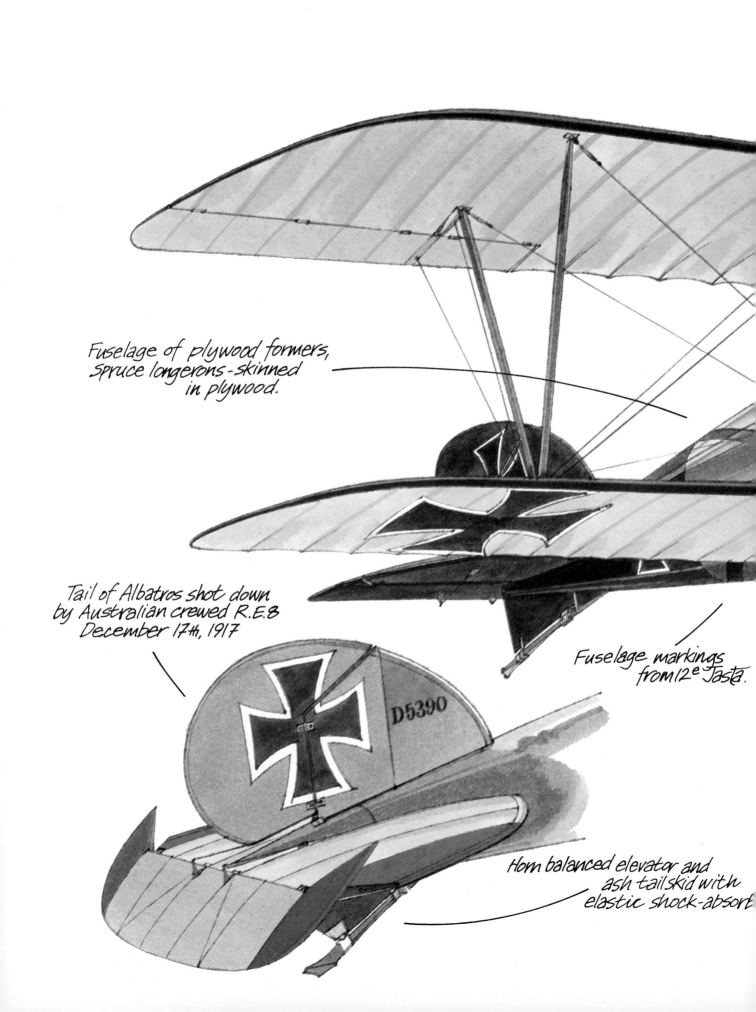

Fuselage of plywood formers, spruce longerons-skinned in plywood.

Tail of Albatros shot down by Australian crewed R.E.8 December 17th, 1917

D 5390

Fuselage markings from 12e Jasta.

Horn balanced elevator and ash tailskid with elastic shock-absorb

ALBATROS DIII

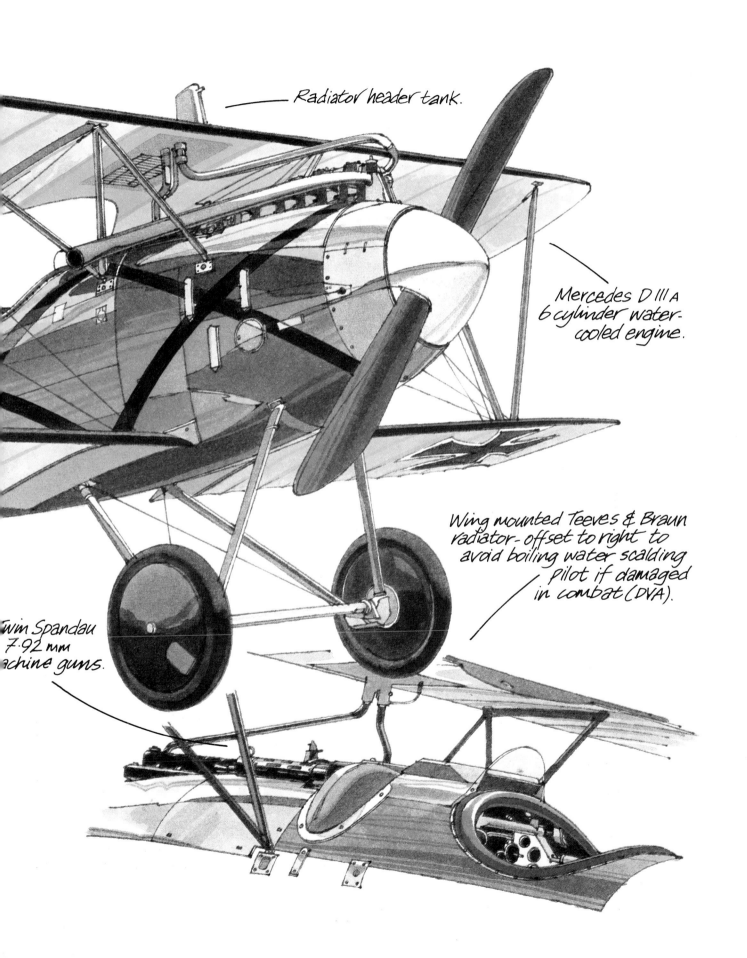

Radiator header tank.

Mercedes D III A
6 cylinder water-
cooled engine.

Wing mounted Teeves & Braun
radiator - offset to right to
avoid boiling water scalding
pilot if damaged
in combat (DVA).

Twin Spandau
7.92 mm
machine guns.

ALBATROS DIII

At the beginning of 1917, the war in the air was going firmly the Allies' way. Bristol Fighters, Nieuport Scouts and Airco D.H.2s were keeping the skies over the trenches clear for the numerous B.E.2s and R.E.8 reconnaissance aircraft that were so essential to the Allied ground forces.

Suddenly the pendulum swung the other way. In six short weeks, beginning in April, Germany regained the upper hand. This was due in part to the success of the formation of German fighting units, the *Jagdstaffeln*. Each *Staffel* or *Jasta* usually consisted of 14 aircraft and was led by a pilot who had already shown outstanding skill and courage.

At this time, too, the Russians began to retreat, freeing more men and equipment including aircraft for the Western Front. But the biggest single influence on the German change in fortunes was the introduction of a new aeroplane: the Albatros D.III.

The D.III was neither significantly faster nor more manoeuvrable than its immediate predecessors, the D.I and D.II. Its uprated Mercedes six-cylinder in-line engine delivered just 10 extra hp. So how did it gain its fearsome reputation that resulted in that fateful period the Allies called Bloody April?

The statistics are unarguable. Between 1 April and 5 May 1917 well over 200 British and French aircraft were brought down, mostly by Albatros D.IIIs, with negligible German losses. It is likely that the German pilots' new-found confidence stemmed in part from their new training and fighting methods, but also from one previously overlooked, but vital factor: improved visibility.

The earlier Albatros fighters – or Albatri as they were occasionally called by the British – suffered from a distinct lack of forward and downward vision. To remedy this serious shortcoming, the Albatros chief designer, Robert Thelen, took a leaf out of a French exercise book; more precisely he studied the Nieuport Scout. The year before, several Scouts had been captured intact and had been sent for evaluation by the inspectors of the Idflieg, the Imperial German Air Service.

Thelen set about making some important changes to the basic layout of his already beautiful fighting aircraft. He adopted a sesquiplane layout, where the lower wing is much smaller in width than the upper. As with the French Nieuports, the result was that the lower wing needed only a single main spar. This led to the adoption of the famous V struts which gave rise to the British pilots' nickname for the Albatros and the French Nieuport – 'V-strutter'.

The single spar arrangement seemed attractive. It saved a considerable amount of weight but it also brought problems, because, under certain conditions of stress, caused by violent manoeuvres, the wing flexed and occasionally failed completely.

The famous Red Baron, Manfred von Richthofen, almost lost his life through exactly this problem. He managed to put his Albatros D.III down in one piece and for a time returned to the D.II. (It is interesting to note that Richthofen's D.II was, in fact, manufactured under licence by Halberstadt, famous for its two-seater reconnaissance aircraft.) But by the beginning of April, the Baron had returned to the D.III. It is not known whether he believed the wing failure to be an isolated incident or whether he had worked out a way of flying the aircraft in combat that would not unduly stress the defective lower wings. The fact remains that Richthofen scored 21 victories against Allied aircraft during April alone.

All the Albatros fighters were noted for their beautiful streamlined fuselages. Thelen accomplished this by making them out of curved sheets of veneer, in a process known as semi-monocoque construction in which, as in a lobster claw, all the strength is in the skin.

One other design detail is worth recording. In order to preserve the Albatros' sleek lines, its Teeves und Braun radiator was mounted in the upper wing centre section, immediately in front of the pilot. This was very quickly moved to one side, after pilots were reported being badly scalded by boiling water pouring from a bullet-ridden radiator.

Von Richthofen was by now in command of the famous *Jasta 11* following the death of his mentor and perhaps the greatest ace of them all, Oswald Boelcke, on 28 October 1916. Boelcke had crashed to his death following a mid-air collision with Erwin Boehme, one of the two leutnants he had selected for future leadership. In an attempt to follow his leader down during a run-of-the-mill dogfight, Boehme's undercarriage caught Boelcke's upper wing tip, causing it to pull away from its struts. The Albatros swung violently out of control. Boelcke fought all the way down and at one stage seemed to have regained some form of control. But at 150m observers saw the Albatros dive steeply into the ground. It could have been the end of an era. However, Boelcke's disciples had learned their lessons well, and Germany's air superiority continued for several more months.

The craving for a hero to worship thrust Manfred von Richthofen firmly into the limelight. The Richthofen legend grew, and not just in his home country. All over the Western Front, Allied pilots could talk of little but an encounter with the Red Baron.

Flying an Albatros D.II, Richthofen actually brought down another victim on the morning of his leader's

SPECIFICATION

Country of origin: Germany.

Manufacturer: Albatros Werke GmbH.

Type: Single-seat fighter.

Year: 1917.

Engine: 175hp Mercedes D.IIIa six-cylinder water-cooled in-line.

Wingspan: 9.05m (29ft 8in).

Length: 7.33m (24ft).

Height: 2.98m (9ft 9in).

Weight: 886kg (1953lb).

Maximum speed: 175km/h (109mph) at 1000m (3281ft).

Ceiling: 5500m (18,000ft).

Range: 320km (199 miles).

Armament: Two synchronized 7.92mm Spandau machine guns.

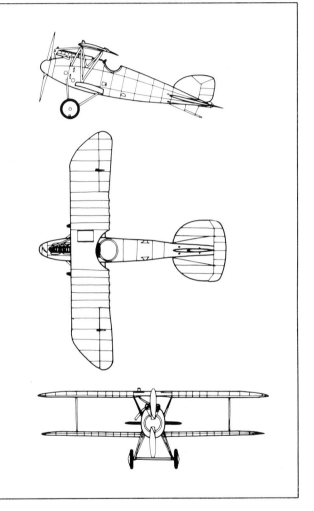

funeral, Sunday 3 November 1916. Von Richthofen took control of *Jasta 11* and began to fly the Albatros D.III. Despite the wing flexing problem that nearly cost him his life, Richthofen's scarlet D.III became the most feared German aircraft over the Western Front.

As had happened so often before in World War 1, the balance of power began to change. This time it was the new Allied S.E.5s and Sopwith Camels that successfully challenged the D.III for number one position. By the end of 1917, the Albatros D.III was being replaced by the D.V. At that time nearly 1000 were in service over the Western Front, with further squadrons seeing duty in Mesopotamia.

The Albatros D.III, with its graceful semi-monocoque fuselage, was one of the most beautiful aircraft of the 1914–18 war. It was also among the most successful.

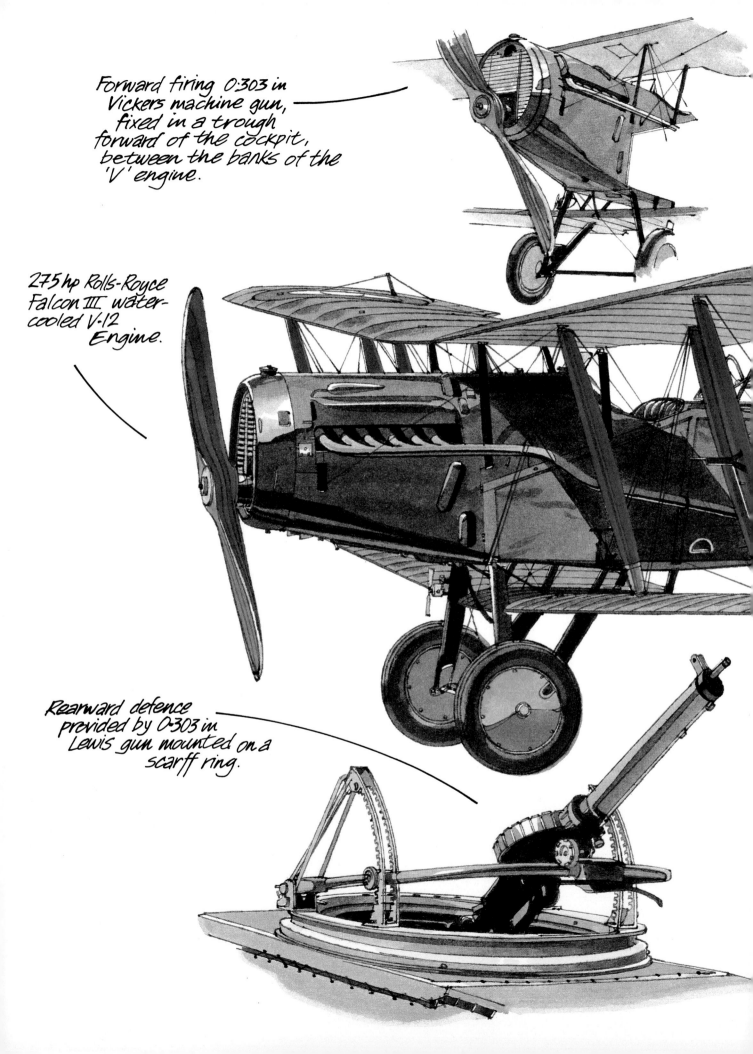

Forward firing 0·303 in
Vickers machine gun,
fixed in a trough
forward of the cockpit,
between the banks of the
'V' engine.

275 hp Rolls-Royce
Falcon III water-
cooled V·12
Engine.

Rearward defence
provided by 0·303 in
Lewis gun mounted on a
scarff ring.

BRISTOL F.2B
FIGHTER

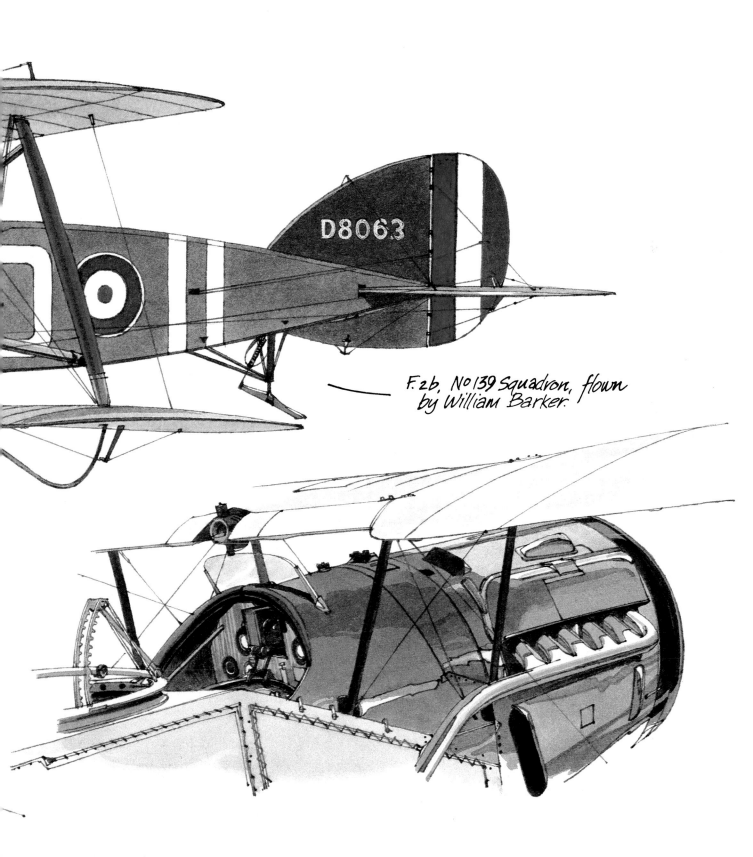

D8063

F.2b, N⁰ 139 Squadron, flown
by William Barker.

BRISTOL F.2B FIGHTER

In 1917, the Bristol Fighter was a very misunderstood aeroplane. On 5 April, six Bristol two-seater fighters of No 48 Squadron took off on the aircraft's first operational mission. Only two returned.

Near Douai the Bristol Fighters had been attacked by five Albatros D.IIIs, the aircraft they had been designed to fight against. But conventional two-seater tactics were hopelessly inadequate against the hard-hitting and highly manoeuvrable Albatros scouts. These dictated that the observer's Scarff-mounted Lewis gun was the main armament, with the fixed forward-firing Vickers used by the pilot as secondary or emergency armament.

That morning, Manfred von Richthofen and four of his crack pilots from *Jagdgeschwader 1* (JG1) proved in the most dramatic way possible that the rear cockpit gunner was no match for a diving attack. Some urgent re-thinking was needed if the Bristol Fighter was not to become one of the greatest flops of the war.

Suddenly the pilots appreciated the fact that the two-seat Bristol Fighter was as fast and very nearly as manoeuvrable as the single-seat Scouts which were much smaller. And that it could be thrown around the sky just like a single-seater. So the Bristol Fighter pilots went on the offensive and started to fly their aeroplanes using conventional single-seat tactics, twisting and turning to get above and behind their opponents (or away from them), and leaving the observer to protect the rear. This tactic was immediately successful and brought to a halt that fateful period for the Allies known as 'Bloody April'.

The Bristol F.2 was designed by Captain Frank Barnwell of the British & Colonial Aeroplane Company. His aim had been to replace the ageing BE.2s that were such easy targets for the German fighters.

Barnwell's early design in March 1916 would have been powered by the 120hp Beardmore. However, at that time Rolls-Royce brought out the much more powerful Falcon I, which could develop 190hp. Barnwell recognised that this extra power would transform his design from a reconnaissance aircraft to a two-seater fighter.

The Bristol F.2A made its first flight on 9 September 1916, and by March 1917 the first aircraft was delivered to front-line squadrons. The F.2A was quickly followed by the F.2B, which had a slightly larger tailplane, some structural changes to the wings and improved cockpit vision. Apart from the first 150 aircraft, the F.2B received uprated versions of the Rolls-Royce Falcon. The Falcon II developed 220hp, but this was quickly followed by the 275hp Falcon III. With this engine, the RFC pilots found they had a magnificent fighting tool.

This change in the Bristol's fortunes was no small

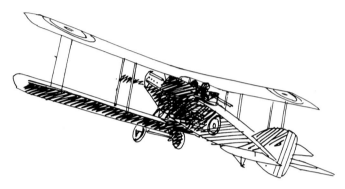

surprise to 'the Hun'. On its first disastrous commitment to battle the new two-seater was closely watched by none other than Manfred von Richthofen, who reported that the Albatros D.III was in all aspects of performance 'undoubtedly superior'. The new Bristol, instantly identified by its fuselage mid-way between the wings, was mentally written off as what a later generation of pilots would have called 'a piece of cake'. Then it suddenly became not merely aggressive but aggressive at both ends, twisting and turning and pumping out lead to targets at front and rear. The crews of these big two-seaters were in the summer of 1917 among the fastest scorers on the Western Front. For example, Capt McKeever and his observer scored almost all their 30 confirmed victories while still flying the original F.2A. Indeed, the Bristol was soon held in such respect that, except for the very top 'crack' circuses, it became a general rule for German pilots never to attack a formation of more than three Bristols, no matter how great their own numerical advantage might be.

With the Falcon III engine the RFC found they had not only all the power they wanted but sweet running and unsurpassed reliability. They were moved, as never before, to write poetry about the sheer joy of flying such a fine machine. At last, it mattered little whether the observer had one gun or, as was usually the case, two — together with as many as eight massive 97-round drums of ammunition, which had to be changed with frozen fingers whilst the Fighter might be flung into a tight turn. Hanging a dozen 20-lb bombs under the lower wing was also no problem, though most of the Bristol's countless missions were various kinds of 'offensive patrol' without seeking surface targets as well.

At one stage production of F.2B airframes outstripped the number of Falcon III engines and, because the need for the Bristol Fighters at the Front was so urgent, several hundred airframes were fitted with the 200hp Sunbeam Arab engine.

One pilot, Major Oliver Stewart wrote, 'The pilot could

SPECIFICATION

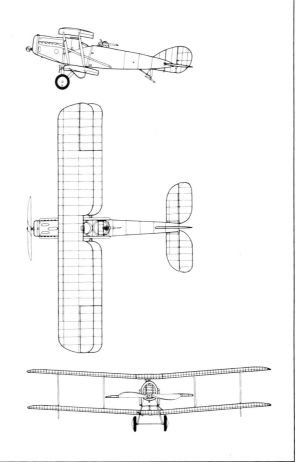

Country of origin: Great Britain.

Manufacturer: British & Colonial Aeroplane Company.

Type: Two-seat fighter.

Year: 1916.

Engine: 275hp Rolls-Royce Falcon III water-cooled V12.

Wingspan: 11.96m (39ft 3in).

Length: 7.87m (25ft 10in).

Height: 2.97m (9ft 9in).

Weight: 1292kg (2848lb).

Maximum speed: 198km/h (123mph) at 1524m (5000ft).

Ceiling: 5486m (18,000ft).

Range: 483km (300 miles).

Armament: One synchronized 0.303in Vickers machine gun, one or two 0.303in Lewis guns.

enter a dogfight and turn almost as quickly and on almost as small a radius as the best single-seater. He could fling his machine about, go into vertical dives, pull it out quickly, turn it on its back, spin it, roll it and generally do every sort of manoeuvre if the need arose. And all the time there was the comfortable feeling that the observer was there with his pair of Lewis guns, watching and protecting.'

Being Major Stewart's observer, however, cannot have been much fun. In fact, the observer's role in all two-seaters was one of the most heroic of the entire war. They had no engine to protect them and they were defenceless against enemy fire; their only protection being their gun. Yet there was no lack of volunteers for the job and indeed they were better off in a Bristol than in anything else.

By the end of the war, 14 squadrons were flying the Bristol Fighter popularly known as the 'Brisfit' or 'Biff'.

Unlike most other Allied aircraft it had stayed in production. It is a tribute to Barnwell's design that Bristol F.2s were produced long after the end of World War 1 and they were still flying in service with the Royal Air Force in 1932.

130 hp Clerget rotary motor, 125 hp at
1250 R.P.M (sea level) giving maximum
speed of 115 mph at 6500 ft.

F6314

Twin synchronised 0·303
Vickers machine guns
mounted in the 'hump'.

SOPWITH F.1 CAMEL

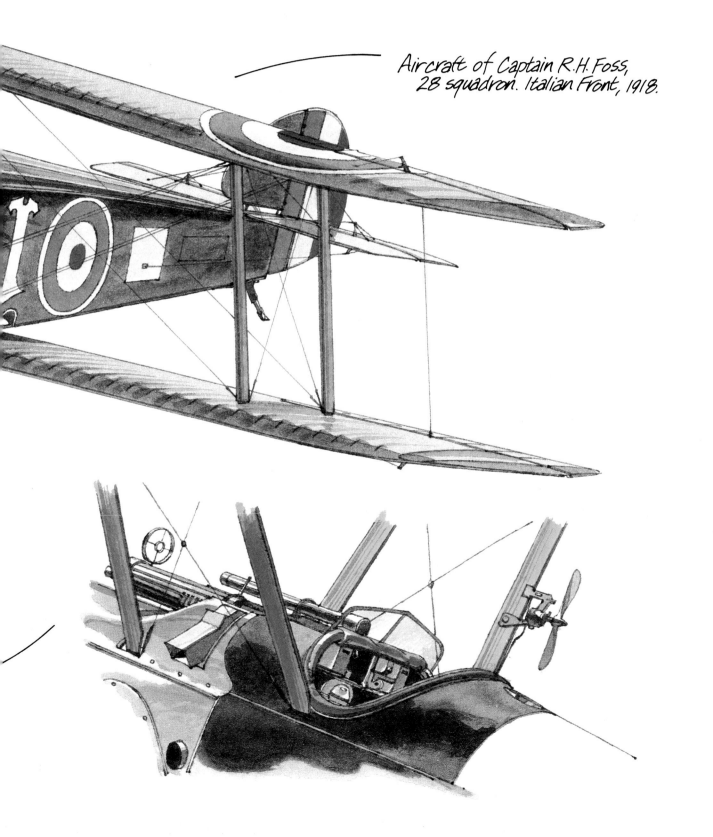

Aircraft of Captain R.H. Foss,
28 squadron. Italian Front, 1918.

SOPWITH F.1 CAMEL

The Sopwith Camel was certainly no camel in the air. It was the top scorer of any single-seat fighter flown by the Royal Flying Corps. The Camel arrived on the Western Front in July 1917 and, in the 18 months that followed up to the Armistice, the Camel was responsible for the downfall of more than 2900 enemy aircraft.

So why was the aircraft called the Camel? This hardly glamorous nickname derives from the humped fairing over the breeches of its twin forward-firing 0.303in Vickers machine guns, fixed immediately in front of the pilot.

It's right and proper that these guns should have given the Camel its name. It was the first time they were fitted as a synchronized pair in a British aircraft. Previously the Dibovsky, Sopwith-Kauper and Constantinesco gears had all been used on the forward-firing gun of the mass-produced Sopwith 1½-Strutter. Most Camels had the Constantinesco gear.

Naturally, these guns gave the Camel impressive firepower. However, a successful fighter has to be manoeuvrable, too. The Camel achieved its fantastic manoeuvrability because of its large rotary engine. The rotary concept was certainly not new. In fact, nearly all aircraft, British, French and German were using rotaries. But the Camel had a relatively short wingspan and an extremely short fuselage. It was powered by a 130hp Clerget or a 110hp Le Rhône engine and since all the weight was concentrated at the front of the aircraft the extra torque that was produced by the cylinders rotating around the fixed crankshaft could be harnessed by skilled pilots to make the Camel turn very tightly indeed. Of course, this torque had its disadvantages, too. The Camel was a difficult aircraft to learn to fly, and several trainee pilots were killed trying to master the same idiosyncracies that could have saved them in action.

Today, though a few real or replica Camels are still flying, only the real ones have rotary engines and nobody is going to hazard these by flying to the limits or doing experiments. Thus, we must rely on the records left by the wartime pilots, and in general they agree that, if one survived the process of conversion to this tricky machine, one was likely to beat the enemy almost every time. The elevator was so sensitive the slightest twitch would send the Camel into sickening undulations, while turning to the right unleashed the pent-up gyroscopic forces so that the stubby machine went round like lightning. It was commonly said that, if a Camel pilot wished to make a 90° turn to the left, the quickest method was to do a 270° turn to the right. In turn this posed problems for anyone trying to get on a Camel's tail: the 'Hun' might take it for granted the

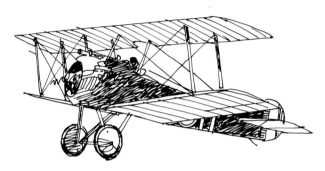

Camel would break to the right, only to find, as he cut off the corner, that he had guessed wrongly.

By the final quarter of 1917 this one type had completely turned the tables on the German fighters and brought the RFC undisputed air superiority over their sectors of the Western Front. One day Capt J.L. Trollope of 43 Squadron (the 'Fighting Cocks') shot down two D.F.W. two-seaters and an Albatros before lunch and three more two-seaters before afternoon tea. This caused quite a sensation, but a few days later Capt H.W. Woollett of 209 (one of the former Royal Navy squadrons transferred on 1 April 1918 to the newly formed RAF) despatched a Fokker, a Pfalz and four unidentified German scouts again between breakfast and tea!

Altogether, 5490 Camels were built, and this figure may include the 300 or so 2F.1 ship's Camels referred to later, although the figure might have been higher. As well as air-to-air fighting, they were used extensively in a ground strafing role. During the battles of Ypres and Cambrai, several squadrons of Camels were converted to drop 25lb bombs and these made regular raids, both on enemy trenches and immediately behind the lines. Camels were used in this way to bring about communications breakdowns. This kind of mission proved far more dangerous than it sounded and many Camels were brought down by well-aimed ground fire.

This led to the development of a special ground attack version of the Camel, the TF.1, or Trench Fighter. Its cockpit was armour-plated and two of its machine guns were angled to fire downwards. The 'Trench' version of the Camel never went into production, but it became the prototype for the successful Sopwith TF.2 Salamander.

Camels also had an illustrious record at sea. A special shipboard version, the 2F.1, was developed and went into operation early in 1918. The wingspan was slightly smaller than the land-based Camel, and it had only one Vickers gun, plus a Lewis gun on the upper wing centre section.

Other·modifications included a detachable rear fuselage and experiments were made with special skids which

SPECIFICATION

Country of origin: Great Britain.

Manufacturer: Sopwith Aviation Company Limited.

Type: Single-seat fighter.

Year: 1917.

Engine: 130hp Clerget 9B nine-cylinder air-cooled rotary.

Wingspan: 8.53m (28ft).

Length: 5.72m (18ft 9in).

Height: 2.59m (8ft 6in).

Weight: 659kg (1453lb).

Maximum speed: 185km/h (115mph) at 1981m (6500ft).

Ceiling: 5800m (19,000ft).

Range: 402km (250 miles).

Armament: Two synchronized 0.303in Vickers machine guns. Could also be converted to carry four 25lb bombs.

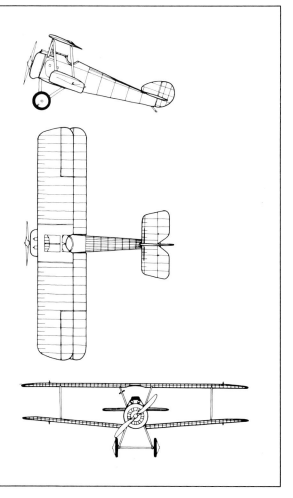

replaced the normal undercarriage and ran along rails fitted to the ship's deck. It was with one of these Camel 2F.1s that Lieutenant S.D. Culley shot down Zeppelin L53 with special incendiary ammunition in August 1918, the last Zeppelin casualty of the war. He took off from a flat lighter towed behind a destroyer.

Some 2F.1s were converted to a dive-bombing role with racks for two 50lb bombs under the fuselage. 340 naval versions of the Camel were built and these flew from an assortment of warships and towed lighters.

But the Camel's greatest single claim to fame was its victory tally of which the most famous was gained by an aircraft of No 209 Squadron, piloted by Captain Roy Brown, who shot down Manfred von Richthofen in his scarlet Dr.1 triplane on 21 April 1918. However, it must be recorded that this success was hotly disputed by a battery of the 14th Australian Field Artillery Brigade and by Australians from the 24th Machine gun Company, all of whom claimed the famous 'Red Baron' for their own.

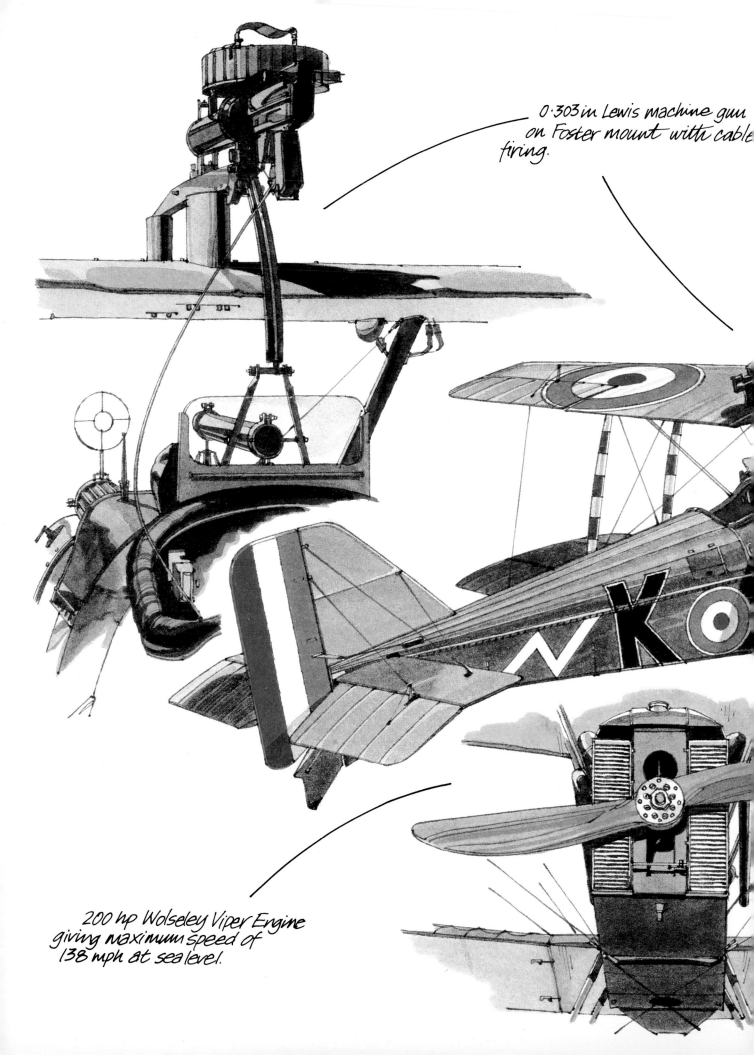

0·303 in Lewis machine gun on Foster mount with cable firing.

200 hp Wolseley Viper Engine giving maximum speed of 138 mph at sea level.

ROYAL AIRCRAFT
FACTORY S.E. 5a

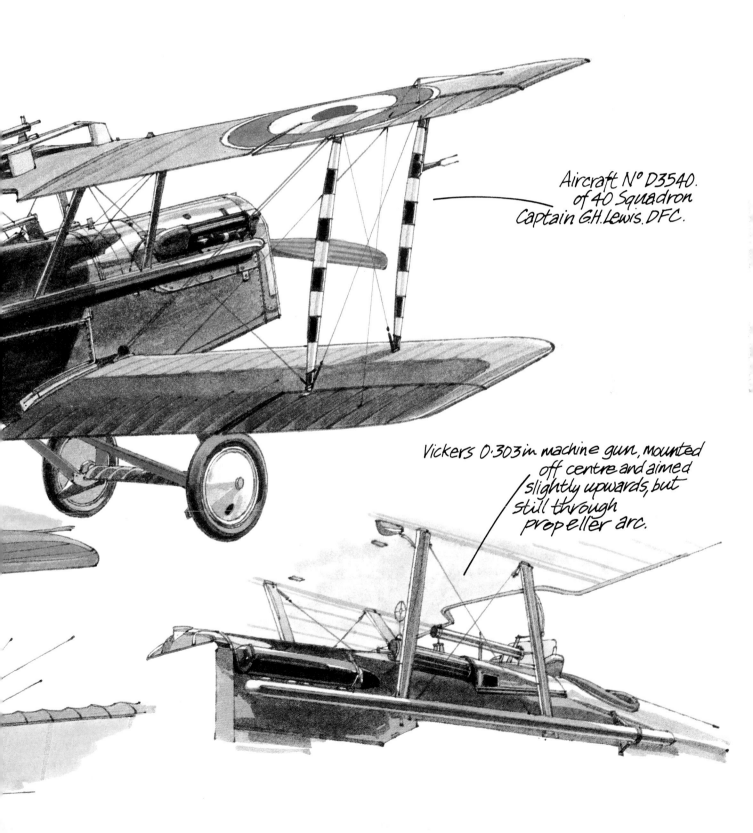

Aircraft N° D3540.
of 40 Squadron
Captain G.H. Lewis. DFC.

Vickers 0.303in machine gun, mounted
off centre and aimed
slightly upwards, but
still through
propeller arc.

ROYAL AIRCRAFT FACTORY S.E. 5a

'The S.E.5 has turned out a dud ... It's a great shame, for everybody expects such a lot from them ... it is a rotten machine.'

Albert Ball wrote these words in the spring of 1917, after he had been dragged back from active service on the Western Front, along with a group of Britain's finest pilots, to form a new fighter group based on the all-important Scout Experimental 5. The 'see-saw' that was taking place in the skies over France had turned once again, this time Germany's way. The Albatros Scouts were faster, had a higher ceiling, could climb quicker and, above all, were out-gunning their Allied opponents.

During the previous winter, the British Air Staff threw down the gauntlet to the fledgling British aircraft industry. 'Build us', they said, 'a single-seater with speed, manoeuvrability and armament superior to the enemy.' The challenge was taken up by the Royal Aircraft Factory, based at Farnborough, and by Sopwith Aviation. That both succeeded is now history. The S.E.5's only serious contender for the best British fighter of World War I was the Sopwith Camel.

The Royal Aircraft Factory's design team of H.P. Folland, J. Kenworthy and Major F.W. Goodden was most impressed with a new aero-engine from Hispano-Suiza. Unlike so many successful engines of this time it did not have rotary cylinders. It was a water-cooled V8. It offered 150hp, a considerable increase over most engines currently available, yet with a weight of only 330lb. As a first step they installed the Hispano-Suiza 8A into the B.E.2c, which was being regularly shot out of the sky by Halberstadts, Albatros and Rolands almost at will. This tremendous upsurge in power transformed the gentle old B.E. But

power alone wasn't the answer. The aircraft required something extra.

The RAF designers went back to the drawing board and produced a tough square-rigged single-seater that made no compromises whatsoever to aesthetics. The S.E.5 was born to fly fast and hard. It gave the pilot excellent vision, but its greatest advantage was its built-in stability. The S.E.5's predecessors, the R.E.s and B.E.s, had needed stability for accurate observation. Now the much faster, more manoeuvrable S.E.5 would turn this into a priceless asset.

If you line your aircraft up behind your target and pull the trigger, you'll destroy your opponent much faster if you have a steady gun platform. That lesson, learned the hard way in the trenches below, was equally valid in the skies above. And so, despite their early protests, Britain's crack pilots began to train on the new aeroplane.

Albert Ball immediately took the Lewis gun off its mounting above the upper wing, preferring to rely on the Vickers with its Constantinesco synchronization. He removed the cumbersome windscreen. He even lowered the seat by 8in. All this was carried out to increase the S.E.5's speed. At the time he believed the aircraft was slower than his beloved Nieuport, although this was not in fact the case.

In time, the British aces began to realise they were on to a winner. Despite its frumpish appearance, they found the S.E.5 was faster and had a higher ceiling than they had believed possible. More important, its fuel capacity gave an endurance of two and a half hours, which was much longer than the Albatros Scouts. So they would be able to climb high and stay high, waiting for the opposition to appear below them.

In March 1917 the S.E.5 was sent to France and had an immediate impact on the war. But within months it was superseded by the S.E.5a with an even more powerful version of the famous engine designer Marc Birkigt's Hispano-Suiza engine, now developing no less than 200hp. Teething troubles with this engine, which were also giving the French problems with the new SPAD, caused the RAF factory to instal a British-built version of the Hispano-Suiza, the Wolseley Viper. This engine also proved troublesome and production was delayed while design defects were rectified.

McCudden, Ball, Bishop, Mannock, and many other British aces found the S.E.5a was at last the aircraft they could fight on equal terms with the German Albatros. Soon after they were delivered, Lieutenant A.P.F. Rhys-Davids, flying with No 5 Squadron, brought down Werner Voss, von Richthofen's famous number two. Although just

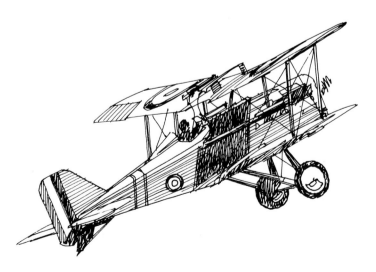

SPECIFICATION

Country of origin: Great Britain.

Manufacturer: Designed at Royal Aircraft Factory. Manufactured at The Austin Motor Company, The Standard Motor Company, Vickers Ltd.

Type: Single-seat fighter.

Year: 1917.

Engine: 200hp Wolseley W4a Viper water-cooled V8.

Wingspan: 8.12m (26ft 7in).

Length: 6.38m (20ft 11in).

Height: 2.9m (9ft 6in).

Weight: 880kg (1940lb).

Maximum speed: 222km/h (138mph) at sea level.

Ceiling: 5944m (19,500ft).

Range: 402km (250 miles).

Armament: One synchronized 0.303in Vickers machine gun, one 0.303in Lewis gun.

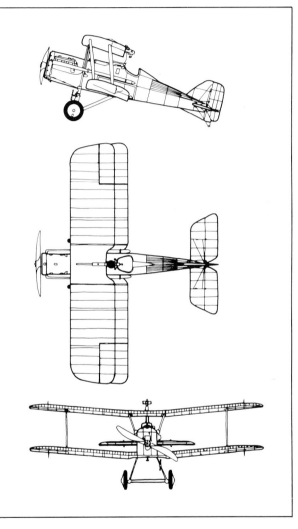

a single victory, it was an enormous boost to Allied morale and an early scalp for the S.E.5a, which, despite its rugged, almost over-simple appearance, was destined to become one of the most successful British aircraft of the World War 1 conflict.

In all, over 5000 S.E.5s and S.E.5as were built, the vast majority being 5as with the more powerful engine. The aircraft remains a lesson to fighter designers of today – speed and manoeuvrability, vital as they are, are not everything. If you cannot deliver your weapons from a stable platform, you are unlikely to achieve your objective. Although the S.E.5a accounted for fewer kills than its great Allied rival the Sopwith Camel, its total victory count ranks as one of the highest per aircraft of the war.

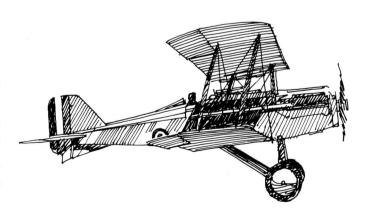

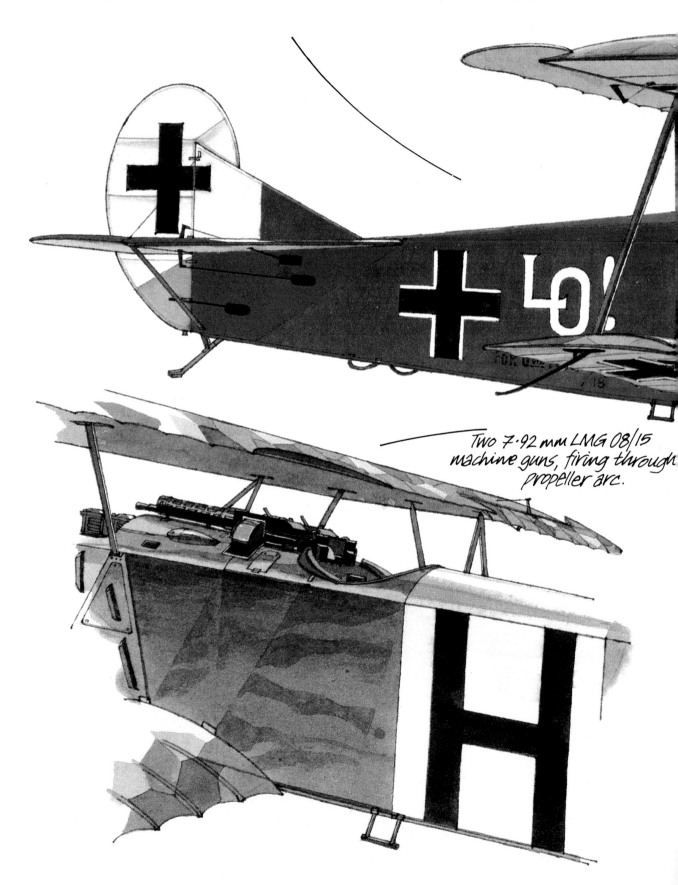

Aircraft 4253 of Jasta 4, Piloted by Ernst Udet
The letters 'LO' were the initials of Lola, the future Madame Udet.

Two 7·92 mm LMG 08/15
machine guns, firing through
propeller arc.

FOKKER D.VII

Mercedes D IIIA Six Cylinder Inline Water-Cooled Engine.
180 hp at 1000 m
Max speed 187 Km/h.

Horn balanced rudder and elevator.

FOKKER D.VII

Only one thing detracted from the Fokker D.VII's reputation. While it was winning battles in the air, the German army was losing the war on the ground. Eventually, when the Armistice was signed in November 1918, the D.VII claimed a further place in the history books by having its own special clause in the agreement. The Allies insisted that all Fokker D.VIIs were to be handed over to them. No other aircraft was mentioned by name, and the Allies took great care that after the war large numbers of this remarkable aeroplane were piled into giant heaps and set on fire. Nevertheless Fokker managed to smuggle 60 trainloads of planes and parts out of Germany into Holland, enabling him to set up his new company.

Towards the end of 1917, Anthony Fokker, conscious of the fact that he needed to re-establish his company's reputation as the leading German aircraft supplier, briefed his famous chief designer, Reinhold Platz, to produce a winner for the competition to choose Germany's next front-line single-seat fighter.

Originally the new Fokker biplane was to be rotary-engined, but structural problems with the wings of the latest Albatros meant that a large number of Mercedes D.III in-line engines became available at short notice. These beautiful engines, which delivered 160hp, were coming off the production line with no particular home for them, so Platz hastily revamped his design. One of these, designated VII, was chosen to represent Fokker at Adlershof airfield near Berlin in January 1918. Some 30 different designs were to be tested exhaustively by Germany's top pilots, and it was obvious that the winner would be assured a large production order.

What was kept very quiet indeed was Anthony Fokker's private fear that the new design would be inferior to some of the opposition in the competition. Brilliant salesman that he was, Fokker began to lobby the pilots before they flew the machine. He decided that he would turn the Fokker biplane's tendency to swing violently into a tactical advantage.

'You will notice a special feature of my ship, Herr Leutnant', he said to ace Oberleutnant Bruno Loerzer, 'is its outstanding ability to turn quickly. Tell the others so they can all benefit.' Like one of its great Allied rivals, the Sopwith Camel, a potential weakness was turned into a tactical advantage. However, the factor that weighed most heavily in the aeroplane's favour was its ability to hang on its propeller. This meant it could fight from below and literally chase an enemy across the sky pumping bullets into it almost at will.

The Fokker D.VII duly won the Adlershof competition

and Anthony Fokker returned to the factory with an initial order for 400 aircraft. It must have been galling for Fokker's great rivals, Albatros Werke, to receive a similar-size order to produce the Fokker biplanes under licence. It is to their credit that the Albatros-produced Fokkers were indistinguishable from the Fokker-built aircraft, despite the fact that they received no detailed plans or designs, but had to work entirely from one completed specimen aircraft.

The production model, the D.VII, entered service in April 1918 and the first batch went, of course, to *Jagdgeschwader I*, Richthofen's famous flying circus. The Red Baron himself, who had tried the new Fokker at Adlershof and had recommended some minor modifications, flew a D.VII on several missions. However, it must be mentioned that he also remained faithful to his first love, the Fokker Dr.I triplane (Dr. standing for Dreidecker or three-winger), in which he tragically met his death on 21 April 1918.

In August 1918, a variant designated D.VIIF was first delivered, powered by a BMW IIIa engine. This developed an extra 20hp which gave it 200km/h performance and improved both rate of climb and service ceiling, cutting the time it took to reach an altitude of 5000m from 38 minutes to just 14.

In many ways, the Fokker D.VII was extremely orthodox. Reinhold Platz had taken all the best features of his earlier designs and built them into an extremely rugged airframe. The flying surfaces, with V-shaped interplane struts, were so well-braced that its pilots never experienced wing flutter even when carrying out the most extreme manoeuvres.

Allied pilots also quickly learned to respect the new biplane, apart, that is, from Major William Barker who managed to shoot down five of them in one epic encounter when he was pitted single-handed against 30

SPECIFICATION

Country of origin: Germany.

Manufacturer: Fokker Flugzeug-Werke GmbH.

Type: Single-seat fighter.

Year: 1918.

Engine: 180hp BMW.IIIa water-cooled six-cylinder in-line.

Wingspan: 8.9m (29ft 2in).

Length: 7m (22ft 11in).

Height: 2.8m (9ft 2in).

Weight: 880kg (1940lb).

Maximum speed: 200km/h (124mph) at sea level.

Ceiling: 6000m (19,685ft).

Range: 246km (153 miles).

Armament: Two synchronized 7.92mm Spandau machine guns.

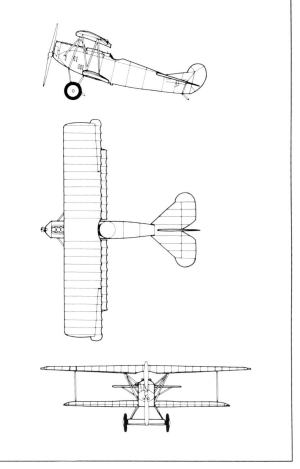

aircraft. This remarkable achievement earned him the respected Victoria Cross.

By the end of the war just 800 Fokker D.VIIs were in action, a small enough number to gain such an awesome reputation.

After the Armistice astute Fokker and his newly assembled staff at the Amsterdam works put the smuggled D.VIIs together and they sold like hot cakes. Among the more than a dozen customers for aircraft assembled from wartime parts were the new air forces of Belgium (occupied during the war) and Switzerland. The home air force bought large numbers for service both in the Netherlands and the East Indies. Even more important, the income from the sales of D.VIIs immediately after the war enabled Fokker to expand the business, build Europe's best-selling airliners and follow the D.VII with a series of even better fighters.

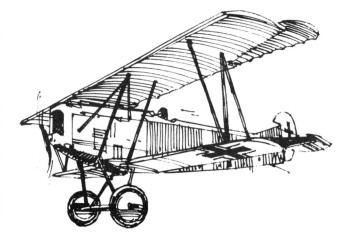

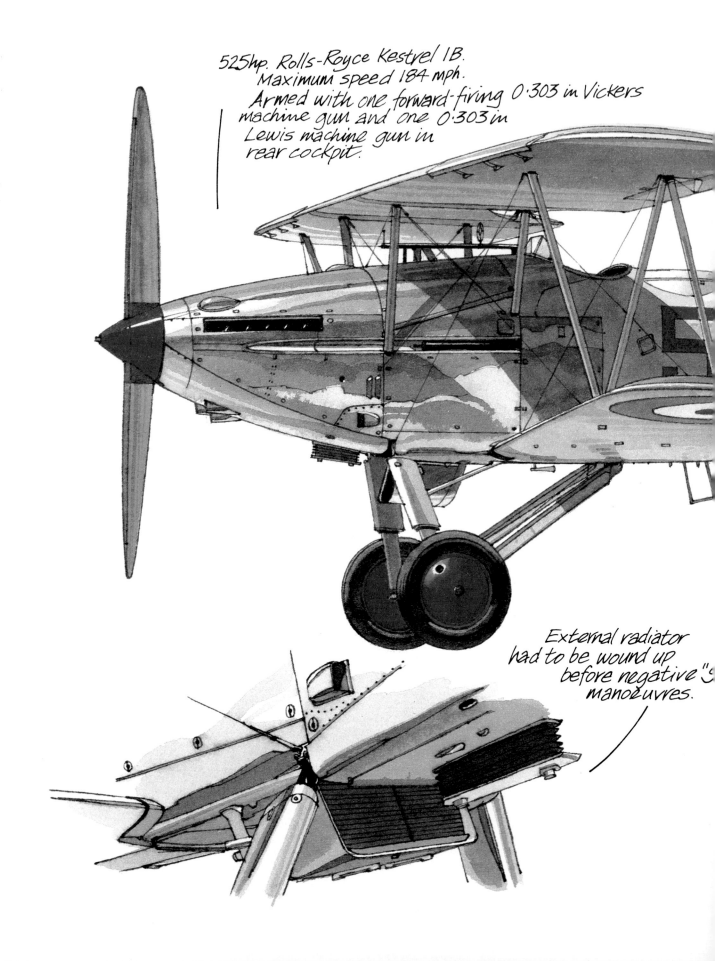

525hp. Rolls-Royce Kestrel IB.
Maximum speed 184 mph.
Armed with one forward-firing 0·303 in Vickers
machine gun and one 0·303 in
Lewis machine gun in
rear cockpit.

External radiator
had to be wound up
before negative "g"
manoeuvres.

HAWKER HART

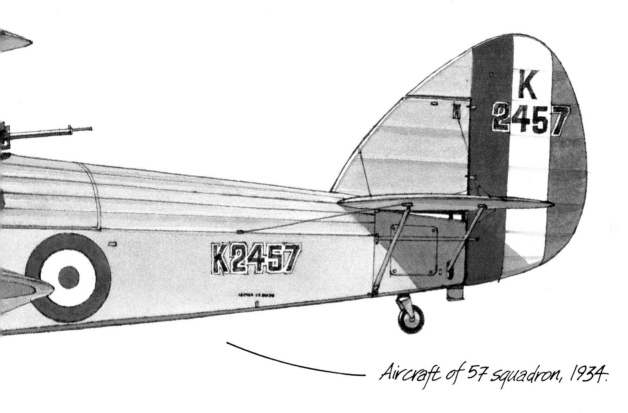

Aircraft of 57 squadron, 1934.

HAWKER HART

The Hawker Hart was designed as a two-seat bomber but something like 3000 Hart variants were built for other purposes. Only a few of these ever saw action. Nevertheless, few people would deny that the Hart has an important place in any history of fighting aircraft. To begin with, it was one of the most beautiful aircraft to come out of the British aviation industry.

The Hart was a favourite of its designer, Sydney Camm. He was the man who designed the famous Hurricane and in the 1950s received a knighthood. The Hart was an important aircraft because it was one of the first bombers designed from the outset to be light, fast and manoeuvrable. In the mid-1920s, the classic bomber was large and cumbersome. It had been designed with one thing in mind – a heavy bombload. Defence was provided by a combination of gun cockpits and escorting fighters.

In 1918 the D.H.4 bomber could outrun all the fighters, and in 1925 the Fairey Aviation Company built the Fox, which could do the same. This embarrassed the Air Ministry, which in 1926 issued a specification for a daylight bomber that would be lighter and more mobile than its predecessors. The Ministry had also recognised that large, relatively slow bombers had no place in the Royal Air Force, unless they could fly at great heights. The turn of those aircraft would come later. Meanwhile, three companies competed for the contract: Avro, Fairey and Hawker.

The Hawker Hart flew for the first time in June 1928. It was soon ranged alongside the Fairey Fox and the Avro Antelope in a series of extensive trials. The Hart duly convinced the Ministry and Hawker was awarded a development contract for 15 aircraft.

The public had a chance to see the sleek new light bomber in July 1929 at the Olympia air show. Its beautiful lines made it the star of the show. The Hart's engine, the Rolls-Royce Kestrel, was a new V12 which developed 525hp and gave the aircraft an excellent maximum speed of 184mph.

Construction was conventional for the day, being metal-framed with a fabric skin. The 15 development aircraft were delivered to No 33 Squadron, RAF, the following January. No 33 Squadron, based at Eastleigh in Hampshire, had been flying Hawker Horsleys. It is a tribute both to the Hart and the personnel of the squadron that they were able to take second place in the RAF's inter-unit contest, despite having just three months' experience on the new aeroplane.

Hawker received orders for a further 151 Harts. Other companies were also appointed to build Harts under licence, and Armstrong Whitworth made 149, Vickers 112

and Gloster 40. For export these were fitted with many other types of engine including air-cooled radials.

From the Hawker Hart came many derivatives. The Hawker Demon was designed as a two-seat fighter, to make use of the aeroplane's manoeuvrability. It was fitted with a supercharged version of the Kestrel engine which boosted its performance up to 585hp. More than 300 were built, most going to the RAF.

Meanwhile, the Fleet Air Arm took delivery of 71 Hawker Ospreys, a float plane or carrier-based variant. A general purpose but extremely tough derivative – the Hardy – was developed for operation in remote places. The Audax, of which no less than 624 were manufactured, was equipped for army co-operation duties, while the Hart (India), as its name implies, was designed for service in hot climates. A special variant, the Hartbees, was developed for South African service and was, in fact, built in Pretoria. These desert variants had a larger radiator, stronger tyres and wheel brakes, and a different version of the Kestrel engine. This developed only a few horsepower less than the heavier engine, so its performance was not adversely affected.

The last major variant was the Hawker Hind bomber, which was introduced in 1934 and began to replace early Harts in squadron service with the RAF in 1936.

Seven RAF squadrons flew the Hart from British airfields, while the Auxiliary Air Force had eight squadrons that were equipped with the type. Harts were still being flown by the RAF on the North-West Frontier in 1939, although at home they had been phased out in favour of the Hind.

It has been said that one of the drawbacks of the Hart was that it was too good. Such was its superiority at first over even the best fighters of the day that to a parsimonious government it became the answer to the problem of how to build a 'one-type air force'. Of course the RAF and Fleet Air Arm never even came near having nothing but Hart variants, but these were so prolific that they stultified the design teams and, to a considerable

SPECIFICATION

Country of origin: Great Britain.

Manufacturer: Hawker Aircraft.

Type: Two-seat day bomber.

Year: 1928.

Engine: 525hp Rolls-Royce Kestrel IB water-cooled V12.

Wingspan: 11.35m (37ft 3in).

Length: 8.93m (29ft 4in).

Height: 3.2m (10ft 5in).

Weight: 2066kg (4558lb).

Maximum speed: 296km/h (184mph).

Ceiling: 6500m (21,320ft).

Range: 740km (460 miles).

Armament: One synchronized 0.303in Vickers machine gun, one 0.303in Lewis gun. Bombload of up to 236kg (520lb) under the wings.

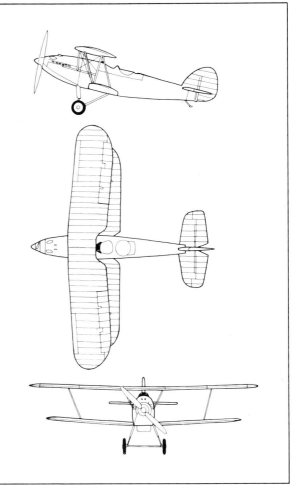

degree, held back the introduction of new technology. After all, the Hart had structure and aerodynamics hardly different from a Camel or D.H.4. The nose looked more pointed and the skeleton was metal rather than wood, but when the final Hectors (an odd version with wings made straight to balance the heavy Napier Dagger 805-hp engine) and Hinds were coming off the line only just before the start of World War II they could be seen to be relics of a bygone age.

The Hart was designed and flown at a time when there was little or no military action around the world and so its bombs were almost never dropped in anger; almost, because the Pegasus-engined Harts built under licence in Sweden finally saw some limited action when they were flown by volunteers with the Finnish Air Force during the 1939-40 Russo-Finnish War.

Pratt & Whitney R-1340-27 9 cylinder Wasp radial air-cooled engine.
Maximum speed 225mph. Armed with two forward-firing
0.30 in Browning machine guns.

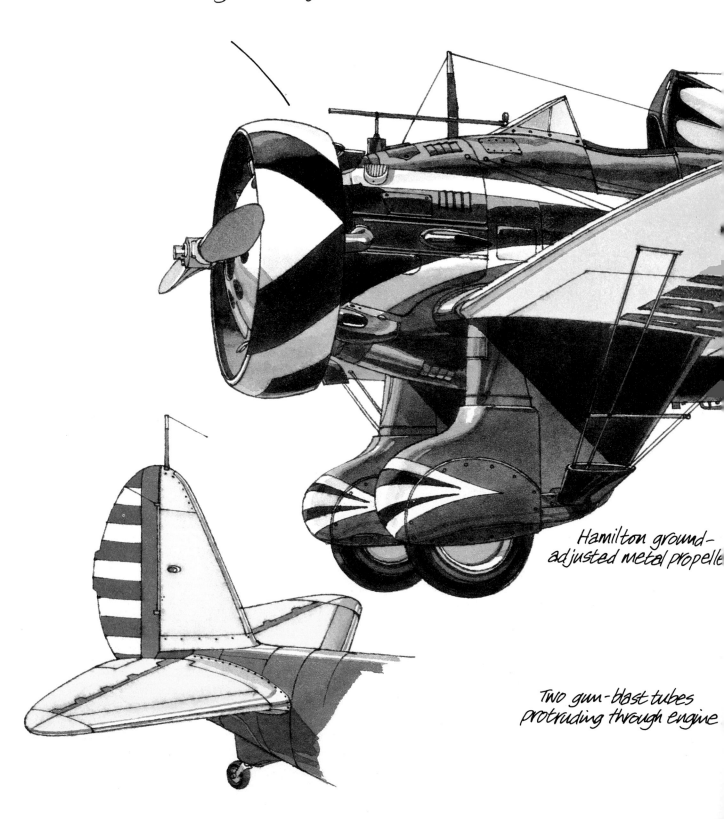

Hamilton ground-
adjusted metal propeller

Two gun-blast tubes
protruding through engine

BOEING P-26

Aircraft of 34th Pursuit
squadron - based at March Field,
California, 1934.

BOEING P-26

The Boeing P-26 was known as the Peashooter. On 7 December 1941, when America was hurled into the war by the Japanese attack on Pearl Harbor, the nickname gained tragic extra significance. In the Philippines the local airforce had some of the last surviving P-26s.

As the hordes of carrier-based Japanese aircraft came in, wave after wave, they were hardly interrupted in their task of escorting the bombers by the handful of Peashooters. And for the amount of damage their two 0.5in machine guns could inflict, they might well have *been* peashooters.

The P-26 was jointly designed in 1931 by the Boeing Airplane Company and the US Army Air Corps, to meet the latter's specification for a pursuit aircraft. However, the Army Air Corps had seen the need to replace their biplane fighters with something a little more modern. Boeing was already producing streamlined aeroplanes with all-metal, stressed-skin structures. Martin was about to fly a bomber which combined the new construction with variable-pitch propellers and retractable landing gear. But the army did not want too many innovations and agreed with Boeing that the new fighters should be a braced-wing monoplane with a fixed undercarriage. The Peashooter first took to the air on 20 March 1932. Its nine-cylinder, 600hp Pratt & Whitney Wasp SR-1340-33 radial engine towed it along at a handy 233mph maximum. Two further prototypes were built, one for static testing and one, in a radical departure, for service testing by operational squadrons. This move was designed to reduce the time lag between first flight and full-scale production. These early flights led to the urgent development of wing flaps to reduce the landing speed. Even with flaps, this proved to

be rather high at 73mph, especially for a fixed-undercarriage aeroplane. One early modification, particularly important for its training role, was the addition of a steel tripod just behind the pilot's head. This became necessary in order to halt the growing number of fatalities caused by P-26s turning over on landing.

Today we can see that, whereas in the 15 years following World War I the only real advance in fighter design was the introduction of more powerful and more reliable engines, by 1933 the entire aerodynamic and structural design was beginning to change. All-metal stressed-skin construction not only made aircraft tougher and better able to stand up to harsh front-line use but it also made it possible to build cantilever monoplanes with quite thin wings, yet without bracing struts or wires. As noted, Boeing and the Army agreed to keep bracing wires on the P-26; it was the last American fighter that would require any.

Another major feature was the use of an air-cooled radial engine. At first glance these flat-fronted engines appear to offer high drag and make high speeds impossible. In practice they offer many advantages. They work well in extremes of temperature, where water-cooled engines overheat or freeze up. Much shorter than other engines, they make fighters more manoeuvrable. Their installed weight in 1933 was often half that of the rival type, with its heavy water-filled radiator and piping, and the latter not only added drag but was vulnerable in combat. In the P-26 the engine was surrounded by a 'Townend ring' which reduced drag. Later radial engines were fully enclosed and as streamlined as those found in any rival engines.

Tooling up for production took most of 1933 and the first production P-26A was completed in December. P-26s were then delivered to no less than 17 squadrons based throughout the United States, the Caribbean and Hawaii.

It was in 1933, following a major exercise at March Field in July, that the strategists in the Army Air Corps concluded that the future role of the single-seat pursuit aircraft would be strictly limited. This view wasn't held universally, but it carried enough weight to delay the commitment to design new single-seaters by several years. Consequently, by the mid-1930s, the P-26 was obsolete by European standards. The little aircraft's importance stems not from its outright performance, but from the fact that it was America's best fighter for many years. What it may have lacked in actual combat ability, it made up for in successfully training American pilots for the giant conflict to come.

SPECIFICATION

Country of origin: USA.

Manufacturer: Boeing Airplane Company.

Type: Single-seat day fighter.

Year: 1932.

Engine: 600hp Pratt & Whitney SR-1340-33 Wasp nine-cylinder radial.

Wingspan: 8.52m (27ft 11in).

Length: 7.28m (23ft 9in).

Height: 3.1m (10ft).

Weight: 1430kg (3153lb).

Maximum speed: 378km/h (235mph).

Ceiling: 8530m (28,000ft).

Range: 580km (360 miles).

Armament: One 0.3in and one 0.5in Browning machine guns or two of 0.5in calibre; provision for 90kg (200lb) of bombs.

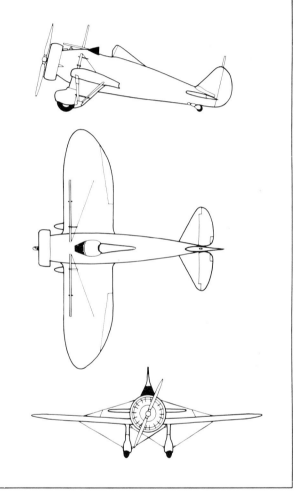

We have hardly mentioned the Peashooter's armament. This is understandable as, by modern standards, it almost didn't exist. Two puny 0.3in fuselage-mounted machine guns meant that the P-26 was heavily undergunned, although later the guns were replaced by larger 0.5in versions.

A final word should go to Major Ira C. Eaker who, when he first flew the P-26, was impressed by its manoeuvrability, loop, roll, climb and dive capability. He went on to say 'All of us who learned our fighter tactics and how to fly and shoot in the little P-26 always . . . had a real nostalgia for this little toy with which we grew to the maturity and experience required for air battles against the Luftwaffe's Focke-Wulf Fw 190 and the Japanese Zero.' It had earned its place in the history of military aviation.

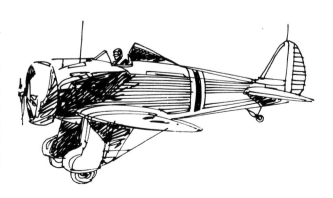

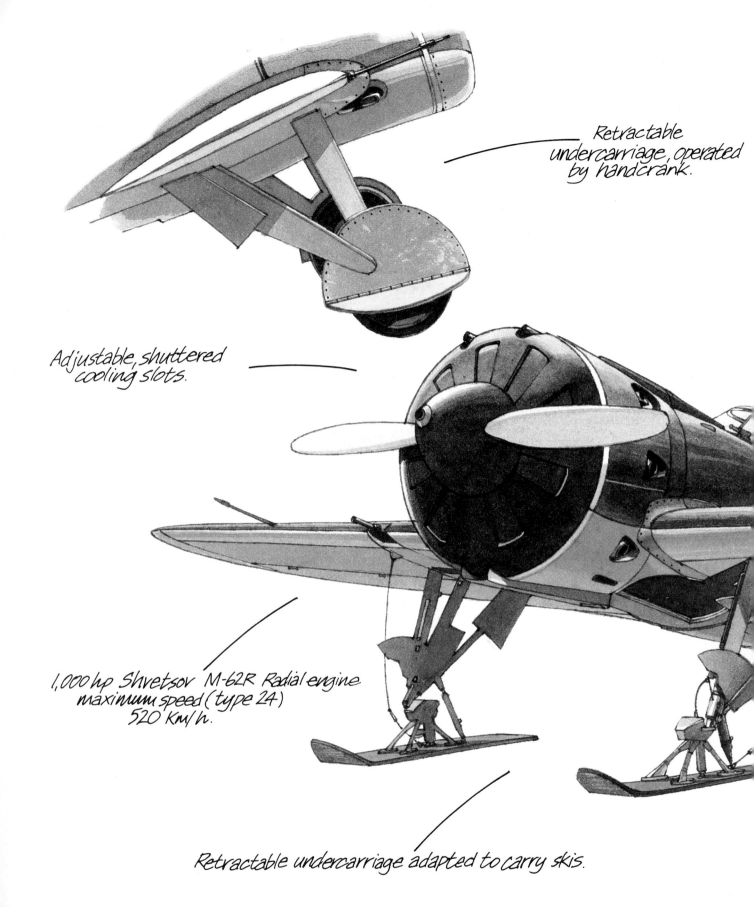

Retractable
undercarriage, operated
by handcrank.

Adjustable, shuttered
cooling slots.

1,000 hp Shvetsov M-62R Radial engine
maximum speed (type 24)
520 Km/h.

Retractable undercarriage adapted to carry skis.

POLIKARPOV I-16

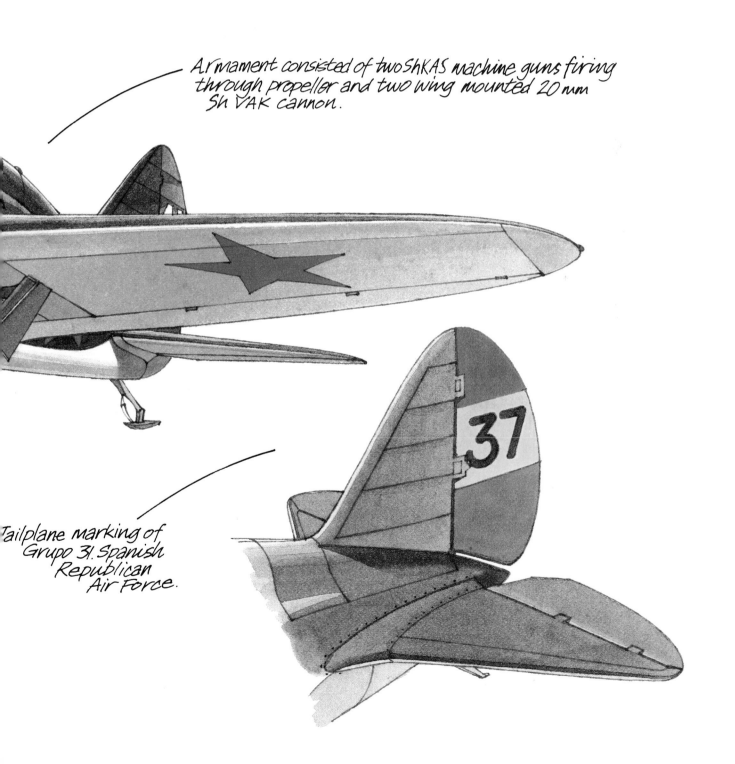

Armament consisted of two ShKAS machine guns firing through propeller and two wing mounted 20 mm ShVAK cannon.

Tailplane marking of Grupo 31. Spanish Republican Air Force.

POLIKARPOV I-16

In the autumn of 1936, the Spanish Civil War was in full swing. Germany and Italy were supporting the Nationalists in strength, with much more modest assistance for the government forces from France and the Soviet Union.

First aircraft on the scene were the German Junkers Ju 52/3ms and the Heinkel He 51 fighters. The best that the Republicans could pit against them were some elderly French Nieuports. However, it was soon realised that Germany and Italy were using the Spanish Civil War to test new aircraft, pilots and strategic theory, so the Republicans were supplied with a variety of aircraft from several countries. These included a few British Bristol Bulldogs, the American Grumman GE-23 and the Russian Tupolev SB-2 bomber.

But by far the most important fighter to see active service over Spain during the early months of the Civil War was a little-known, but remarkable Russian mono-plane called the Polikarpov I-16. Nikolai Polikarpov designed the I-16 as an alternative to his highly successful biplane, the I-15. The squat little single-seat monoplane made its first flight on 31 December 1933.

It should have set the world alight, but no one in the West was looking. At the time it was first delivered to the Soviet Air Force, the Polikarpov I-16 was easily the most advanced single-seat fighter of its time. It was a cantilever wing monoplane, needing no drag-inducing bracing struts to support the wing. It also had a fully retractable undercarriage and a variable-pitch propeller. True, it was an ugly little beast compared with the elegant biplanes of the time, but its performance was outstanding. The *Rata* (Rat) as it became known by the Nationalists – the Republicans called it the *Mosca* (Fly) – was astonishingly manoeuvrable for a fast monoplane. It had a high rate of roll, it looped with absolute precision and it could out-climb and out-dive the Heinkel biplanes at will.

If it was not the ideal gun platform, the I-16 made up for this with its ability to get itself in a 'killing' position much quicker than its steadier opponents. Being so tiny and with such a large proportion of its flying surfaces being aileron, rudder or elevator, the I-16 was a very sensitive aeroplane to fly. It was definitely not one for beginners, although it's interesting to note that over 1000 two-seat trainer versions were built.

The I-16's undercarriage was retracted manually with a handcrank located between the pilot's feet. With the undercarriage extended, the aircraft became extremely unstable at slow speeds and could easily be stalled, if it wasn't flown all the way down on to the ground.

The first consignment of Polikarpov I-16s to Spain numbered nearly 500, although only 200 or so were ever operational at one time. However, they had an immediate impact on the agile but slow Heinkel He 51s.

Armament generally consisted of two 7.62mm ShKAS machine guns firing through the propeller arc, with two more in the wings. In later types, the wing machine guns were replaced by two ShVAK 20mm cannon. Even later models had under-wing rails to carry two RS-82 rockets. The little I-16 was such an immediate success that the Nationalists were supplied with the Italian Fiat CR.32. Even then, the I-16 proved equal to the task, with the Republican aces such as Captain Andres Garcia Lacalle able to build up an impressive number of victories. Foreign pilots, who were flying with the Republicans and who rejoiced in the superb handling qualities of the I-16, included American Frank Tinker and Russian A.K. Serov.

It was not until the Messerchmitt Bf 109 arrived, which was later to achieve a certain notoriety among the pilots of the RAF, that the Polikarpov I-16s became outclassed, although they achieved reasonable results against the early 109s. But that didn't stop them being used in other theatres of war.

Polikarpov I-16s saw active service with the Chinese in the Sino-Japanese War of 1937-9, and finally were thrown in at the deep end in 1941 by the Russians against the full might of the Luftwaffe. Despite the increased power of their uprated Shvetsov radial air-cooled engine, they were, of course, hopelessly outclassed against the Messer-schmitts. It was only the gallantry of the Russian pilots, who sometimes deliberately flew straight into their opponents, that stopped the Germans from winning total air superior-ity on the Eastern Front.

In all, around 8600 examples were built, including trainers, the last ones entering service as late as 1942. It is a tribute to this little aeroplane's toughness, cheapness and fire-power that it remained the most numerous Soviet fighter until 1943.

From our distant viewpoint we can assess the I-16 fairly, and may find it difficult to understand why it was difficult in World War II. At that time, such was the absence of

SPECIFICATION

I-16 (24)

Country of origin: Soviet Union.

Manufacturer: Polikarpov Design Bureau.

Type: Single-seat fighter.

Year: Prototype, 1933, Type 24, 1941.

Engine: 1000hp Shvetsov M-62R nine-cylinder air-cooled radial.

Wingspan: 9m (29ft 6in).

Length: 6.13m (20ft 1in).

Height: 2.56m (8ft 5in).

Weight: 1912kg (4215lb).

Maximum speed: 520km/h (323mph) at sea level.

Ceiling: 9000m (29,500ft).

Range: 402km (249 miles); 700km (435 miles) with auxiliary tanks.

Armament: Two ShKAS 7.62mm machine guns, two ShVAK 20mm cannon.

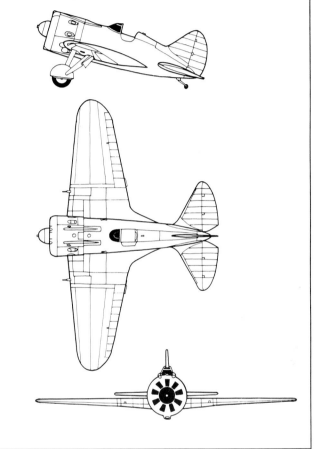

contact with the Soviet Union, it was widely thought by the Western Allies that the I-16 was quite a new design, and that Rata was its real name instead of a derogatory epithet applied by a Spanish enemy. Throughout World War II not one Western pilot is known to have flown an I-16 (though Free French pilots flew all the later Soviet fighters), and the I-16 was almost written off as archaic. So perhaps it was, though at the time of its design it was by far the most modern fighter in the world. Unquestionably, just as the Hart held back newer types in Britain, so did the continued development of the I-16 hold back the introduction of less tricky and more powerful fighters in the Soviet Union.

To a considerable degree the I-16 resembled the Sopwith Camel, in that it was short, stumpy, tricky to fly and dangerous to an inexperienced pilot, yet at the time it was designed quite the best fighter in the world.

Subsequent development, and especially the introduction of outstanding machine guns (firing 50 per cent faster than any others in use) and reliable high-velocity 20mm cannon, served to mask the basic fact that other nations were getting into production with such machines as the Bf 109 and Spitfire, which outclassed the Polikarpov.

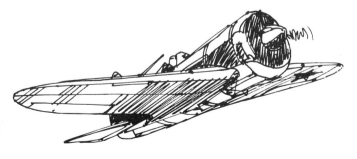

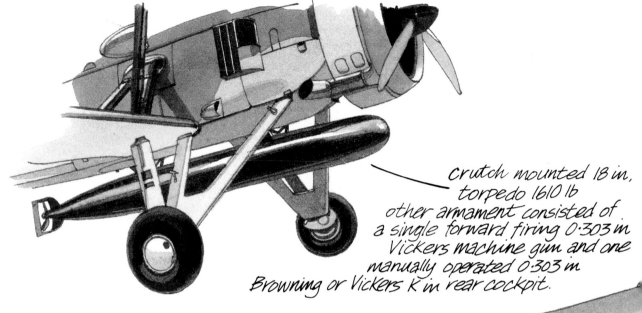

crutch mounted 18 in.
torpedo 1610 lb
other armament consisted of
a single forward firing 0·303 in
Vickers machine gun and one
manually operated 0·303 in
Browning or Vickers K in rear cockpit.

750 hp Pegasus engine, (Mark II and later)
Maximum speed 138 mph. Range with full load 547 miles.

FAIREY SWORDFISH

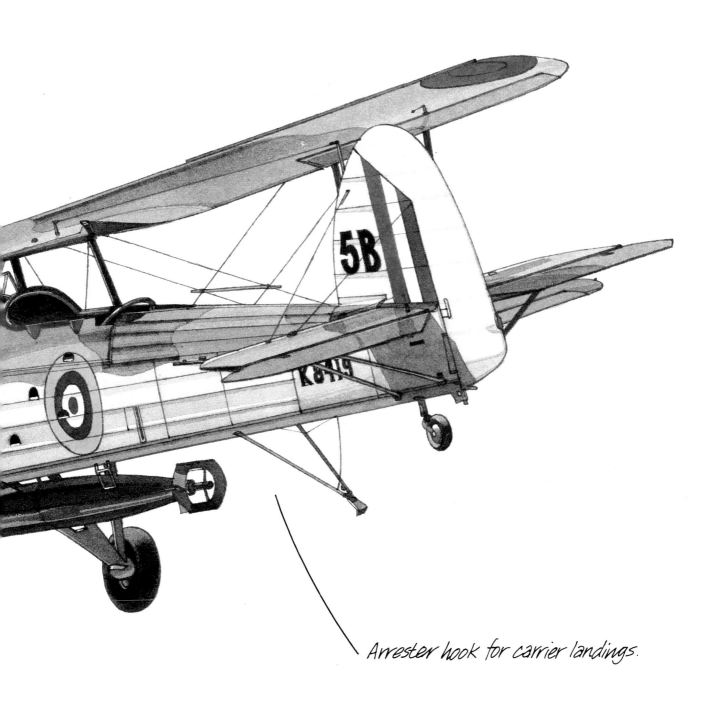

Arrester hook for carrier landings.

FAIREY SWORDFISH

As darkness fell on the evening of 10 November 1940, the Italian fleet was lying at anchor in the great harbour of Taranto. The crews relaxed, secure in the knowledge that for this night, at least, the war was a very long way away.

Hours later, three battleships, the *Littorio*, the *Conte di Cavour* and the *Caio Duilio* were all beached, out of action, or at the bottom of the sea. They had been destroyed by a lumbering biplane that was considered obsolete even before it was built: the Fairey Swordfish.

The Swordfish was first flown in April 1934; it had been designed to a specification (S.38/34) that called for a two/three-seat long-range torpedo-carrying bomber. It was powered by a single 690hp Bristol Pegasus IIIM3 nine-cylinder radial engine. Armament – if you ignored the all-important torpedo – was woefully inadequate, comprising a World War 1-style combination of forward-firing 0.303in Vickers and rear-mounted Lewis gun. It was hardly a match for the multiple guns and cannon of the Messerschmitt and Focke-Wulf fighter monoplanes it had to combat.

Nevertheless, the Swordfish inspired a fierce loyalty in the men who flew it. A long patrol over the North Atlantic in winter must have been one of the worst experiences of the entire war.

Yet the crew who had to carry out these missions, pilots and navigators, have nothing but praise for the 'Stringbag', as the Swordfish was called.

Most Swordfish squadrons were carrier-based and, for this purpose, the Swordfish was ideal. The very qualities which labelled it obsolete were indeed its hidden strengths. The low stalling speed gave its pilots every chance to land safely even in severe weather. That said, sorties were flown in conditions that made flying almost impossible. The decks of the auxiliary carriers could be plunging 50 or 60ft up and down in heavy seas. There was no way, either, that these hastily converted merchant ships could heave-to, as they would then become instant prey for the ever-present U-boats.

Apart from Taranto, the exploits of the Swordfish are legion. It was a Swordfish that delivered the torpedo that crippled the steering gear of the *Bismarck*, allowing the British Home Fleet to catch and eventually sink the great warship. One Swordfish squadron, based in Malta, destroyed an average of 50,000 tonnes of enemy ships each month during 1942.

So much for success stories. It also has to be recorded that the Stringbag had its share of failures too. Not least of these was the desperate attempt by the Allies to halt the breakout of the pride of the Germany Navy, the *Scharnhorst*, the *Gneisenau* and the *Prinz Eugen*, from Brest in northern France on 12 February 1942. Swordfish sent up to attack the German fleet were shot out of the sky, both by the naval guns and by umbrella cover provided by massed Focke-Wulf Fw 190s.

Only three crew men returned, and the great ships were not even damaged. As a result of this action the Swordfish's leader, Lieutenant-Commander Eugene Esmonde was posthumously awarded Britain's most distinguished medal, the Victoria Cross.

The Swordfish was an extremely large aeroplane with a wingspan of 45ft 6in, length 35ft 8in and a height of over 12ft. These dimensions should have made it clumsy and awkward to handle. But the reverse was the case. Time after time Swordfish pilots escaped from much faster, more heavily armed opponents by their superior agility. Along the coast of Norway, Fleet Air Arm pilots learned to entice Messerschmitt Bf 109 pilots deep into the heart of fjords, twisting and turning close to the cliff sides. Not only would the Swordfish escape; the faster, but less manoeuvrable monoplanes would sometimes become jammed in the narrow fjord and come to grief.

The Swordfish was built in conventional biplane style with an all-metal fabric-covered airframe, but its powerful Pegasus radial allowed a fair amount of armour plating to be fitted forward of the cockpit area. The propeller was a massive three-bladed affair, no less than 12ft in diameter. Wings had to be folded manually.

In all, 2391 Swordfish were built, well over half of them by Blackburn Aircraft. The last aircraft were delivered in June 1944. From 1943 all Swordfish carried rails for 8 rockets and many had a closed cockpit and radar mounted between the landing gear.

To look back at this truly great machine from a distance of 40 years we can see that it represented perfect fitness for purpose in all respects except survivability against either modern fighters or large warships, whose murderous fire caused severe (sometimes 100 per cent) casualties among attacking Swordfish. Its good points were its

SPECIFICATION

Mk I

Country of origin: Great Britain.

Manufacturer: Fairey Aviation Company.

Type: Two-seat torpedo bomber.

Year: 1935.

Engine: 690hp Bristol Pegasus IIIM3 air-cooled nine-cylinder radial.

Wingspan: 13.87m (45ft 6in).

Length: 10.87m (35ft 8in).

Height: 3.76m (12ft 4in).

Weight: 3400kg (7496lb).

Maximum speed: 222km/h (138mph).

Ceiling: 5867m (19,250ft).

Range: 880km (547 miles) with torpedo.

Armament: One synchronized 0.303in Vickers machine gun and at the back one Vicker's K or Lewis 0.303in machine gun. One 18in (457mm) torpedo or 680kg (1500lb) bomb load or eight rockets.

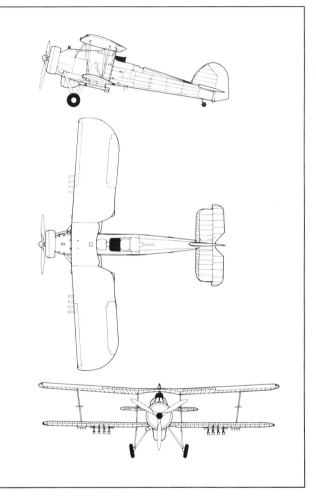

absolutely robust, easily repaired generous-sized airframe, reliable engine and amazingly docile qualities. It became routine to fly when all other carrier-based aircraft were grounded. In a foul winter blizzard, at night, a 'Stringbag' could be hauled off the deck at maximum weight at just over 50 knots and flung into a tight climbing turn just above the sea with complete assurance. The well-muffled crew then might rumble along to a target six hours away and still do their work and slam back on the pitching deck in the certain knowledge that they would make the arrival on deck first time, unfailingly pick up a wire and that the mighty widespread landing gears would take the strain. What aircraft but Swordfish could have taken off from the torpedoed escort carrier *Nabob* despite the fact that the short flight deck was sloping upwards towards the bows at over 20 degrees?

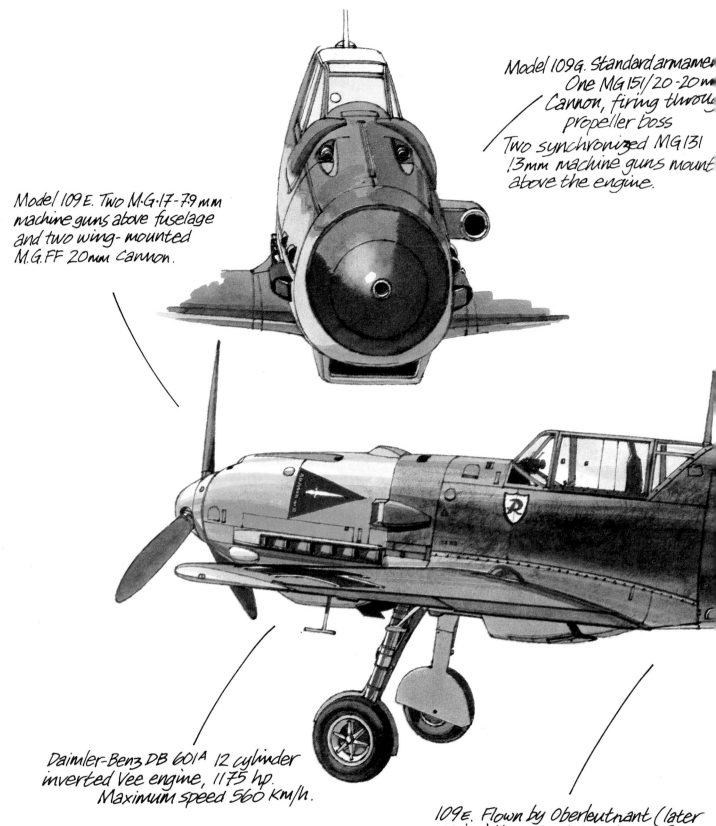

Model 109G. Standard armament
One MG 151/20-20 m
Cannon, firing throug
propeller boss
Two synchronized MG131
13mm machine guns mount
above the engine.

Model 109E. Two M.G.17-7.9 mm
machine guns above fuselage
and two wing-mounted
M.G.FF 20mm Cannon.

Daimler-Benz DB 601A 12 cylinder
inverted Vee engine, 1175 hp.
Maximum speed 560 Km/h.

109E. Flown by Oberleutnant (later
Major) Helmut Wick. Belgium 1940
56 Victories.

MESSERSCHMITT Bf 109

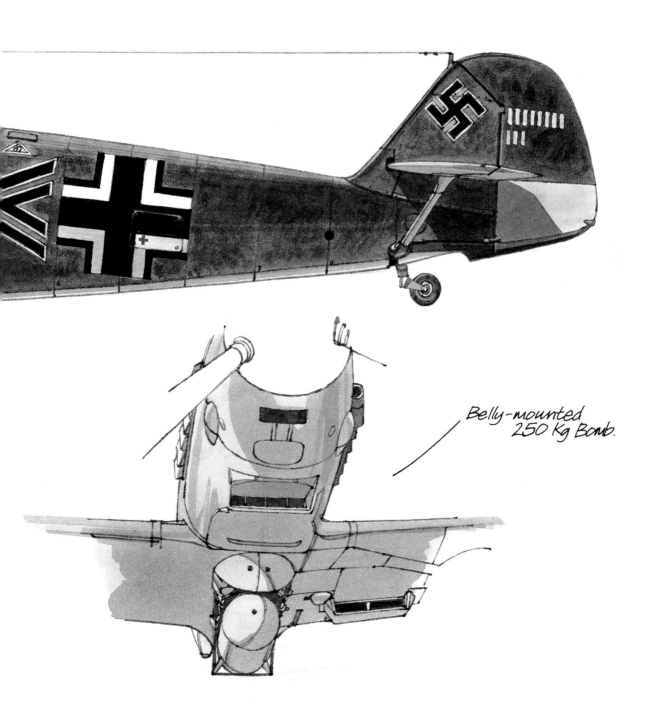

Belly-mounted
250 Kg Bomb.

MESSERSCHMITT Bf 109

The legendary story of the Messerschmitt Bf 109 began in 1933 when the German Air Ministry announced a competition for a new fighter. Very reluctantly they allowed Willy Messerschmitt to take part. They thought his entry would come last. The prototype Bf 109 flew in late May 1935, powered by a British Rolls-Royce Kestrel engine because the Jumo 210 was not ready. Having seen it, the officials almost laughed. The rakish small-wing monoplane looked more like a racer. Luftwaffe procurement chief Ernst Udet proclaimed: 'That thing will never make a fighter!' That was before he flew it.

Subsequently the 109 so turned the tables on its detractors that by the start of World War II it was the standard single-seat fighter of the Luftwaffe. It swept opposition from the sky all over Europe, was built in larger numbers than any other single type of fighter, and shot down approximately twice as many aircraft as any other aircraft in history.

The Bf 109 cut its fighting teeth several years previously, during the Spanish Civil War. The He 51 biplanes of the German Kondor Legion were being severely mauled by the faster and much more deadly Polikarpov I-16s supplied to the Republicans by the Soviet Union. However, when in 1937 the Kondor Legion was re-equipped with some of the first production Bf 109s, the tables were turned with a vengeance.

Only a handful of Bf 109s saw service in Spain, but they were so superior to anything then in the sky that their effect was tremendous. Meantime, back in Germany, a totally unrelated Messerschmitt racer, with a specially boosted engine, set a world speed record which stood unchallenged for 30 years. The Nazi propaganda machine called the racer the 'Messerschmitt 109R' to give the impression that it was a version of the fighter.

Following the Spanish conflict, the next serious test for the Bf 109 came when 200 of them formed the spearhead of Germany's attack on Poland on 1 September 1939. The Poles had around 160 fighters, mostly their own PZL P.11c gull-winged monoplanes, and something like the same number of modern bombers. When the smoke cleared, Germany had lost fewer than 80 fighters, while Poland's casualties totalled some 350 aircraft, although around 120

of these (both fighters and bombers) had been interned in neutral Rumania.

So Messerschmitt's new fighter was flying high, but a little under one year later, when the Battle of Britain began in earnest in August 1940, the hitherto victorious Bf 109 finally met with some real opposition. One of its problems was that it had an operational endurance over southern England of only 20 to 30 minutes, and the Hurricanes and Spitfires of the Royal Air Force proved to be formidable adversaries.

On the day planned for the Luftwaffe's major assault in the Battle of Britain, code-named *Adlertag* (Eagle Day), 30 Messerschmitt Bf 109Es, headed by Major Günther von Maltzahn, took off from Dinan and set a course for the sky high over Dorset. One of the pilots in the second wave of fighters, Leutnant Heinz Pfannschmidt, very quickly found himself in the worst kind of trouble.

The Spitfires of 609 Squadron had scrambled from Warmwell to intercept the raiders and were already airborne and waiting. Pfannschmidt was caught in the gunsight of a Spitfire flown by Pilot Officer D. M. Crook, and a two-second burst from eight 0.303in Browning machine guns sent the German machine spiralling crazily down to crash in the waters of Poole harbour.

This was the first recorded shooting-down on *Adlertag* of a Bf 109; but it proved, as the Battle of Britain progressed, to be the first of hundreds. The Luftwaffe was forced to accept the simple truth that the Bf 109 was not at all suitable as a bomber escort. Its range was far too limited.

So its role was switched to that of defensive fighter and fighter-bomber. With the introduction of the improved Bf 109G, the type took on a whole new lease of life. It was in a Bf 109G-14 that Major Erich 'Bubi' Hartmann scored most of his unrivalled total of 352 confirmed 'kills', and Bf 109Gs and Ks remained largely unchanged right to the end of hostilities in May 1945.

From the start of development, the 109 excelled in most flight manoeuvres, its climb and dive capability was unrivalled and general handling at low speeds exceptional. Spinning trials showed behaviour better than any existing German biplane fighter, and even the much-criticised narrow landing gear was a deliberate design feature with many advantages. At high speeds the control forces increased dramatically, until at speeds near 644km/h in a dive, the rate of roll was almost zero, unless the pilot was very strong. Oddly, trivial deficiencies such as the lack of a rudder trimmer – which made flight very tiring when trying to fly straight at high speed – lasted almost to the end of production in 1944. Many experts on the 109

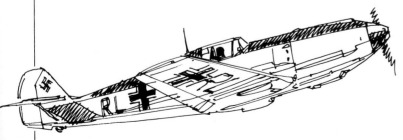

SPECIFICATION

Bf 109E

Country of origin: Germany.

Manufacturer: Messerschmitt AG.

Type: Single-seat fighter-bomber.

Year: 1939 (prototype 1935).

Engine: 1175hp Daimler-Benz DB601A liquid-cooled V12.

Wingspan: 9.87m (32ft 4in).

Length: 8.64m (28ft 4in).

Height: 2.28m (7ft 5in).

Weight: 2505kg (5523lb).

Maximum speed: 560km/h (347mph).

Ceiling: 10,500m (34,450ft).

Range: 700km (435 miles).

Armament: Typically two synchronized 7.92mm MG 17 machine guns above engine and two MG FF 20mm cannon in wings.

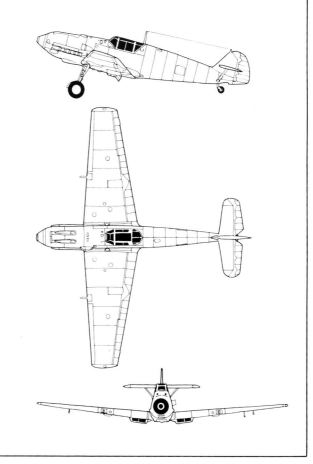

considered the 1941 version, the 109F, the nicest to fly. Many stuck to it in preference to the more powerful, heavier and much more heavily armed 'Gustav', the 109G, which was far more numerous than all the other versions added together.

A little-known fact about the Bf 109 is that in 1939 the German High Command, worried by Britain's naval superiority, ordered a sea-borne version of the fighter for operation from the aircraft carrier *Graf Zeppelin*. The main structural difference, apart from the fitting of an arrester hook and catapult spools, was an increase in wing span of 108cm, folding down for hangar storage to an overall width of 4.95m. This naval version was designated the Bf 109T.

Though it was on the losing side, the Messerschmitt Bf 109 was probably the most important fighter of World War II. Not only did it shoot down far more aircraft than any other type in history, but it also, initially backed up by no other fighter except the big twin-engined Bf 110, took on the air forces of Spain, Poland, Denmark, Norway, the Netherlands, Belgium, France, Yugoslavia and Greece and eliminated them as fighting forces.

It is calculated that some 30,500 were produced, and this figure does not include those which were built in Czechoslovakia for service with the Czech Air Force and Israel, or those built by Hispano in Spain. Many of these Spanish post-war productions, known as Ha-1109s and Ha-1112s, were still on active service as late as the mid-1950s, and one curious aspect of this longevity is that the wheel had turned full circle. The final Iberian version, the Ha-1112 was powered, as was the original prototype, by a British Rolls-Royce engine, in this instance a Merlin. These in fact acted the part of Daimler-Benz powered Bf 109Es in the film *Battle of Britain*.

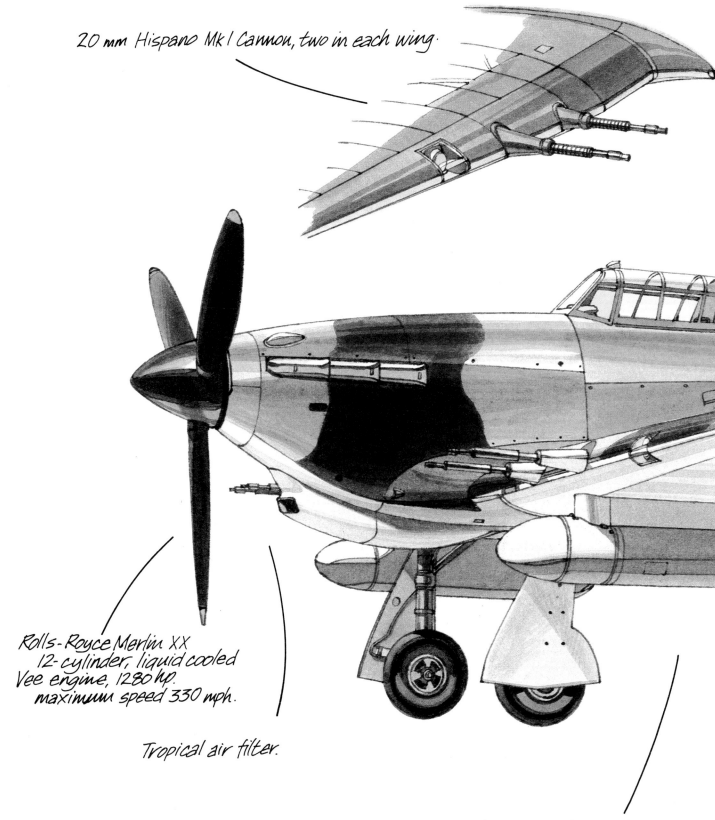

20 mm Hispano Mk I Cannon, two in each wing.

Rolls-Royce Merlin XX
12-cylinder, liquid cooled
Vee engine, 1280 hp.
maximum speed 330 mph.

Tropical air filter.

40 gallon long-range fuel tank,
two carried.

HAWKER HURRICANE

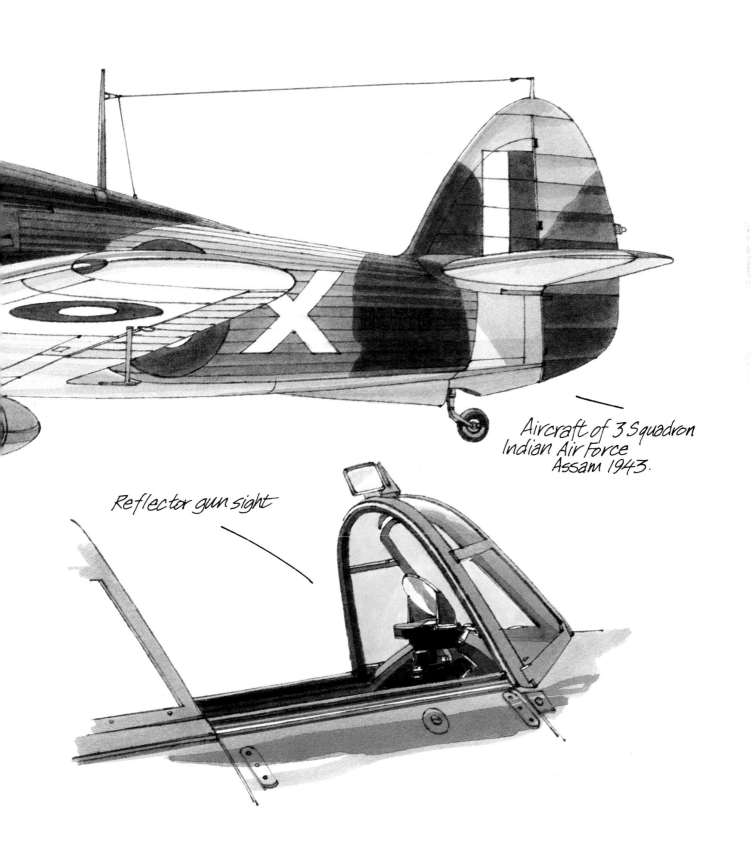

Aircraft of 3 Squadron
Indian Air Force
Assam 1943.

Reflector gun sight

HAWKER HURRICANE

If ever one aircraft could be said to have saved a nation, it was the Hawker Hurricane during the summer and autumn of 1940.

No one can ignore the immense contribution that was made by the Supermarine Spitfire in the Battle of Britain, but by virtue of the fact that there were far more Hurricanes in service at that time and that these aircraft recorded a greater number of victories, for once the magnificent Spitfire has to take second place.

In July 1940, Adolf Hitler reluctantly came to the conclusion that Britain was not going to be reasonable and surrender, and so he gave orders for an invasion fleet to be assembled. One important objective remained before an invasion could proceed: control of the skies over the English Channel. This could be achieved only through the destruction of the RAF's Fighter Command.

The Battle of Britain was about to begin. It was a battle that, if viewed objectively, the Luftwaffe should have won easily, for they were able to draw on far greater numbers of battle-hardened pilots and proven aircraft. However, the RAF had one important psychological advantage. They were fighting over their home territory. This meant that a parachute descent or a forced landing would not result in imprisonment for the duration of the war, but a quick return to squadron service.

Another crucial factor was that, whereas Britain had just one objective – survival – Hitler ordered the Luftwaffe to

undertake a number of different tasks. These included the destruction of British fighter bases and the all-important radar stations, attacks on Allied shipping in the Channel and (in due course) indiscriminate bombing of Britain's capital city, London.

From the outset, things didn't go well for the British. Although the Hurricane pilots were steadily outscoring their opponents, the rate of attrition of both men and machines meant that Air Chief Marshal Dowding had to switch his limited squadrons around, trying to fool the Germans that he had greater resources. This pattern continued throughout August and it was only poor German intelligence that hid the true desperate plight of Fighter Command from Reichsmarschall Hermann Goering.

At the beginning of September Fighter Command was on the verge of defeat when, amazingly, the Luftwaffe switched their attacks away from the fighter bases and on to London. This piece of unbelievably inept strategy was almost certainly the result of pure accident. On 24 August German Heinkel He IIIs and Junkers Ju 88s mistakenly dropped their bombs over London's East End instead of their intended target, the oil storage tanks on the estuary of the River Thames. Immediate retaliation by British Bomber Command was a raid on Berlin, which caused Hitler to order the destruction of Britain's cities, starting with London.

With the pressure off their airfields and with greatly increased aircraft production, Fighter Command appeared to have absorbed the worst that Germany could throw at them. It certainly seemed so to the authorities in Berlin, where on 17 September, Hitler ordered the dispersal of the invasion fleet. The threat of an immediate landing was over.

So much for the facts of the Battle of Britain. What about the modest single-seater fighter that had done more than any other to influence its outcome? Sydney Camm, who was responsible for the beautiful Hawker Hart, designed the Hurricane in 1934-35. Despite its modern appearance, the Hurricane was a compromise in terms of new ideas and traditional construction methods. Instead of using a light metal-skinned monocoque body, it retained the tubular metal cross-braced fabric-covered structure used on between-the-war biplanes. However, a stressed skin metal wing was designed even before the prototype had its first flight on 6 November 1935, and this wing came into production at the start of the war.

The Hurricane was so well received that a first production order for 600 aircraft was made; although the Hawker directors had decided to produce 1000 aircraft in

SPECIFICATION

Mk I

Country of origin: Great Britain.

Manufacturer: Hawker Aircraft.

Type: Single-seat fighter.

Year: 1937.

Engine: 1030hp Rolls-Royce Merlin III liquid-cooled V12.

Wingspan: 12.19m (40ft).

Length: 9.55m (31ft 5in).

Height: 4m (13ft 1in).

Weight: 3397kg (7490lb).

Maximum speed: 519km/h (322mph).

Ceiling: 10,365m (34,000ft).

Range: 813km (505 miles).

Armament: Eight 0.303in Browning machine guns.

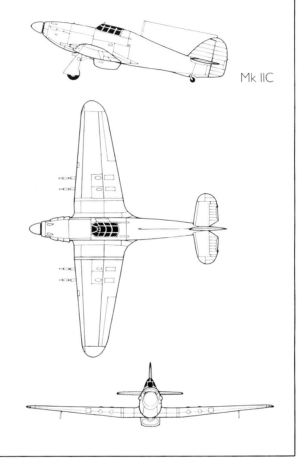

Mk IIC

early 1936, long before the official order was received. The engine was Rolls-Royce's marvellous V12 Merlin, the same engine that powered the Spitfire. The obsolete wooden two-bladed propeller was replaced in 1940 by a constant-speed three-blader making it more efficient at altitude.

There is no doubt that in almost every aspect of performance, the Hurricane was marginally inferior to its main opponent, the Messerschmitt Bf 109. The 109 could out-climb, out-dive and out-roll it, but the Hurricane had two important assets. It could fly a tighter-radius turn, allowing it to get inside the Messerschmitt during dogfights, and it provided a steady gun platform for its eight 0.303in Brownings. At the same time, it could absorb a lot of punishment without falling out of the sky. In June 1940, the Mk II Hurricane reached Fighter Command, fitted with an uprated Merlin XX 1280hp engine. These changes made

the Hurricane far more versatile and gave it the performance necessary for its wider role in other war theatres. These included Europe, North Africa, Malta, the Far East, and the Soviet Union which received nearly 3000 aircraft, some fitted with skis.

In all, 14,231 Hurricanes were built, 1451 of them in Canada. There can be no doubt that it was one of the most important fighters of World War II.

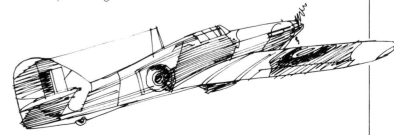

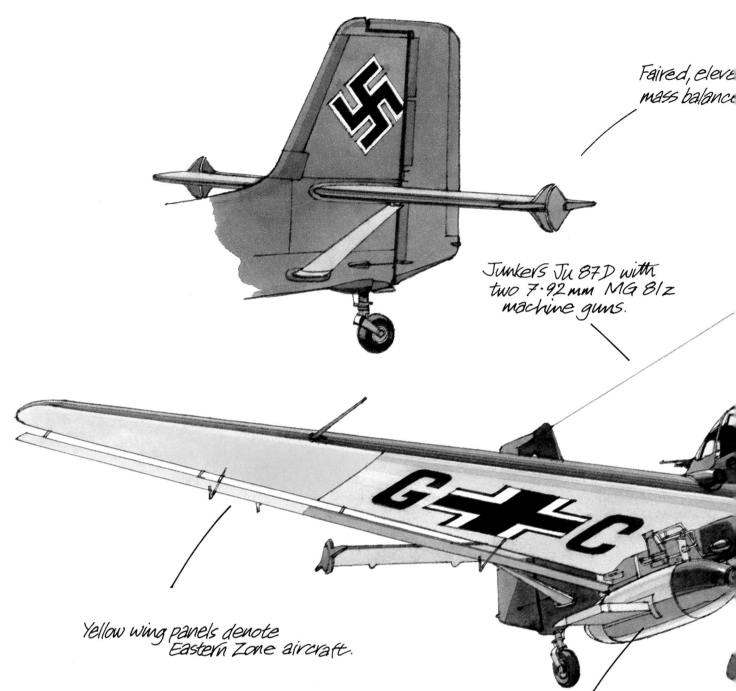

Faired, eleve
mass balance

Junkers Ju 87D with
two 7·92 mm MG 81z
machine guns.

Yellow wing panels denote
Eastern Zone aircraft.

Two pod-mounted 37mm Flak cannon carried.

JUNKERS Ju 87
'STUKA'

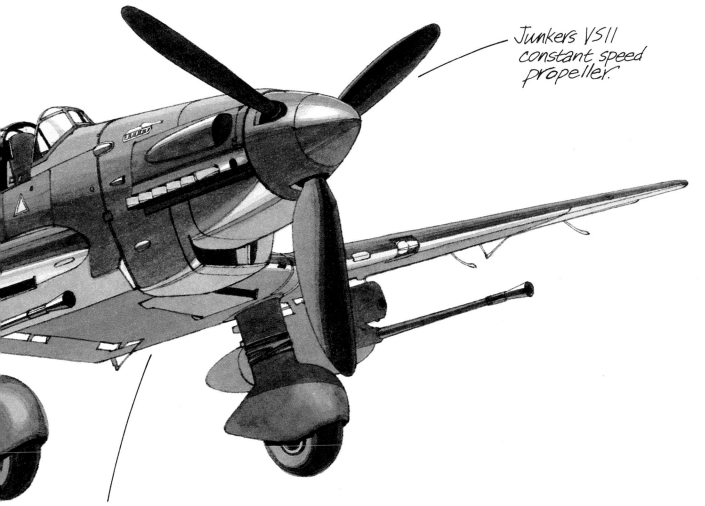

Junkers VS11
constant speed
propeller.

1500 hp Junkers Jumo 211P liquid-cooled
inverted V12 engine.

JUNKERS Ju 87 'STUKA'

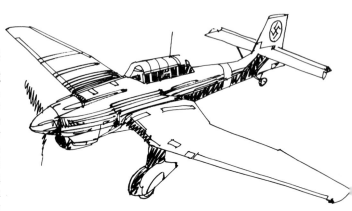

In spite of the fact that it was really good at only one thing, and virtually useless in almost any other capacity, the Ju 87 was undoubtedly the most feared Luftwaffe aircraft during the early part of the war. Universally known as the 'Stuka', which was an abbreviation of *Sturzkampfflugzeug*, the German for dive-bomber, its large fixed undercarriage and odd cranked wings gave it an appearance of ugly menace. This, sometimes coupled with the banshee screaming of dive-activated sirens (said to have been fitted following a suggestion made by Hitler himself), had a powerful psychological effect. The Stuka probably struck more terror into the hearts of more people than any other air-to-ground attack weapon, not excluding the V1 flying bomb.

The history of aviation is riddled with ironies: the first prototype of this scourge of Britain's ground and sea forces was fitted with a British engine, the Rolls-Royce Kestrel. German interest in dive-bombers began in World War 1, and it never really waned much during the following years of 'peace'. Junkers had been one of the pioneers of all-metal combat aircraft in World War 1, but until well into the 1930s used corrugated skins which caused high drag. By 1934, when the RLM (air ministry) issued its definitive dive-bomber specification, the company had made the transition to smooth stressed skin.

Karl Pohlmann led the Ju 87 design team, and the ungainly prototype of this aircraft was flown at the end of 1935. Faulty design of the tail assembly took a year to rectify, so that it was not until November 1936 that the pre-production Ju 87A-0 left the Dessau factory and finally took to the air. The resulting Ju 87A-1 was put into production in 1937, with huge 'trousers' over the main landing gear, and when it first saw action, with the Legion Kondor in Spain, the unprecedented precision of its bombing shocked the Republican forces considerably. In all but the worst weather conditions, the Ju 87A-1s were able to place their single large bombs (250kg) with devastating accuracy. Both physically and metaphorically, the Stuka had arrived with a bang.

The Ju 87 did indeed embody much that was modern in aircraft design. All were stressed-skin machines with the Junkers high-lift double-wing flap/aileron system, and all were fitted with hinged dive brakes beneath the outer inverted gull wings. New VDM constant-speed propellers were fitted, holding engine rpm at a safe level even in dives of 60° or 70°. Red lines painted on the cockpit side windows at angles of varying degrees with the horizon gave the pilot an indication of the steepness of the dive, and the aircraft was aimed at the target using the sight of the single fixed gun. However, in 1937 and 1938,

sometimes due to ground mist, or pilot black-out or simply because of pilot error, several Stukas failed to pull out of their dives in time and crashed.

But for several more years, up to 1942, the Stuka continued to revel in its reputation of colossal striking power and its reign of terror went unchecked. With the introduction in 1938 of the spatted Ju 87B, the excellent Jumo 211 engine, with direct fuel injection, replaced the previous Jumo 210, approximately doubling the power, and a simple autopilot was installed in order to help eliminate the fatal hazard of failure to pull out of a dive.

The Ju 87B was a far better all-round performer than its predecessor, and its shrieking appearance over battlefields when World War II broke out was guaranteed to create maximum panic. In the four-week Blitzkrieg on Poland the effect of the Ju 87B can only be described as shattering. It was responsible for wiping out most of a Polish infantry division during an attack on the railway yards at Pyotrkow. Ju 87Bs also carried out the destruction of all but two of the main surface ships of the Polish navy, and they ravaged Polish forces during close ground conflicts, often with the German troops only 100 metres away.

In some ways, 1940 was a very good year for the Stuka. In April a flight of the long-range Ju 87R version played a major role in Operation *Weserübung*, the invasion of Norway. An attack over Norwegian waters resulted in the sinking of several important Allied warships. In May, almost every Stuka in the Luftwaffe took part in the massive German drives through the Low Countries and France. Later, they were to press south through Yugoslavia and on to Greece and Crete.

But in another and perhaps more important respect, 1940 was also the year during which the hitherto unstoppable Stuka suffered its first real defeat. From mid-August, Stuka activity in the skies over Britain was forced to cease. The devastation of virtually defenceless ground forces was one thing: fighting in the air was something else, and to the Spitfires and Hurricanes, the

SPECIFICATION

Ju 87B

Country of origin: Germany.

Manufacturer: Junkers Flugzeug-und Motorenwerke AG. and Weser Flugzeugbau.

Type: Two-seat dive bomber.

Year: 1938.

Engine: 1200hp Junkers Jumo 211 Da liquid-cooled V12.

Wingspan: 13.8m (45ft 3in).

Length: 11.1m (36ft 5in).

Height: 3.9m (12ft 9in).

Weight: 4250kg (9370lb).

Maximum speed: 390km/h (242mph).

Ceiling: 8000m (26,250ft).

Range: 600km (373 miles).

Armament: Two 7.92mm MG 17 fixed forward-firing machine guns in wings, one 7.92mm MG 15 swivel mounted machine gun in rear cockpit. One 500 kg bomb below fuselage, two 50kg bombs under each wing.

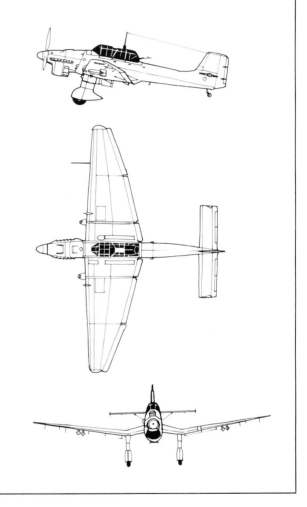

Stuka was almost a sitting duck. Huge numbers were destroyed with ease.

However, this crushing rout of the Stuka in the Battle of Britain was by no means an indication that its usefulness was at an end. Far from it. Ju 87s went on to be deployed with considerable success in many other theatres of war, and one proud unit continued right up to the Allied victory in 1945. Ju 87Ds, with longer span, more power and an 1800kg bombload, saw a great deal of action over the Eastern Front. These greatly improved versions were fitted with heavier armour and better firepower for service as low-level close-support aircraft, though dive bombing continued against specific targets. The Ju 87G series, urged upon the Luftwaffe chiefs by the most famous Stuka pilot, Hans-Ulrich Rudel, was armed with two 37mm Flak 18 tank-busting guns each with a magazine of six rounds. All Stukas could be fitted with skis for winter take-offs and landings, and Ju 87s went on with their harassment of Russian armour and infantry until the end of that long campaign. Finally, Rudel was credited with a battleship, a cruiser, a destroyer, hundreds of lesser ships and over 800 vehicles including 519 tanks.

In September 1944, the German High Command issued an order that all aircraft production other than that of fighters was to cease immediately. Only then did the Weser factory, which built the Stuka, stop turning out their Ju 87s, having by this time reached a total of just over 5700. With the possible exception of Rudel, not even the men who flew it could deny that the Stuka was a rather ugly brute; but equally, no one will ever forget it.

Aircraft in colours of 152 Squadron, Burma.

MT557 UM⊙E

Armed with Four 0·303 in Browning Mk II machine guns and two 20 mm British Hispano cannon.

SUPERMARINE
SPITFIRE

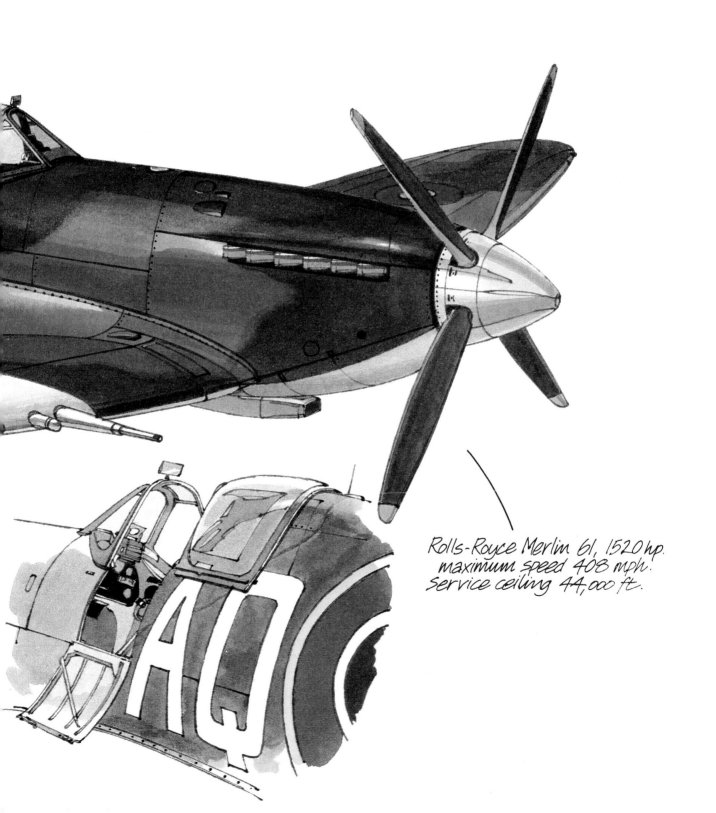

Rolls-Royce Merlin 61, 1520 h.p.
maximum speed 408 m.p.h.
service ceiling 44,000 ft.

SUPERMARINE SPITFIRE

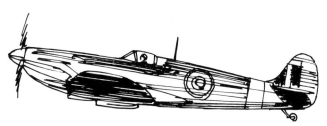

To the British, the Spitfire was more than an aeroplane; it was a symbol. After the fall of France, when Britain stood alone and Germany was poised to launch a massive invasion across the English Channel, Britain's only protection seemed to be a handful of Spitfires and their incredibly brave pilots.

This was quite untrue, because at that time Fighter Command had many more Hawker Hurricanes in service than Spitfires, and they performed just as well as their more illustrious counterparts. But, that said, the Spitfire proved to have far more potential for development. It was perhaps the finest fighting aeroplane of World War II, if not of all time.

So much has been written about the Spitfire and its rightful place in history that it would serve little purpose to add yet more glowing, impassioned passages to the legend. Instead, we will take a factual look at this marvellous aeroplane, from its inception to its final days in post-war service.

Like so many aircraft, the Spitfire was a response to a need. That this need was recognised by only a few, not least its designer, Reginald Mitchell, makes the Spitfire's early history all the more remarkable.

In Britain, the early 1930s was a time not merely of peace, but of a wish to disarm and certainly not invent new weapons. With hindsight, it is easy for historians to see the obvious pointers to World War II, but at the time, politicians and other opinion formers were all desperately trying to paper over the cracks in international harmony. In Britain there was no way that large sums could be committed to a military aircraft programme.

Money *was* being spent on aircraft design in the United States and Germany where stressed-skin metal construction was leading to faster and more efficient bombers and passenger-carrying aircraft. The casual observer could have been forgiven for thinking that, in 1930, the only advanced technology in the British aircraft industry was concerned with the next year's Schneider Trophy race, which had popular appeal comparable with winning the World Football Cup today.

By 1934 plans were well advanced in Germany for a single-seat fighter that would prove to be one of the most significant weapons of the conflict to come – the Messerschmitt Bf 109. In the Soviet Union the Polikarpov I-16 already existed and almost all other advanced countries were issuing specifications for equally advanced single-seaters.

It was then, in the summer of 1934, that the British aircraft industry woke up. At the Air Ministry young Squadron Leader Ralph Sorley worked out that future

fighters would need eight machine guns. And at Vickers-Supermarine, Reginald Mitchell tore up his programme to improve the F.7/30 Spitfire, which was already flying, and began the design of a completely new single-seat fighter, the Type 300, which would eventually also be named the Spitfire.

Mitchell had designed the S.5, S.6 and S.6B seaplanes that had won the final three Schneider Trophy races, bringing the trophy to Britain for keeps. This experience helped, but the real keys to the success of his new fighter lay in different directions.

First was his choice of powerplant. The Rolls-Royce P.V.12, later named Merlin, prompted him to design the smallest airframe that could be accommodated around it. More important, perhaps, was his choice of wing aerofoil section, the NACA 2200. Wind-tunnel tests as early as 1927 had shown him that this section, coupled with an elliptical plan-form, would give the low drag characteristics necessary for a world-beating fighter design.

In March 1936 Mitchell's Spitfire made its first flight, from what is today Southampton airport. It was a winner from the start. Within four months the Royal Air Force had placed an initial order for 310 aircraft. At first, production was painfully slow. Supermarine had to divide their time between the Spitfire and the Stranraer and Walrus flying boats, and were designing a large bomber. Moreover the 'Spit' was difficult to make, and Britain had not yet realised they were likely to go to war.

As late as August 1938, when it entered service, many elements within the RAF were undecided about the value, and the potential, of the Spitfire. The Hawker Hurricane, superficially similar but designed along more conventional lines, being larger and of traditional technology, had beaten the Spitfire into service. It was much easier to make and to repair, and was considered by many to be superior. The Spitfire eventually answered its critics effectively.

The Spitfire Mk I, of which more than 1500 were built at Southampton, was powered by the Rolls-Royce Merlin II which developed 1030hp. Armament was at first only four 0.303in Browning machine guns, but after the start of the war all eight were fitted. From autumn 1940 a few had four Brownings and two Hispano 20mm cannon, which became standard on most later versions. A further

SPECIFICATION

Mk VB

Country of origin: Great Britain.

Manufacturer: Supermarine Aviation Works Ltd.

Type: Single-seat fighter.

Year: 1941.

Engine: 1440hp Rolls-Royce Merlin 45 liquid-cooled V12.

Wingspan: 11.23m (36ft 10in), clipped 9.93m (32ft 7in).

Length: 9.12m (29ft 11in).

Height: 3.48m (11ft 5in).

Weight: 3016kg (6650lb).

Maximum speed: 602km/h (374mph).

Ceiling: 10,820m (35,500ft).

Range: 756km (470 miles).

Armament: Two 20mm Hispano cannon and four 0.303in Browning machine guns plus two 250lb bombs under 'Universal' wing and one 500lb bomb or drop tank under fuselage.

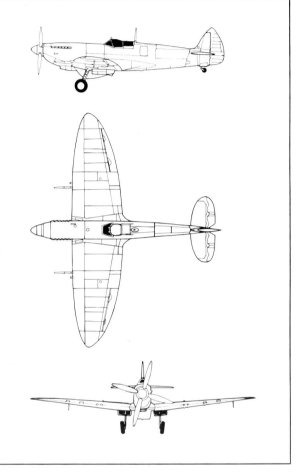

920 Mark IIs were built at Castle Bromwich, near Birmingham. Like many Mk Is some had the 1175hp Merlin XII. These helped to see Britain through the dark days of 1940 and, in the early months of 1941, began to take the air war back across the English Channel to France.

Further developments into specialised high-altitude and photo-reconnaissance versions followed, alongside continuous development of the Merlin engine. The Spitfire certainly proved more than a match for its main rival, the Messerschmitt Bf 109. The German mainstay could out-climb, out-dive and equal the Spitfire for sheer speed at low altitudes (below 20,000ft). But it was less manoeuvrable and the early Spitfires' superior rate of turn enabled them to hold their own in a dogfight.

During 1941, Spitfire pilots, now flying the 1440hp Merlin 45 powered Mk V, found that they were being out-fought by a completely unknown adversary with a radial engine. This was eventually identified as the Focke-Wulf Fw 190.

By sheer chance, Rolls-Royce had already produced a totally new Merlin, the Mk 61, with two superchargers in tandem. For take-off it gave 1565hp, and at high altitudes it gave double the power of the Spitfire I engine. This new engine was rushed into production and fitted to the Spitfire V, turning it into the Mk IX, with 4-blade propeller, long nose, twice as many exhaust stubs and twin underwing radiators. The Mk IX took on the 190 and won.

The Spitfire, in all its 22 different Marks, continued to be built until March 1948. By then no less than 20,346 aircraft (excluding prototypes) had been built. Alongside the Spitfires were Seafires, flown from aircraft carriers by the Fleet Air Arm.

Symbol of a nation's courage, there will never be an aircraft like it.

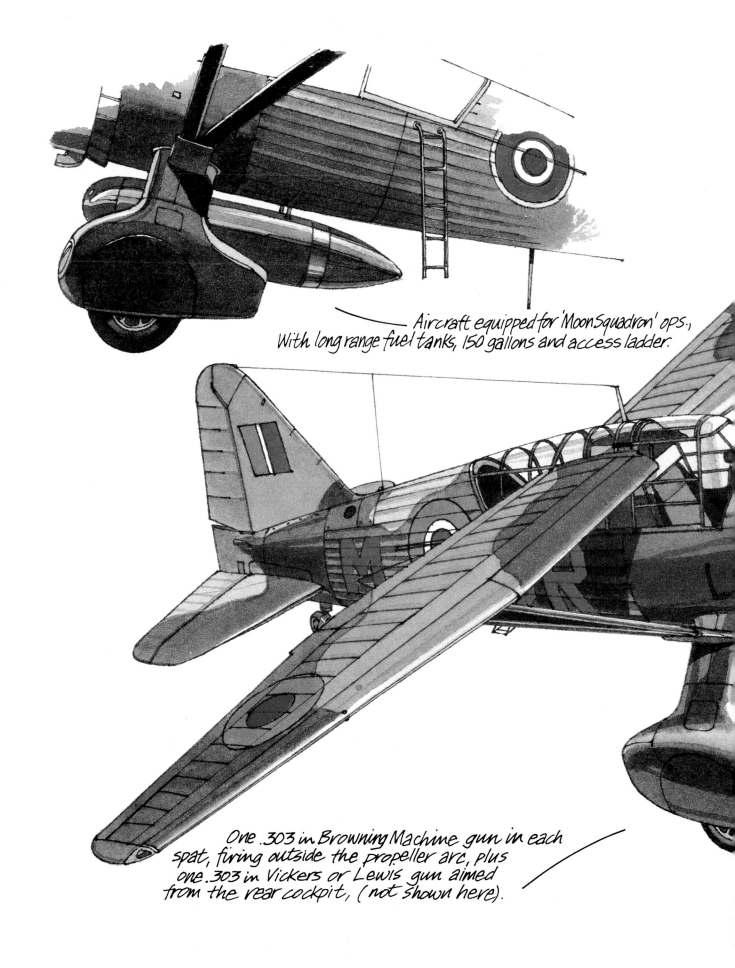

Aircraft equipped for 'Moon Squadron' ops.,
With long range fuel tanks, 150 gallons and access ladder.

One .303 in Browning Machine gun in each
spat, firing outside the propeller arc, plus
one .303 in Vickers or Lewis gun aimed
from the rear cockpit, (not shown here).

WESTLAND LYSANDER

9 Cylinder Bristol Perseus XII sleeve valve radial engine
905 bhp – maximum speed 237 mph.

Alternative armament of two
250 lb bombs could be carried
on stub wings.

WESTLAND LYSANDER

It is still several hours before dawn. The Moon, partly obscured by clouds, is giving hardly any light at all. There is little wind. The silence is almost complete. The man, standing in the shadows of the wood, glances nervously at the luminous dial of his watch. There it is... the faint murmur of a Bristol Mercury XII radial, the sound he has been waiting for. He steps forward into the tiny clearing and begins to flash his torch beam into the darkened sky.

The Westland Lysander circles overhead once only, drops steeply over the trees and bumps down on to the clearing in the forest, its massive Elektron box under-carriage absorbing the shock with hardly a creak. How it manages to pull up before crashing into the trees on the far side is a mystery known only, perhaps, to Teddy Petter, the designer.

As it taxies back into the wind, the man runs forward. The canopy is already in the open position. Even before he has clambered up the ladder, thoughtfully bolted to the fuselage side, and into the rear seat, the 'Lizzie' is rolling forward. Within an incredible 165 yards, it is airborne. The trees flash below, inches away. The year is 1943 and another Allied agent is snatched from the Gestapo.

The prototype Lysander flew for the first time on 15 June 1936. At that time the Lysander was intended purely for 'army co-operation', a role which in World War II hardly materialised. Snatching, or 'inserting' courageous individuals in enemy territory had not been thought of, and few who witnessed that uneventful maiden flight could have guessed at the heroic place in military history the Lizzie would claim for itself. Two years later, almost a year before war was declared, the Lysander was operational with the Royal Air Force. Its earliest wartime duties, which began in France just eight days after the outbreak of war, were relatively mundane, mainly carrying supplies to the British Expeditionary Force.

In November 1940, the Lysander made its first clandestine landing in northern France in support of the resistance movement. A special long-range version had been developed, the Mk IIIA. Its extra fuel load meant in theory that it could carry just one passenger, but there are many recorded instances of the Lizzie IIIA bringing out no less than four passengers in an emergency.

The Lysander had a very wide range of speed, from a healthy maximum of 237 mph down to a surprisingly low 55mph. At this speed it was highly manoeuvrable, and in a strongish breeze it could land almost vertically. It owed its outstanding short take-off and landing performance not only to its powerful engine – in addition to the Bristol Mercury XII, it was also fitted with an 870hp Mercury XX and a 905hp Perseus XII – but also to the leading-edge slats along the entire wingspan of 50ft. These had the effect of smoothing out the airflow at very steep angles of attack, thus delaying the otherwise inevitable stall at very slow speeds. These slats opened and closed automatically, foreshadowing the powerful slats used in the latest jet airliners in service today.

Although never designed as an acrobatic aeroplane, the Lysander could be looped quite spectacularly. This was, of course, frowned on by the authorities, but several pilots put the Lizzie through quite a tough aerobatic schedule during off-duty moments. Slow barrel rolls were possible, although if the procedure was speeded up, there was a danger of losing the leading-edge wing slats. It says something for the Lizzie that pilots who were forced to endure hours of deadly serious and highly dangerous 'taxi' works would want to climb back into the same cockpit for some light relief that would have severely overstressed other similar airframes.

Of course, when the Lysander was designed it was fondly thought that 200-mph aircraft with the odd machine gun might survive in war (another in this class was the Battle). The Lysander was never pitted head-on against the Luftwaffe, except on brief occasions such as the front-line resupply of the beleaguered garrison at Calais, so its vulnerability was not demonstrated in the same brutal ways as with the Battle. Its good qualities were its STOL (short take-off and landing) capability, its reliability and its generous size, which put it almost in the same class as the Swordfish in being able to carry almost anything. For example the belly had a shackle for a 150-gallon long-range tank, and on one occasion a motorcycle laden with supplies was hung there quite successfully because it was urgently wanted by a French force under General Leclerc in the Western desert. The bomb 'wings', resembling those of today's attack helicopters, were also designed to drop supply containers but not the large wooden beer casks which in 1944 were often flown to front-line troops in Normandy.

Among the oddball Lysanders were one with a swept-forward wing and another that looked like two aircraft in close formation. The Stieger wing, designed by H.J. Stieger, was much smaller in span than the regular 50ft,

SPECIFICATION

Mk II

Country of origin: Great Britain.

Manufacturer: Westland Aircraft Ltd.

Type: Two-seat army co-operation.

Year: 1936 (first flight prototype).

Engine: 905hp Bristol Perseus XII nine-cylinder sleeve-valve radial.

Wingspan: 15.24m (50ft).

Length: 9.29m (30ft 6in).

Height: 4.42m (14ft 6in).

Weight: 2685kg (5920lb).

Maximum speed: 381km/h (237mph).

Ceiling: 8077m (26,500ft).

Range: 966km (600 miles).

Armament: One 0.303in Browning machine gun in each wheel spat and one 0.303 in Lewis, Vickers K or Browning gun (armament not always installed).

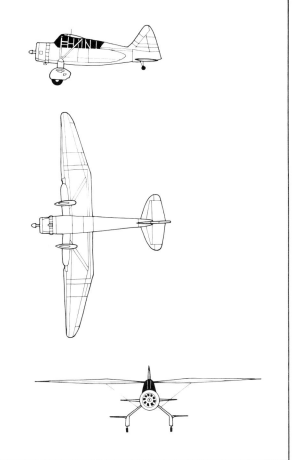

but its 38ft had constant chord (width) so area was not much less. It had full-span high-lift slats and flaps, and actually generated more lift than the original model, reducing landing distance in most conditions to a mere 150ft. As there was no room for ailerons, lateral control was effected by spoilers, which were then a radical idea but which today are found on most of the latest fighters and airliners. As for the Dalanne Lysander, this used an enormous tailplain, with twin fins on the tips, in an arrangement tried in France in the 1930s. The aircraft was virtually tandem-winged, and it was built not to get much greater flexibility, but to fit a four-gun tail turret, just as in RAF heavy bombers.

In all, 1670 Westland Lysanders were built, 225 of them in Canada. They were withdrawn from active service in 1944. Their job, which they had carried out supremely well, was over.

Twin 12·7mm Breda
machine guns
400 rounds
per gun.

Fiat A 74R. IC 38 14 cylinder
radial engine. Air cooled
Maximum speed 439 km/h

FIAT CR.42
FALCO

Aircraft of 20° Squadriglia, 46 Gruppo, 15° Stormo Assalto
Fighting at El Alamein, late 1942

FIAT CR.42 FALCO

This was the last great fighter biplane. Born into an age where cantilever low-wing monoplanes, such as the Messerschmitt Bf 109 and Supermarine Spitfire, were already showing the world that, for biplanes, the war was over, the Fiat Falco had no right to exist.

Over five years and nearly 1800 aircraft later, the Falco had proved, in the most emphatic way possible, that it had every right, not merely to exist, but to be remembered as one of the finest biplanes of all. The Falco, or Falcon, was designed by Ing. Celestino Rosatelli as a development of his equally famous CR.32 which was to perform so well for the Nationalists in Spain. At first it is hard to see why Ing. Rosatelli clung to the high-g, high-manoeuvrability concept of the mid-1930s biplane. Although far more manoeuvrable than a monoplane, out-and-out speed was already proving more valuable in air-to-air combat. Many observers believed that the design itself, and particularly the Italian Ministero dell'Aeronautica's acceptance of it for volume production, were not merely the result of short-sightedness, but of a total bankruptcy of ideas.

A closer look at the thinking of the time – it was only 1936, remember – shows that many air strategists believed there was still plenty of room for biplanes with a high rate of turn to fight alongside the quicker monoplanes. This opinion was justified by the enormous interest shown when the Falco was first exhibited to the world. Its appearance was at least a year later than it should have been, because Fiat had to wait for the arrival of its A74 RC.38, 14-cylinder, two-row air-cooled radial engine, around which the airframe had been designed. At last the first test flight of the Falco was made by Comandante Valentino Cus in early 1939. The wait, it seemed, had been well worthwhile. After some three hours' flying Comandante Cus declared the Falco to be 'the ultimate pilot's aeroplane'. It was apparently capable of every conceivable manoeuvre and cheerfully stood up to everything Cus threw at it during the entire prototype test programme.

An early Government contract called for the construction of 200 aircraft and it is interesting to note that the prototype was actually included in this number.

The Fiat engine was a good example of radial piston engine technology. It was derived from the famous World War 1 series of designs from the Gnome and Le Rhône factories. It delivered 840hp at ground level for a maximum of three minutes and could sustain 828hp at 3800m. Propulsion was via a three-bladed Fiat-Hamilton constant-speed propeller. The Falco's airframe was the epitome of sturdiness. The sesquiplane wings were steel and light alloy covered in fabric, with ailerons on the upper wing only. The Warren-Truss type interplane bracing was

similar to that used on earlier Rosatelli designs. The fuselage framework was steel tube, with dural formers making the oval section. It was fabric covered behind the cockpit and panelled with alloy up front.

Armament consisted of two 12.7mm Breda-SAFAT heavy machine guns mounted ahead of the cockpit, and a somewhat antiquated San Giorgio Type B reflector sight was fitted. The Falco's pilots were given some up-to-date instruments, but no radio, and, significantly, no armour protection.

The first Falcos to see action were not Italian, but Belgian. One month before Italy entered the war in June 1940, Falcos of the 3ème and 4ème *Escadrilles* of the Belgian Aéronautique Militaire fought a brave, but brief battle against the might of the Luftwaffe. Shortly after Italy declared war, a 12-strong force of CR.42s from 23° Gruppo (3° Stormo) attacked a quiet airfield in the Alpes-Maritimes. Fayence, now better known as a national gliding centre, was totally unprepared for the attack and many French aircraft were destroyed. Similar Falco attacks on other airfields in southern France gave the Italians mastery of the Mediterranean skies.

All this prompted the Ministry to order follow-up contracts for a further 300 aircraft. The government was not deterred by the Falco's early experiences in Northern Europe when they were deployed by the Corp Aereo Italiano to support the Luftwaffe in attacks on Britain. The first raid on Ramsgate was quite successful, but, shortly after, 40 Falcos escorting 10 Fiat B.R.20s were intercepted over Harwich by 30 Hurricanes. The result was disastrous for the Falcos, with five bombers and three escorts destroyed, without loss by the Hurricanes. However, any thoughts that the Falco might be finished as a fighting machine were premature. Falcos showed their mastery of certain kinds of combat in Greece, Mesopotamia, Albania, Ethiopia and throughout North Africa and the Mediterranean. Finland and Hungary had both put them to singularly effective use, strafing the exhausted,

SPECIFICATION

Country of origin: Italy.

Manufacturer: Fiat.

Type: Single-seat fighter.

Year: 1939.

Engine: 840hp Fiat A.74 R1 C.38 14-cylinder two-row radial.

Wingspan: 9.7m (31ft 10in).

Length: 8.26m (27ft 1in).

Height: 3.59m (11ft 9in).

Weight: 2295kg (5060lb).

Maximum speed: 439km/h (273mph) at 6000m (19,700ft).

Ceiling: 10,200m (33,500ft).

Range: 775km (482 miles).

Armament: Two 12.7mm Breda-SAFAT machine guns (CR.42bis).

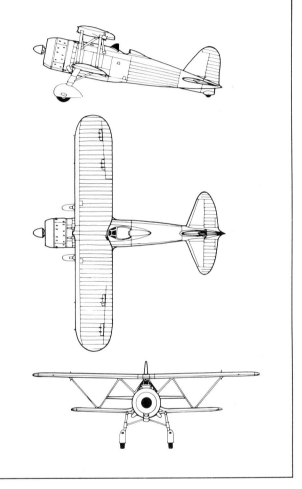

retreating Russian troops during the bitter summer of 1941.

Throughout its entire production career, the Falco was hardly changed, apart from minor modifications at squadron level to convert some aircraft to carry 100kg bombs. The Germans were not slow to recognise the particular advantages of the Falco for supporting troops fighting partisans in difficult territory. After they wrested control of the Italian aircraft industry in 1943, they placed a further contract for 200 CR.42s to be flown by the Luftwaffe.

One or two Falcos remaining in Italy after the war were converted to make excellent two-seat fighter-trainers, and these were still flying in the 1950s. For an aeroplane that was obsolete before it was designed, the Fiat CR.42 Falco proved to be one of the most determined fighters of the war.

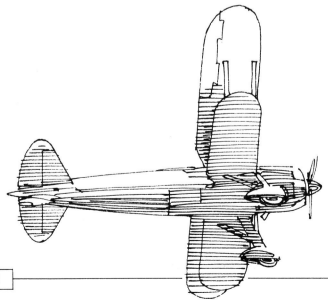

One 20mm ShVAK Cannon and one 12·7mm machine gun, portside only.

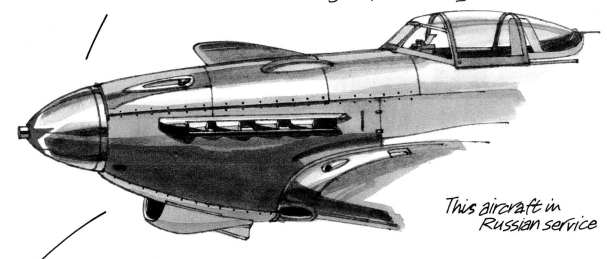

This aircraft in
Russian service

Yak 900 Klimov Vee·12 liquid cooled engine VK 105 P.F. 1260 hp.

Armour glass rear screen.

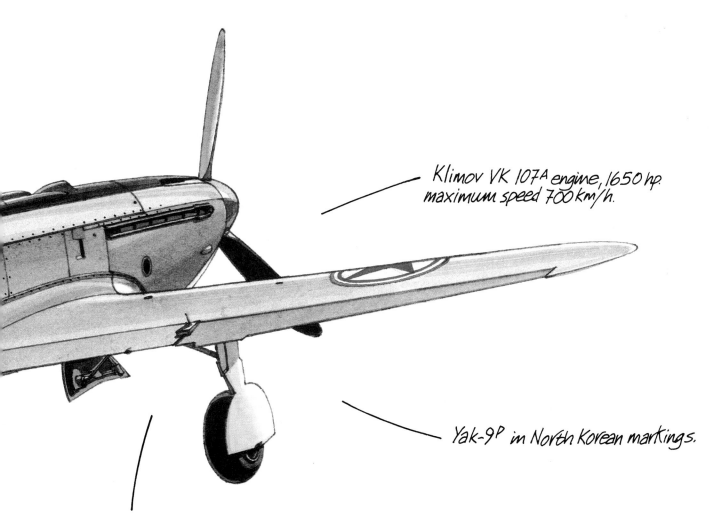

Klimov VK 107A engine, 1650 hp.
maximum speed 700 km/h.

Yak-9P in North Korean markings.

One 23mm VYa-23V Cannon firing through propeller boss.
Two 12.7mm UBS machine guns in upper cowling.

YAK-1 to YAK-9

Soviet aircraft take their designation from the designer rather than the manufacturer. In 1925, Aleksandr S. Yakovlev began to design gliders, but ten years later he embarked on a study of fighters, and when in 1938 the Soviet government had an urgent need in this field he quickly came up with the Ya-26 *Krasavec* (beauty) prototype which flew in March 1939. This wood-and-tubular-steel fighter was typically Russian in having a huge engine in a small airframe, with very limited armament. Soviet pilots, often badly trained, found it difficult to fly at first, and many Yak-1 production fighters crashed. Production was in full swing by the German invasion of 22 June 1941, but by October 1941 production had to be transferred 1600km from Moscow to Kamensk-Uralskii, east of the Urals. By the end of that year output had not only been restored but increased enormously, and eventually more Yaks (all types) were built than any other fighter in aviation history, accounting for 60 per cent of all Soviet fighters built during 1941-45. In about 18 months the Yak was the subject of so much rapid development that the Yak-9 actually entered service in the winter of 1942.

Originally designated the 7DI, the Yak-9, while retaining its wooden skin, incorporated portions of light alloy structure which gave it a greater fuel capacity. This, together with very many detail improvements, enabled its pilots to meet the German Bf 109Fs and Gs in the terrible battle of Stalingrad on roughly equal terms. In fact, the Yak's only problem was its relative lack of firepower. In 1944, when the smaller Yak-3 dogfighter entered service, its performance was so impressive that the Luftwaffe command issued orders to its pilots that engagement with this fighter was to be avoided at all costs. In 1944, the Normandie-Niemen Group (a Soviet-based Free French squadron) scored a total of 273 kills against the Luftwaffe, all gained on Yak fighters given to the group by the Soviet Union; over one-third were attributable to Yak-3s. Later still, the remarkably durable Yak-9 was employed against its former allies in the 1950-53 conflict in Korea.

The basic essence of Yak design was robust simplicity,

an overriding requirement caused by the harsh Russian climate and a need to remain operational over vast snowbound areas, far from industrial facilities, with the minimum of servicing. Instruments and other delicate systems were restricted to absolute essentials such as rev-counters and pressure-meters, and the indispensable coolant thermometer. There were no gyroscopic indicators at first other than that showing turn and bank. Fuel gauges were located in the tops of the tanks in the wings, but this posed much less of a problem than might at first be supposed. From mid-1942 the Yak-1M had a very advanced cockpit canopy, reinforced at the front and rear with thickened armoured glass, which afforded the pilot improved all-round vision, particularly to the rear, which helped save many lives. The Yak-9 was the first single-seat fighter in the world to have this invaluable facility, just one of many that made this aircraft so well-loved by the men who flew it.

Aleksandr S. Yakovlev designed his innovative aeroplane with the pilot always in mind: another safety factor was a system by which the fuel tanks received the burnt exhaust gases purified through a filter as they gradually emptied, so that the omnipresent danger of an explosion during aerial combat was vastly reduced. And, although the aircraft in practice spent most of their life at low and medium altitudes, each had an oxygen mask on a hook at the cockpit's left side. This often incorporated a radio telephone headset but, as wearing this restricted head movement, most pilots preferred to fly in silence and rely upon the good all-round vision. Many Yaks had no radio. Curiously, pilots also needed to unbuckle their seat-straps which, unlike those of Western aircraft, held the pilot's shoulders rigidly fixed. Stranger still, this tight harness design was never modified, not even in the Yak-3.

The Yak-9s and -3s did, however, embody many improvements, not least being that of firepower. A 20mm ShVAK rapid-fire cannon firing through the hub of the propeller was standard on most Yaks, with one or two heavy BS machine guns above. A few Yak-9Ts and -9Ks had enormous anti-tank cannon. Some had a 45mm gun, but because of the recoil and tendency to jam, this was soon replaced with a 37mm cannon. This installation was used to great effect during and after the Battle of Kursk, but it too demanded certain care in operation because the recoil reaction served to reduce airspeed. On at least one occasion a pilot turned this drawback into an advantage by firing the cannon to act as a brake on a too-short icy landing strip.

Although it closely resembled the Yak-9 in silhouette, the Yak-3 was a lighter, faster and an even more elegant

SPECIFICATION

Yak-3

Country of origin: Soviet Union.

Design bureau: Aleksandr S. Yakovlev OKB.

Type: Single-seat fighter.

Year: 1944.

Engine: 1260hp Klimov VK-105PF-2 liquid-cooled
V12.

Wingspan: 9.2m (30ft 2in).

Length: 8.5m (27ft 10in).

Height: 2.4m (7ft 10in).

Weight: 2670kg (5900lb).

Maximum speed: 720km/h (448mph).

Ceiling: 10,800m (35,450ft).

Range: 815km (506 miles).

Armament: One 20mm ShVAK cannon and two
12.7mm BS machine guns.

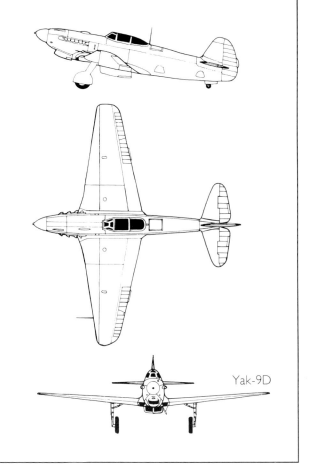

Yak-9D

aircraft. Weighing only 2670kg in full battle order, it had an astonishing rate of climb, held beautifully firm in tight turns, and generally performed with tremendous vivacity. British pilots who flew both machines compared it very favourably with the Spitfire. Inevitably though, the early batches of this remarkable aircraft had their teething troubles, and perhaps the most disconcerting of these concerned the undercarriage retention gear. Having apparently hooked back into the retracted position, the undercarriage would often, when the pilot put on a sudden burst of speed, drop down suddenly with a juddering thud.

But thanks to continued design efforts this and other faults were always quickly remedied. Yak-9s and -3s went on long after the end of World War II to be flown by a wide variety of air forces in many parts of the world. The Yak-9 trainer was produced in Poland in 1946. The Normandie-Niemen Group were permitted to retain

their Yak-3s and took them back to France when hostilities ceased: one example is preserved in the Musée de l'Air at Le Bourget. Last of the wartime Yaks, the -9U, was retained in Germany and ironically, used for the 'buzzing' and harassment of Western aircraft during the Berlin Airlift, when the Russians attempted to isolate that city in 1948-49.

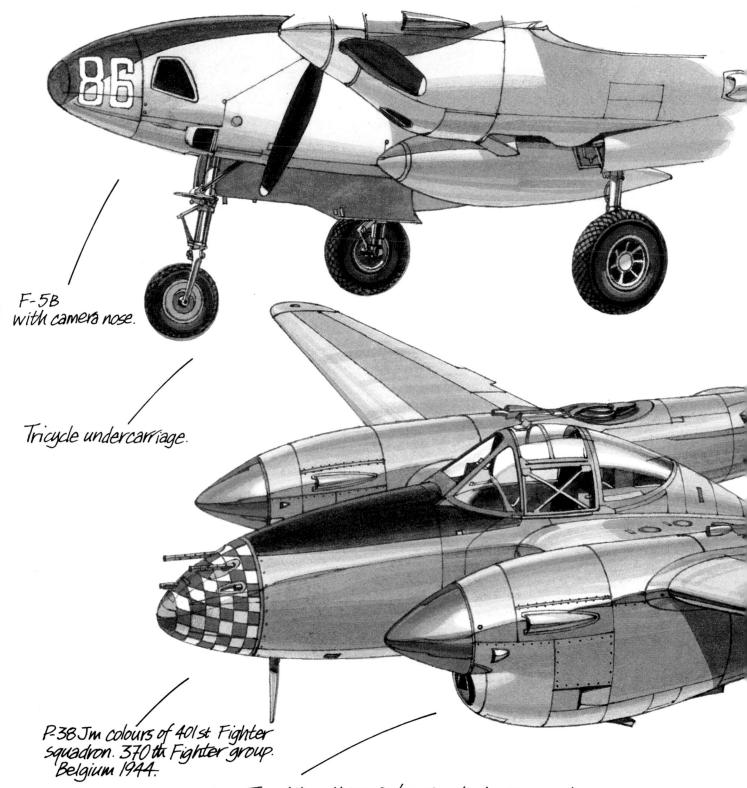

F-5B
with camera nose.

Tricycle undercarriage.

P-38 Jm colours of 401st Fighter
squadron. 370th Fighter group.
Belgium 1944.

Two Allison V-1710-89/91 12 cylinder Vee engines.
1425 hp. 422 mph maximum speed.

LOCKHEED P-38 LIGHTNING

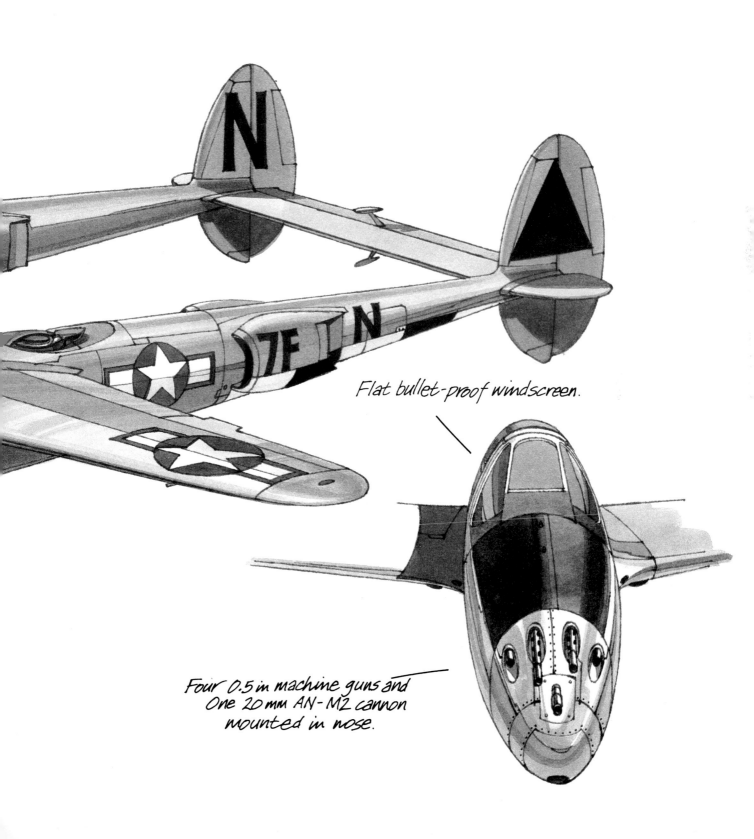

Flat bullet-proof windscreen.

Four 0.5 in machine guns and
One 20 mm AN-M2 cannon
mounted in nose.

LOCKHEED P-38 LIGHTNING

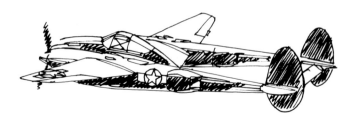

Just as North American Aviation had never before produced a fighter until it designed and built the widely acclaimed Mustang, Lockheed had never built a production military aircraft. Then, in the early weeks of 1937, the company accepted an exceedingly challenging specification from the US Army for a long-range interceptor capable of 360mph at medium height, and a flight endurance of not less than one hour. What emerged was first designated the Model 414 and then the XP-38.

Although the word 'unique' is overworked and often misused, this aeroplane, developed to satisfy the US Army's visionary requirement, fully justified that description. Conceived in the main by Hall Hibbard, it was revolutionary in appearance and it embodied a very large number of 'firsts'. It was the first fighter to have a tricycle nosewheel undercarriage, the first single-seat fighter to have twin engines, the first fighter of twin-boom configuration to enter service, the first squadron fighter with turbochargers or handed (opposite-rotation) propellers, the first fighting aircraft known to have encountered the compressibility problem near the speed of sound, and it soon became the first to be fitted with power-boosted controls.

With an unloaded weight of 14,100lb it was heavier than a loaded Blenheim, Britain's standard light bomber in 1939. This and some other aspects of its design prompted doubts in the minds of more than one US Army expert: they saw vulnerability and risk in the layout of the Allison engines, which had ducts leading to and from the turbochargers in the tops of the tail booms, and further pipes linking the engines to coolant radiators fitted on to both sides of the booms well behind the wing.

Nevertheless, the first prototype flew on 27 January 1939, and soon astounded the aircraft community by smashing the record for a US transcontinental flight. It completed the coast-to-coast dash in a staggering 7h 2min – but was destroyed when it undershot the runway on landing at New York's Mitchell Field. This unfortunate end to a magnificent performance did nothing to dampen enthusiasm for the XP-38, and doubts as to cost and risk still voiced by some sectors of Army opinion were firmly overcome.

The rapidly growing factory at Burbank, California, began to turn out P-38s with one 37mm cannon and four 0.50in machine guns in the nose of the central nacelle. This concentrated firepower may have prompted the German Luftwaffe later to dub the P-38 *der gabelschwanz Teufel*, the fork-tailed devil.

A British order in 1940 for 670 ran into problems of export prohibition of the new features, which specified removal of the turbochargers and even of the opposite rotation of the 'handed' propellers. Lockheed's warning that these modifications would impair performance was well and truly fulfilled. Predictably, the RAF rejected the aircraft, sending it back with a name which stuck – the Lockheed Lightning. The P-38E introduced the 20mm M-2 gun, with twice the amount of ammunition possible with the 37mm. It was with the aid of this weapon that a P-38E shot down a Focke-Wulf Fw 200C over the sea near Iceland, minutes after the USA entered the war – the first of many Lightning kills.

Subsequently, the P-38 was constantly engaged in the thick of the action in several theatres of war. It served in North Africa, North-West Europe and, of course, in the Pacific, where P-38 pilot and top-scoring USAAF air ace Major Richard Bong shot down 40 enemy aircraft. In April 1943, in the same war zone, P-38s flew more than 500 miles from their base in Guadalcanal to make a precision interception of the G4M bomber carrying the great Japanese Admiral Yamamoto. The G4M still lies in the Bougainville jungle, and formation leader Tom Lanphier later became a Lockheed test pilot.

The main 1942 versions were the P-38F, which could carry two 1000lb bombs or drop tanks, and the P-38G with new 1325hp engines. During the span of their wartime career, the many types of P-38s were modified, often in the field, to carry out an extremely wide range of duties. In the mass-produced P-38J the intercoolers were removed from the wings and refitted under the engines in order to provide room for an extra 55 US gallons of fuel: this changed the appearance. The hydraulically boosted ailerons of later J types helped enormously to improve manoeuvrability and cut down on pilot fatigue. With its higher emergency power, the P-38L was able to carry 4000lb of bombs, or ten 5in rockets, and formations of this version made numerous bombing attacks under the direction of a lead-ship whose special droopsnoot (the P-38 had several quite distinctive nose shapes) housed a bomb-aimer with a Norden sight. The type F-5 was developed as a fast photo-reconnaissance aircraft; the P-38M was a two-seater nightfighter fitted with an ASH radar pod, and Lightnings were even used to tow gliders.

SPECIFICATION

P-38J

Country of origin: USA.

Manufacturer: Lockheed Aircraft Corporation.

Type: Single-seat long-range fighter.

Year: 1943.

Engines: Two 1425hp Allison V-1710-89/91 liquid cooled V12.

Wingspan: 15.9m (52ft).

Length: 11.5m (37ft 10in).

Height: 3.9m (12ft 10in).

Weight: 9800kg (21,600lb).

Maximum speed: 680km/h (422mph).

Ceiling: 13,500m (44,000ft).

Range: 3640km (2260 miles) (with drop tanks).

Armament: One 20mm Hispano cannon and four 0.5in Browning machine guns. Could carry two bombs of up to 726kg (1600lb) each or ten rockets.

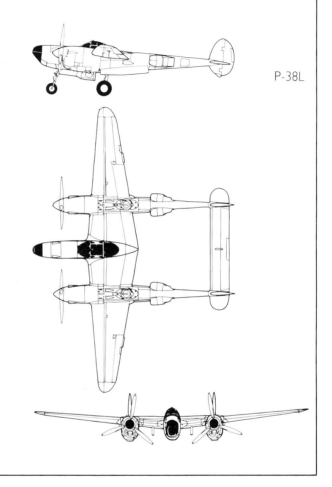

P-38L

They operated on skis and, carrying a brace of stretchers, served as fast ambulances.

But of all this bewildering catalogue of types, the one that saw most action was the powerful long-range P-38J. Its 1425hp engines gave it a top speed of 420mph, and it was capable when equipped with drop tanks of escorting US bombers from England to Germany and back.

Some aviation historians take the view that Lightnings were never really good at close-combat fighting, but they were undeniably among the very best long-range interceptors and escorts, and their superabundance of other qualities sets them firmly in the front rank of World War II aircraft.

In August 1945, when US production finally ceased, the total number of Lightnings delivered into service was 9942. They vanished from the USAAF in a matter of weeks, but served in many other air forces. Immediately after the war, the IMAM company of Italy rebuilt a number of P-38L fighters, fitting them with a separate instructor's front cockpit for employment by the Aeronautica Militare Italiano as dual-control trainers. The F-5E, one of the final photo-reconnaissance models, was used in Peking by the Chinese Nationalists in 1945 and the Free French flew large numbers of P-38s of several types.

Revi 16^B reflector gunsight

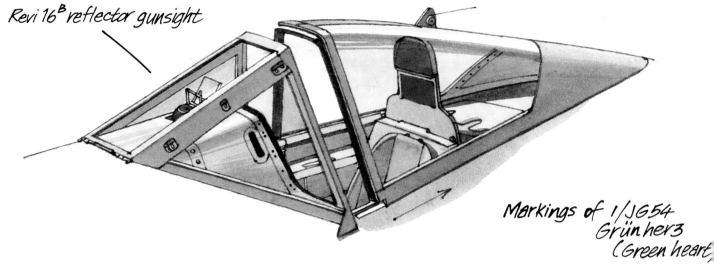

Markings of 1/JG54
Grün her3
(Green heart)

Yellow underwing panel denotes aircraft
serving on the Eastern front.

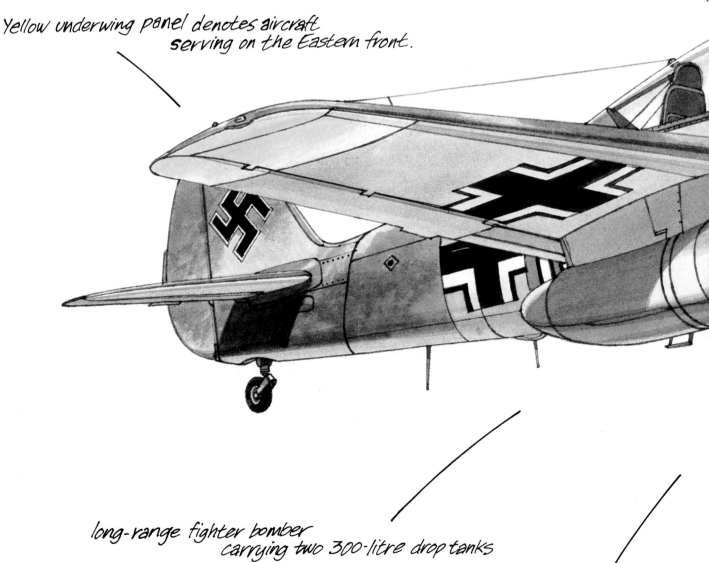

long-range fighter bomber
carrying two 300-litre drop tanks

Armament consisted of two fuselage mounted MG 131 machine-guns
and two MG 151 20mm Cannon mounted in wing roots.

FOCKE-WULF Fw 190

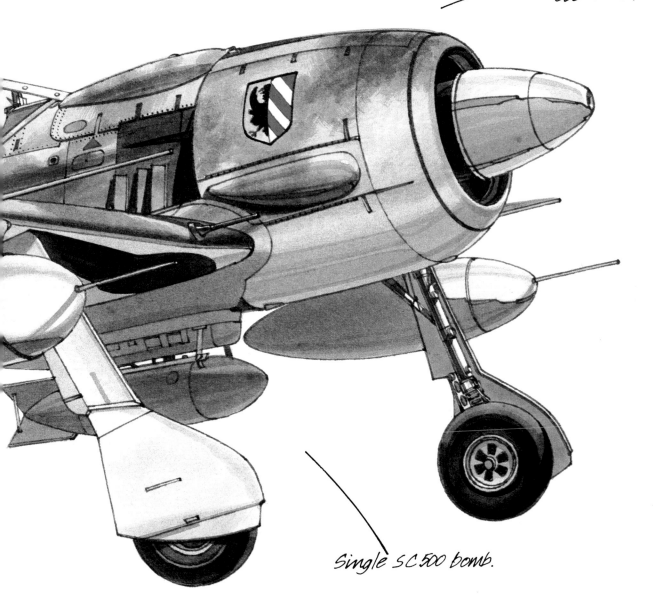

B·M·W·8 01D, 14 cylinder two-row radial engine, 1700 hp maximum speed 656 km/h.

Single SC 500 bomb.

FOCKE-WULF Fw 190

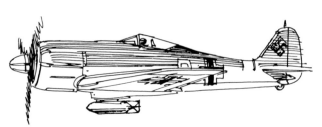

When in 1937 Focke-Wulf of Bremen was asked to design a new fighter which might eventually supersede the Messerschmitt Bf 109, there was a strong body of opinion in the upper echelons of the RLM (German air ministry) that the project, headed by Kurt Tank and R. Blaser, was a costly waste of time. Nothing, they said, could possibly compare with their marvellous Bf 109.

Undaunted by the controversy, the Tank and Blaser team set out to design and build what was to become probably the most versatile small warplane of World War II. Almost unbelievably, British Intelligence had no inkling of its existence, despite the fact that the first three months of flight testing took place at Bremen airport before the war! Having met the Fw 190s in combat, the RAF had wrongly assumed them to be captured Curtiss Hawk 75s, American-built aircraft of earlier vintage and quite similar appearance. The RAF pilots who were on the receiving end knew better!

Out of the blue, on 23 June 1942, the Adjutant of III/JG2 landed his Fw 190A-3 on an RAF airfield by mistake. Close examination of their prize gave rise in RAF circles to considerable consternation. Although built to take a large and heavy radial engine, the neat little airframe was of masterly compact design, and one which readily lent itself to fast and simple manufacture. So much so that by the end of 1943, components were being turned out in no fewer than 24 different factories. It was an extraordinarily effective aircraft, one notable feature being that almost everything was electric.

The Fw 190 was the first production type armed with the new Mauser MG 151/20 cannon, in addition to MG FF cannon and machine guns. Many Luftwaffe pilots considered the Fw 190 a much better all-round aircraft than the Bf 109, which virtually all of them had flown previously. It had heavier combat protection, certain advantages in low-level manoeuvrability, handled far better and was able to carry greater offensive armament. As the series progressed, this came to include incredibly heavy bomb loads (including the SC 1800 bomb 1,800kg), rocket clusters, and the largest torpedoes, so that its potential for air-to-ground attack surpassed that of any other single-engined aircraft of the day. The Fw 190 replaced the Ju 87s as quickly as pilots could convert.

Looking at its disadvantages, those fighter pilots who remained loyal to the Bf 109 complained of the Fw 190's relative lack of performance at high altitudes. This was not a serious drawback, because almost all the fighting over the Eastern, Tunisian or Italian fronts took place at low and medium heights. The main design changes were directed towards the provision of longer endurance and an

ever-greater versatility in firepower. These efforts were so successful that as early as late 1942, the Fw 190 was widely recognised by both sides as being the Luftwaffe's star performer in the field of tactical attack.

But, and notwithstanding its multiple repertoire, the Fw 190's performance as a straight fighter aircraft was formidable, to say the least. Apart from having a slightly larger turning circle, it could out-do the Spitfire V on every count, and especially in that vital battle tactic, the fast half-roll and dive. The Fw 190 came to the RAF as a very nasty shock, and the only good which emerged from the encounter was a further speeding-up of development at Vickers Supermarine. Even so, it was not until the introduction of the Mk IX that the Spitfire could begin to meet the Fw 190 on more or less equal terms.

Still in its role of air-to-air combat machine, the Fw 190's first really large-scale action – and one which made its name a byword – took place on 12 February 1942 when the battle-cruisers *Scharnhorst* and *Gneisenau*, together with the heavy cruiser *Prinz Eugen*, made a daring run up the English Channel.

Operating in relays, almost 200 Fw 190s, backed up by a much smaller number of Bf 109s, provided a massive umbrella for the little flotilla, and a British attack on the ships was pitifully unsuccessful. Naval air squadrons of obsolete Fairey Swordfish offered such slow targets that the Fw 190 pilots were actually forced to lower their flaps and even their landing gear in order to slow down long enough to hold the lumbering Swordfish in their gunsights.

Not one single bomb or torpedo found a target, the Swordfish were massacred, and all three German warships reached their home ports unscathed, except for damage caused by mines laid by the RAF in their path.

Before their victory in the English Channel, the Fw 190s were operating in growing numbers in theatres of war as widely separated as the Soviet Union and North Africa. And, as successive modifications allowed for the carrying of more and heavier bombloads, it was seen increasingly over Britain on hit-and-run missions.

Various other ideas for ways in which to use this highly adaptable aeroplane never reached fruition. Some members of a diverse family of Mistel (mistletoe) aircraft involved an Fw 190 carried pick-a-back to a long range target on a Junkers Ju 88 packed with explosives and

SPECIFICATION

Fw 190 A-8

Country of origin: Germany.

Manufacturer: Focke-Wulf Flugzeugbau GmbH.

Type: Single-seat fighter-bomber.

Year: 1942 (prototype 1939).

Engine: 1700hp BMW 801D 18-cylinder air-cooled radial.

Wingspan: 10.5m (34ft 5in).

Length: 8.85m (29ft).

Height: 3.95m (13ft).

Weight: 4900kg (10,800lb).

Maximum speed: 656km/h (408mph).

Ceiling: 11,410m (37,400ft).

Range: 900km (560 miles).

Armament: Typically two 13mm MG 131 heavy machine guns above engine, two 20mm MG 151/20 cannon in wing roots and two MG 151/20 30mm MK 108 cannon in outer wing panels. Bombload: one 500kg bomb below fuselage and four 50kg bombs under wings.

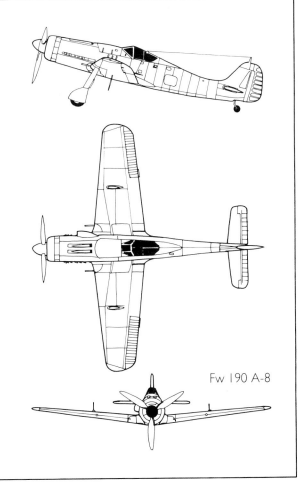

Fw 190 A-8

guided after release by the pilot of the Fw 190. On the other hand the prolonged effort to improve high-altitude performance eventually led, in September 1944, to the start of deliveries of the Fw 190D-9, or 'Dora-9'. Allied pilots called it the 'long-nosed 190' because it had a long liquid-cooled Jumo 213A engine, with a circular frontal radiator. To balance this the fin was enlarged and the rear fuselage lengthened. The D-9 was faster at all heights than earlier 190s, and it led to Kurt Tank's masterpiece, designated for him personally, the Ta 152. This was just coming into service at the final German collapse.

It seems curious in retrospect that production of the successful Fw 190 never even came close to that of its predecessor the Bf 109. By the end of the war, the comparative totals amounted to 30,500 for the Bf 109 and about 19,450 for the Fw 190, respectively.

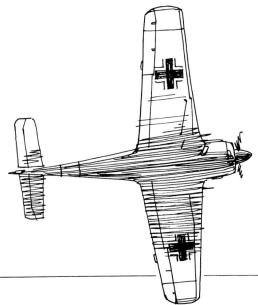

Two fuselage-mounted
7.7mm machine guns and two
wing-mounted 20mm Navy Type 99
Mk I cannon.

Nakajima NK IC Sakae 14 cylinder radial
air-cooled engine, 950 hp.
Maximum speed 534 Km/h.

A6 M5c of Nº221 Naval Air Corps
(A land-based unit)

MITSUBISHI A6M
ZERO-SEN

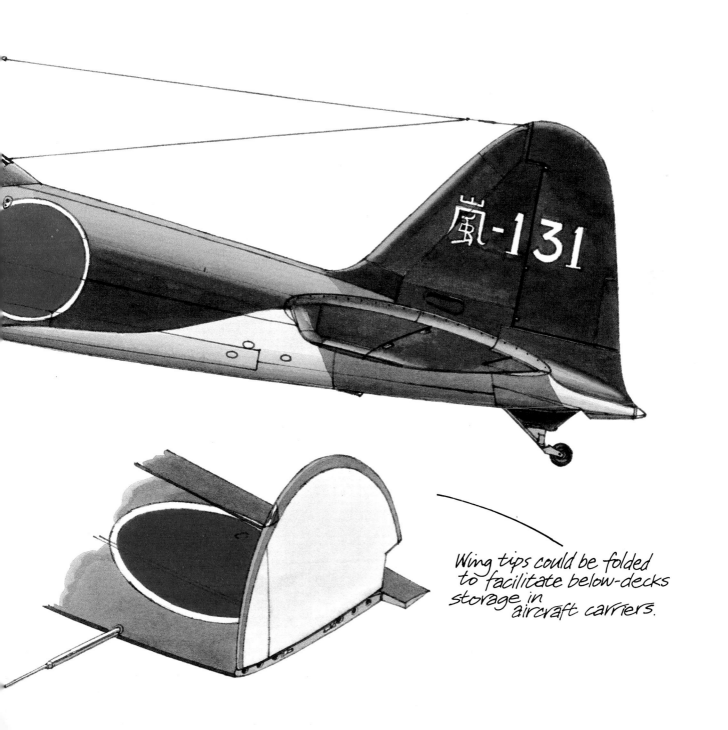

Wing tips could be folded
to facilitate below-decks
storage in
aircraft carriers.

MITSUBISHI A6M ZERO-SEN

This famous aeroplane, more commonly known as the Zero or Zero-Sen, was as important to Japan as the Spitfire was to Britain. Both aircraft came to represent the fighting spirit of a nation, and few earned their lasting fame with greater distinction.

The Zero was designed for the Imperial Navy to replace the Mitsubishi A5M, a splendid little fighting aeroplane designed by one of Japan's most famous aviation engineers, Jiro Horikoshi. The A5Ms were flown operationally during the Sino-Japanese war where, in 1937, they destroyed ten Chinese aircraft in a single dogfight over Nanking. A curious indifference on the part of the Western powers to this and other exhibitions of Japanese aircraft efficiency resulted in a most unpleasant shock to American and British staff when, just four years later at Pearl Harbor, the serious threat of the next-generation Mitsubishi product was stunningly brought home to them. The fact that a previously ignored light carrier-borne fighter was able to fly rings round the latest US land-based fighters seemed totally unbelievable.

Horikoshi's basic brief when he and his team set out in 1937 to create the A6M was for a hard-hitting, long-range naval aircraft with a speed of 500km/h. He produced a lightly built but very clean and efficient machine capable of exceeding the speed required and with outstanding manoeuvrability. A final design using an improved engine was put into production in 1940 and, before official trials were even half-completed, two squadrons with 15 aircraft were sent to China for testing under battle conditions. They decimated all opposition (destroying 99 enemy aircraft for the loss of only two of their own) and provided the West with its first real inkling of what this previously unknown machine was really capable of.

General Claire Chennault, commander of the American Volunteer Group, the Flying Tigers, reported on the Zero; but his timely warning of its potential threat appears to have been ignored by Washington bureaucracy. The devastating attack on Pearl Harbor came on Sunday 7 December 1941, when more than 400 A6M2s and -3s were flying from Japanese carriers, and further large numbers were being delivered as they rolled off the production lines. It very soon seemed to the Allies that the skies were full of Zeros. Their range and endurance were amazing and their unrivalled all-round performance enabled them to sweep away the mainly second-rate fighters that dared to oppose them. Not until the summer of 1943, when Zeros were finally outclassed by American F4U Corsairs and, from late August, F6F Hellcats, was the myth of their apparent invincibility dispelled.

Before then, however, the Zero reigned supreme and

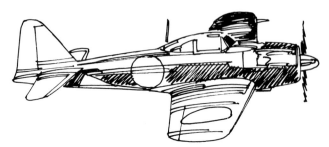

its innumerable exploits in the Far East might best be exemplified by an account of one famous engagement in April 1942. Operating from an airstrip at Lae in New Guinea, a flight of nine Zeros led by the Imperial Japanese Navy's 'ace' pilot Saburo Sakai crossed the Owen Stanley range of mountains at a height of over 4875m for an attack on the Allied airfield at Port Moresby. In a dogfight over the target Sakai's Zeros clashed with four Bell P-39D Airacobras of the USAAF. Sakai shot down two of the Airacobras, and his two wingmen bagged one each. The battle was over within minutes with the Zeros emerging unscathed. Other long-range attacks saw these Zeros in action as far afield as the Philippines, Singapore and the Bay of Bengal.

The fitting of a drop tank boosted fuel capacity to 710 litres and this was sufficient to give the Zero, with its small economical engine, an unparalelled range (for a fighter) of almost 3200km and, when one considers the fact that this would involve both man and machine in an endurance of *six to eight hours*, the proliferation of Zero myths becomes more understandable.

After the 1942 Midway conflict, which saw the sinking of four of Japan's major aircraft carriers, Zeros were largely land-based. The Mitsubishi designers made desperate efforts to adapt and improve the type. It was especially outclassed at high altitudes, but an attempt to rectify this failure by fitting the A6M4 with a turbocharged engine proved abortive, and the A6M5 was rushed into production at both Mitsubishi and its biggest rival, Nakajima, in the summer of 1943. But the new machine was only slightly better than those which preceded it. Its wings were strengthened for steeper and faster diving, and it was fitted with separate engine exhaust stacks and an increased variety of armament combinations.

Unfortunately, none of these additional sophistications equipped the Zero to compete effectively with its new rival Allied opponents and, although production of the A6M5 continued right up to the end of hostilities, the brilliant Sun of the Japanese Zero was at last beginning to set. Perhaps its only advantage at this stage of the war was that, flown by an experienced pilot, it might still

SPECIFICATION

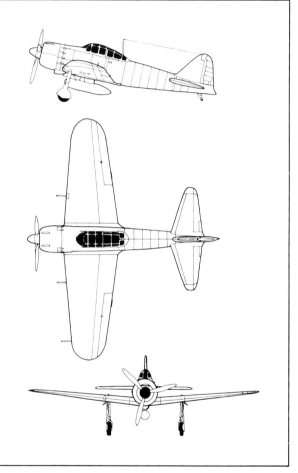

Country of origin: Japan.

Manufacturer: Mitsubishi Jukogyo Kaisha.

Type: Single-seat fighter.

Year: 1941.

Engine: 950hp Nakajima NK1C. Sakae 12 14-cylinder two-row radial.

Wingspan: 12.0m (39ft 5in).

Length: 9m (29ft 9in).

Height: 2.9m (9ft 6in).

Weight: 2800kg (6160lb).

Maximum speed: 534km/h (332mph).

Ceiling: 10,300m (33,790ft).

Range: With drop tanks 3110km (1940 miles).

Armament: Two 20mm Type 99 Model 1 cannon in wings, two 7.7mm Type 97 machine guns in upper fuselage, wing racks for two 60kg bombs.

outmanoeuvre most of the current opposition, if only in the evasive sense.

The Zero was never regarded as a versatile aircraft, but an A6M2-N seaplane version was built at Koizumi by Nakajima to serve as a convoy escort, and the Sasebo and Hitachi companies between them produced the A6M2-K dual-cockpit trainer. These were the only two operational models ever to depart from the basic design shape, and the function in each case was non-aggressive. In its death throes the Zero was used to perform what must be the

absolute and ultimate act of aggression: that of a suicide or *Kamikaze* attack. Together with Yokosuka MXY-7s, which were the only aircraft ever to be built in numbers for pilot-suicide attacks, and almost all other available aircraft, Zeros packed with high explosive carried out around 1900 *Kamikaze* sorties (as against some 5000 normal bomber raids) and their score of hits at Okinawa alone was 24 ships sunk and 200 damaged. All sinkings were of American ships, and of those damaged only four were British. The heavily armoured flight decks of British aircraft carriers proved to be an invaluable defence against suicide aircraft.

Figures for total production vary slightly, but all are around the 10,450 mark and it is generally agreed that Zeros made up not less than 80 per cent of all single-seat fighters put into service with the Imperial Japanese Navy in World War II.

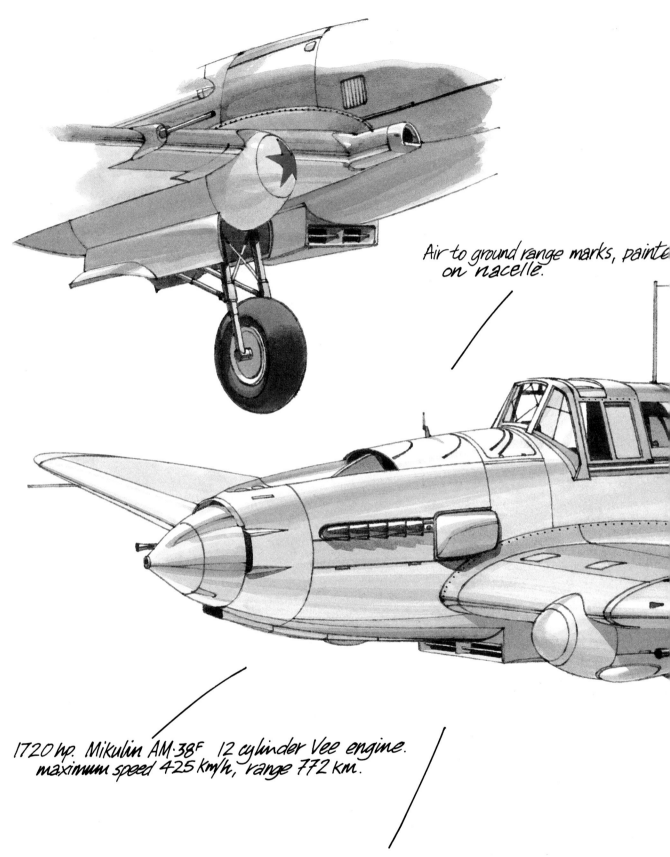

Air to ground range marks, painted on nacelle.

1720 hp. Mikulin AM·38F 12 cylinder Vee engine. maximum speed 425 km/h, range 772 km.

Forward fuselage and crew area constructed of 5 to 12 mm armour plate

ILYUSHIN Il-2
STORMOVIK

Aircraft shown in winter camouflage.

Two pod-mounted 37mm NS37 cannon.

ILYUSHIN Il-2 STORMOVIK

To every outward intent and purpose, the Ilyushin Il-2 Stormovik, which made its first flight on 30 December 1939, was just another single-seat ground-attack aircraft bearing a strong resemblance to a British counterpart, the ill-fated Fairey Battle. It was armed with two 20mm cannon and two 7.62mm machine guns fixed into the wings, and had underwing racks for bombs and/or rockets. With a top speed when 'clean' of around 450km/h, an operational ceiling of 6500 metres and a range of 600km, it appeared to be a rather mundane specimen.

It was nothing of the kind, and any resemblance to the Fairey Battle was literally *less* than skin-deep. The Battle was an unmitigated disaster: the Il-2 Stormovik, together with its subsequent version the Il-10, was an absolute runaway success. The British machine was a death-trap, but the Stormovik was marvellously safe because its designers had sacrificed a lot of payload in order to encase the cockpit and engine areas with a massive 700kg of protective armour plating. Small wonder that its pilots loved the Stormovik. It was a real survival machine.

Almost immediately after its maiden flight, the original prototype was modified to take a new and more powerful engine. Then, after further trials, the aircraft went into full production in March 1941, just three months before the German invasion in June. The Stormovik rapidly settled down to the business of tackling the German tank units and, had the aircraft been available in greater numbers, that first big German onslaught might well have been slowed to a crawl. The Il-2, fitted quickly with an extremely powerful new 23mm gun, knocked out tanks and ravaged infantry, and generally made its presence hard felt. Production was pushed to the limit and, when the aircraft was honourably retired many years later, the number of Il-2s put into service exceeded that of any other warplane anywhere in the world. The final production total was 36,163.

So much for ground attack. In the air, the Il-2 was faced from the very beginning with mighty opposition. In spite of its protective armour plating, the German Bf 109 was a devastating adversary and Il-2 losses were high. Something had to be done, and quickly. In October 1942 the Bf 109 problem was remedied with much success by the introduction of the Il-2M3 which had a cockpit enlarged to accommodate a rear-gunner: an unpleasant surprise for the Luftwaffe, and one which greatly reduced the Bf 109s' supremacy in dogfights over the Front.

Not long afterwards, and certainly in plenty of time for the important Battle of Kursk in mid-1943, the calibre of the Il-2's main guns was increased to 37mm. This gave them sufficient stopping power to take out Panther and

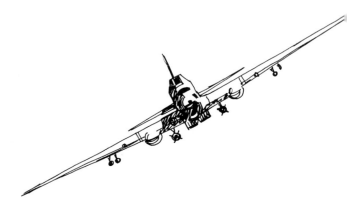

Tiger tanks from the rear, thought by the Germans to be virtually invincible. The Stormovik proved them wrong and, as it was now capable of giving the Bf 109 a very stiff contest as well, it had rapidly become a force to be reckoned with.

By this time Russian factories were turning out the improved Stormoviks at the rate of 300 a week. The autumn of 1944 saw the introduction of the Il-10 series, a completely new design. The new model incorporated changes in engine installation, and the landing gear was altered so that it turned at an angle of 90° on retraction to lie flush inside the wings instead of in bulged fairings. These and other important modifications reduced the overall drag by a factor of something like 50 per cent and so vastly improved performance. The Stormovik had come of age. It had also become much celebrated, and very widely known. Different sides gave it different names. The Germans called it *Schwarzer Tod* (Black Death), but to those who flew it, the aircraft was always known affectionately as *Ilyusha*.

The Il-2s, and later the Il-10s, were deployed in every Russian theatre of war, but undoubtedly its most effective role was on the Eastern Front. Thanks to its ability to survive well at low altitudes, it was able to launch its attacks at heights often under 90m. This capability gave it two tremendous advantages: an element of complete surprise as it seemed to appear out of nowhere, and the ability to rake the thinner rear armour of enemy tanks and armoured emplacements with horizontal fire, the angle of maximum damage.

Stormovik pilots had a favourite tactic, known to friend and foe alike as the Circle of Death. Swooping in very low, the aircraft would streak down on one side of the target, curve across its front, and traverse again to attack from the rear. This way, a flight of several aircraft would form a continuous circle, attacking again and again until their ammunition was exhausted. During the Battle of Kursk, just 20 minutes of this murderous circling cost the German 9th

SPECIFICATION

Il-2M3

Country of origin: Soviet Union.

Design Bureau: Sergei V. Ilyushin OKB.

Type: Two-seat armoured close-support aircraft.

Year: 1941.

Engine: 1720hp Mikulin AM-38F liquid-cooled V12.

Wingspan: 14.6m (47ft 11in).

Length: 12m (39ft 5in).

Height: 3.4m (11ft 2in).

Weight: 6360kg (14,021lb).

Maximum speed: 425km/h (264 mph).

Ceiling: 6000m (19,680ft).

Range: 772km (480 miles).

Armament: Two 23mm VYa cannon and two
7.62mm ShKAS machine guns in wings, and racks
for eight 82mm rockets and four 100kg bombs;
one 12.7mm UBT defensive gun in rear cockpit.

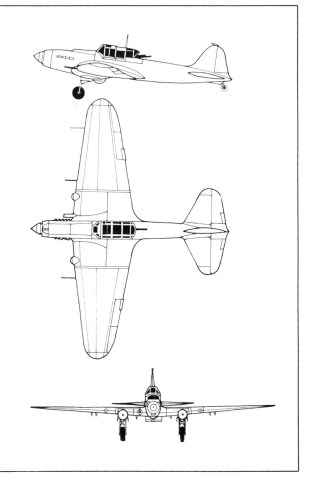

Panzer Division 70 of the latest tanks. By this same
manoeuvre, the 3rd, 9th and 17th Panzer Divisions lost no
fewer than 580 Panthers and Tigers, with the latter
Division suffering most heavily. The 17th Panzer Division
began the battle with 300 'invincible' tanks: the Stormoviks
reduced this number to 60. It was a stunning victory.

There can be no doubt at all that the Stormovik was a
truly outstanding aircraft, probably the best ever of its
type. It was safer for its pilot in combat than any other
similar machine, and fully trained pilots are undoubtedly as
valuable as the aeroplanes they fly. So in this respect alone,
the Stormovik, with by far the lowest casualty rating of any
Soviet machine, made a vitally important contribution. It
was also responsible for saving the lives of countless
Russian infantry, as relfected by Stalin's oft-quoted remark:
'. . . this aircraft is as essential to the Soviet Army as air and
bread'.

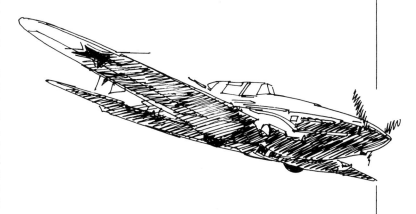

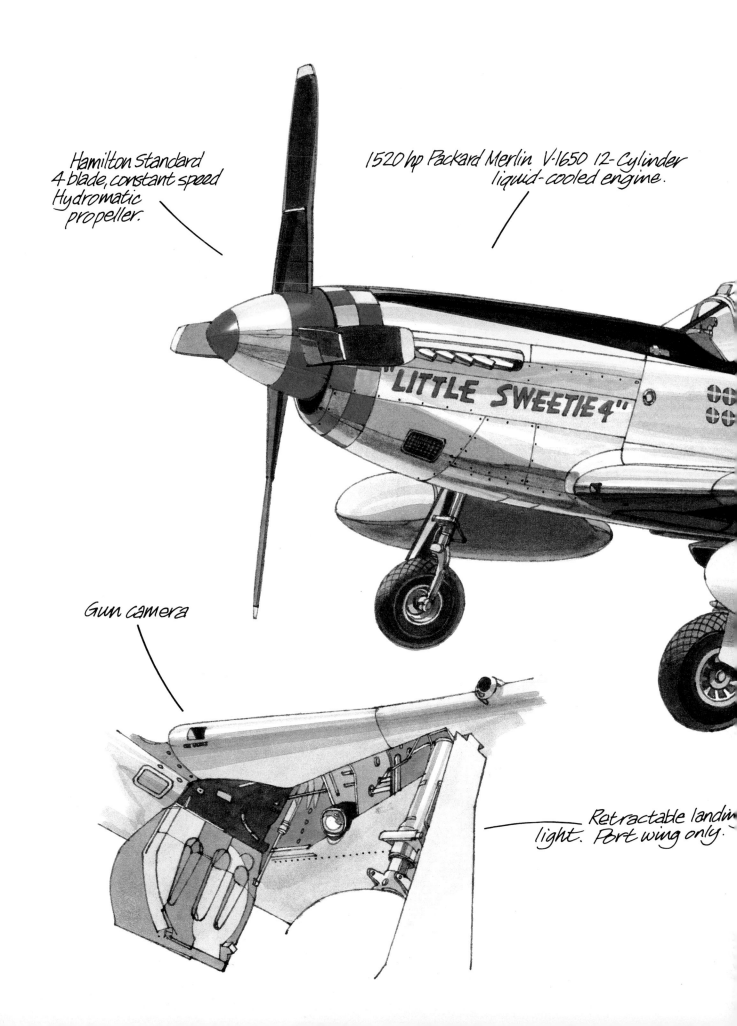

Hamilton Standard
4 blade, constant speed
Hydromatic
propeller.

1520 hp Packard Merlin V-1650 12-Cylinder
liquid-cooled engine.

"LITTLE SWEETIE 4"

Gun camera

Retractable landing
light. Port wing only.

NORTH AMERICAN P-51
MUSTANG

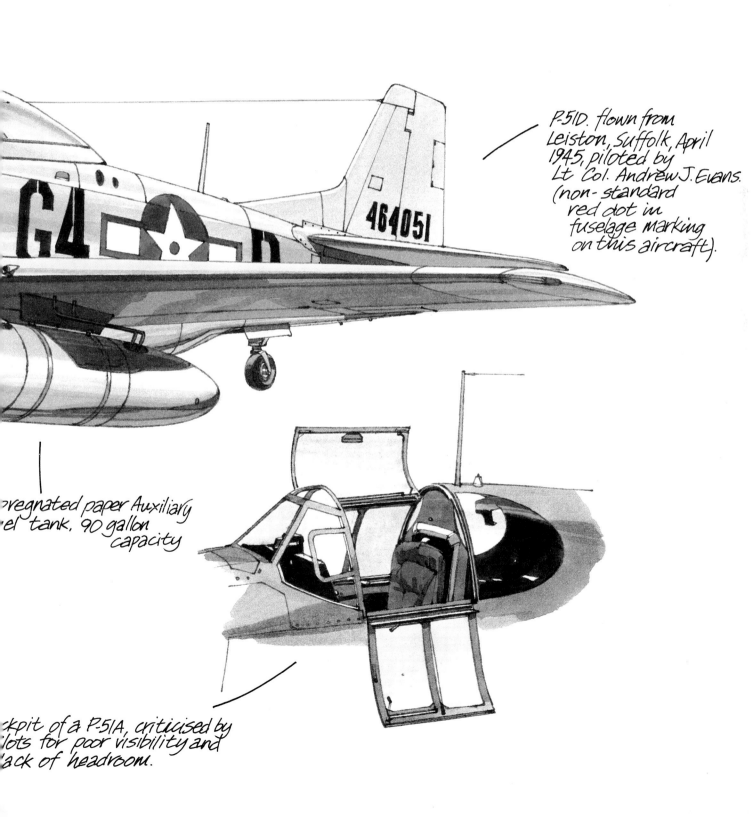

P-51D. flown from
Leiston, Suffolk, April
1945, piloted by
Lt. Col. Andrew J. Evans.
(non-standard
red dot in
fuselage marking
on this aircraft).

464051

G4

regnated paper Auxiliary
el tank, 90 gallon
capacity

kpit of a P-51A, criticised by
lots for poor visibility and
ack of headroom.

NORTH AMERICAN P-51 MUSTANG

Some aviation historians, and certainly those pilots who flew them, subscribe most strongly to the proposition that the North American P-51 Mustang was the greatest piston-engined fighter of World War II. Be that as it may, few, if any, aircraft had a more intriguing history.

In 1939, the British, badly in need of more combat aircraft, asked the North American Aviation company to build for them, under licence, the Curtiss Hawk 87. The Americans were willing to comply, but said they could build a new and better machine. They not only could... they did, and they carried out the assignment with astonishing speed. They designed, built and test-flew a prototype within 17 weeks! Considering NAA had never built a fighter before, this was an incredible feat.

When this, the first of all Mustangs (known then as the NA.73X), took to the air on 26 October 1940, it was new from nose to tail. It was about the size of the Spitfire and had about the same power, yet it had heavier armament (four 0.5in and four 0.300in guns or four 20mm cannon), three times the fuel capacity and higher speed! It had only one real drawback: the Allison engine delivered only moderate power at anything over medium altitudes. Most of the first Mustangs and USAAF P-51s and F-6s with the Allison engine were therefore used as low-level fighter, attack and reconnaissance aircraft.

In 1942 it was suggested that the altitude-limitation problem might be overcome by fitting a Rolls-Royce Merlin engine. NAA not only agreed, they did a huge amount of redesigning, and the end result exceeded all expectations. This revitalised Mustang was designated the P-51B.

The birth could not have been more propitious. Allied bombers raiding targets deep inside Germany in daylight were having to go it alone, and the cost in lost aircraft was cause for grave concern. When the first of the P-51Bs arrived in England at the end of 1943, they were welcomed with profound relief. To facilitate long-range escort duty, this revolutionary Mustang was fitted with an extra rear-fuselage tank and with drop tanks, first of 75 US gallons and later of 108 US gallons capacity under each wing, permitting a round-trip range of about 1700 miles. This was sufficient to accompany the heavy bombers on their longest raids. Once the tanks were dropped, the P-51Bs could deal on pretty even terms with any Bf 109 or Fw 190 or indeed any other piston-engined German fighter.

The rate of bomber losses fell sharply as more and more Mustangs were delivered into service. Reichsmarschall Goering, head of the German Luftwaffe, said that when he saw these fighters over Berlin, he knew the war

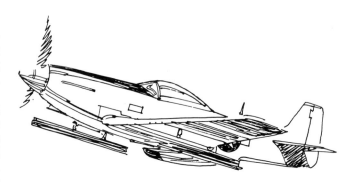

was lost. But still further design improvements were yet to come. The P-51's flush hinged canopy offered limited rear vision, and it was decided that a sliding bulged design of the type made by the Malcolm company in Britain would be much better. The conversion proved to be an easy one, and modifications were carried out in the field. By spring 1944, even this had been replaced by one of the first teardrop or blister canopies.

The P-51D models had two more 0.5in wing guns, increasing the armament to six machine guns with an additional 620 rounds of ammunition. Strengthened mainplanes allowed for the fitting of racks for two 1000lb bombs. The power to fly the slight extra weight was to come from a new Packard-Merlin engine known to the British as the Merlin 68.

First arrivals in England of the P-51D were met with great excitement, though careful check flights demonstrated that this new Mustang was, in fact, not quite such a good performer as the P-51Bs already in service. It was fractionally slower to climb, about 3mph slower in level flight and directional control was not so good due to the reduced side area of the rear fuselage. A few experienced pilots preferred to stick with the previous model, but the P-51D was fitted with an added dorsal fin which restored the aiming accuracy. Six Bazooka-type rockets, three slung under each wing, were fitted to a few P-51s used for attack missions.

A very much more striking type was built towards the end of the war, the P-82 Twin Mustang. This extraordinary aircraft was basically two lengthened Mustangs joined together by new centre wing and tail surfaces, with new landing gears. The Twin went on to become one of the standard long-range night and escort fighters of the Korean war, where three of them became the first North Korean Air Force victories. Conversely, Mustang Twins of the USAF inflicted the first losses to the other side, when several Soviet-built Yak-9s were shot down during the first two days of the conflict.

By 1943 North American Aviation's design team were

SPECIFICATION

P-51D

Country of origin: USA.

Manufacturer: North American Aviation, Inc.

Type: Single-seat fighter-bomber.

Year: 1944.

Engine: 1520hp Packard V-1650 V12 (licence-built Rolls-Royce Merlin 61 series)

Wingspan: 11.3m (37ft 1in).

Length: 9.8m (32ft 4in.)

Height: 4.17m (13ft 8in).

Weight: 5260kg (11,600lb).

Maximum speed: 703km/h (437mph).

Ceiling: 12,770m (41,900ft).

Range: 3930km (2440 miles).

Armament: Six 0.5in Browning MG 53-2 machine guns and wing racks for two 1000lb bombs.

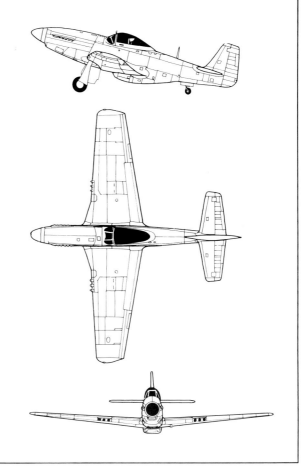

busy with a revised airframe which was planned to reduce structure weight. Gradually the Light Mustang became almost a new type, though it remained only a paper project until 1944 when it went ahead as the N.A.105. A pure interceptor, the new model was built in three forms, the XP-51F ultralight model, the XP-51G with six instead of four guns, more fuel and a British Merlin 145M and five-blade propeller, and the XP-51J with highly boosted Allison engine and no inlet below the spinner. All had straight leading edges made possible by the very small wheels, and speeds reached 494mph. Out of this effort came a further model, the N.A.126, and this went into production as the P-51H. This was the standard Mustang at VJ-day, but orders were cancelled overnight and output stopped at the 555th P-51H, to make total output, 15,586 including 266 P-51Ds made in Australia.

Other types of this versatile aeroplane continued in service long after World War II was over. The USAAF and Air National Guard picked the Mustang as standard post-war piston-engined fighter-bomber, though it was not the P-51H that was selected but the mass-produced P-51D. Called F-51D from 1947, they saw intensive use in Korea, formed the backbone of the infant Israeli air force and served with many other countries. Even today the USAF has supported the manufacture of new piston and turboprop Mustang versions by the Cavalier company, and the Piper Enforcer is currently flying with the USAF as an economical attack aircraft derived from the Cavalier Turbo Mustang III!

Today, more than 40 years after its creation, the Mustang is one of the aircraft most avidly sought after by civilian flying buffs, and it is confidently expected that the legendary P-51 will be ranging the skies well into the next century.

Pressurised cabin, altitude 42,650 ft

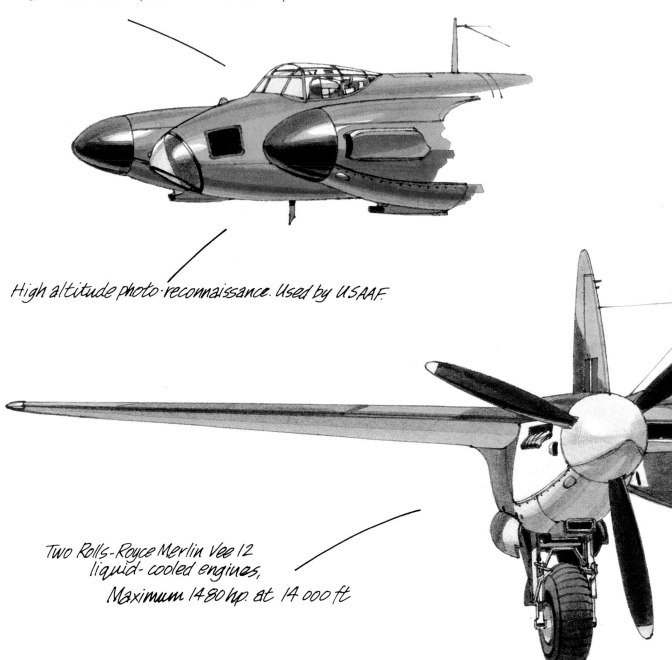

High altitude photo-reconnaissance. Used by U.S.A.A.F.

Two Rolls-Royce Merlin Vee 12
liquid-cooled engines,
    Maximum 1480 hp. at 14 000 ft

de HAVILLAND MOSQUITO

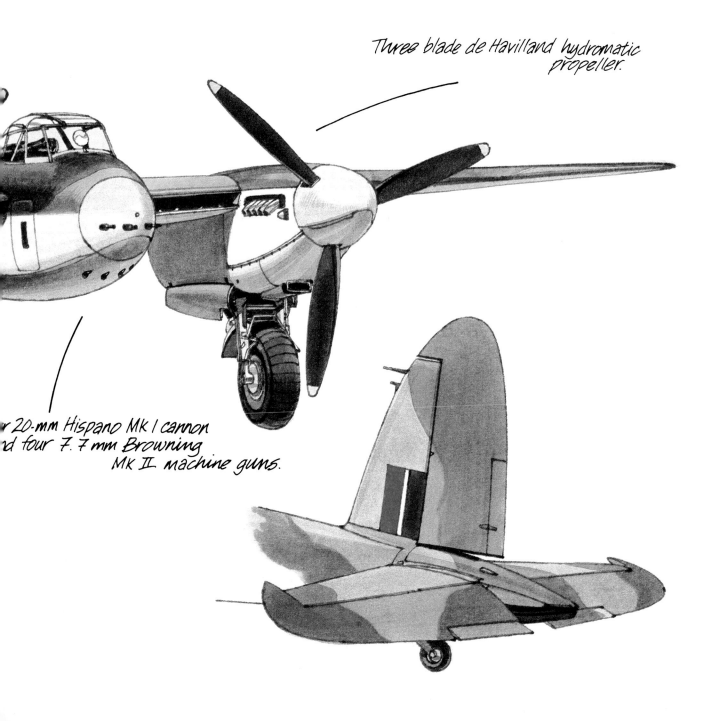

Three blade de Havilland hydromatic propeller.

r 20-mm Hispano Mk I cannon
d four 7.7 mm Browning
Mk II machine guns.

de HAVILLAND MOSQUITO

Perhaps the most amazing fact about this phenomenal combat aircraft is that from the very first day of its conception nobody but its creators wanted anything to do with the idea, and it was not until January 1940, after three whole years of dogged persistence by Sir Geoffrey de Havilland and his colleagues C. C. Walker and R. E. Bishop that a specification was reluctantly issued. Even then, the programme was cancelled twice by production czar Lord Beaverbrook and, when at last a prototype was flown in November, almost another whole year had gone by.

The problem was that almost everyone then in authority thought the de Havilland people were mad. Patterned in 1937 on the new Albatros transport, the D.H. 98 Mosquito was originally conceived as a fast light bomber. Out of this beginning grew the revolutionary idea of a machine whose twin Merlin engines would provide it with such great speed as to make any defensive armament unnecessary. The airframe was to be constructed entirely of wood, using balsa and plywood sandwich strengthened by rigid panels and stringers of spruce. The very thought of an unarmed bomber, much less a wooden one, provoked incredulous snorts and a shaking of heads. Royal Air Force bigwigs simply did not want to know. Had they been less reactionary, and had the Mosquito been put into production when it was first mooted, the war might not have lasted so long.

As things were, the first operational flight did not take place until September 1941, when a single Mosquito reconnaissance version made an unarmed run to take a series of aerial photographs of the French Atlantic coast. Messerschmitt Bf 109s attempted to intercept it, but this strange new aircraft outran the German fighters with such derisive ease that their pilots must have been astounded. It is safe to say that the RAF pilot was equally impressed, and two months later 105 Squadron took delivery of its first few B.IV bombers. Curiously, though, these did not go into action until May 1942, when they did so with a 2000lb bombload. From this point on, however, it must have been perfectly obvious to everyone concerned in aerial warfare that what they had in this radical aircraft was something very special indeed. Continued bomber development resulted in 1943 in the B.XVI, which was equipped with a pressure cabin and a bomb-bay sufficiently enlarged to take a 'cookie' weighing 4000lb, as big as those carried by the much-heavier Lancasters.

Back in May 1941, the first Mosquito F.II night fighter version took to the air. It had airborne radar, four cannon under the floor and four machine guns in the nose, and this impressive array of firepower when allied with the aeroplane's great speed of 400mph made it the scourge of all opposition. But this range of armament was only the first of numerous variations, which included mines, depth charges and rockets, and even a six-pounder 57mm gun internally mounted low on the centreline.

This most versatile of all British aircraft could be, and was, equipped to hit any kind of target at any time of night or day, and it did so with comparative impunity. Its unprecedented combination of speed, range and destructive power made it practically invincible, probably the most fearsome nuisance-weapon ever to harass the German forces. Unmatched as a daytime intruder it was also perfect, when fitted with Oboe precision navigational aids, for putting down accurate marker flares at night for a following bomber stream.

By 1941 de Havilland were developing Mosquitoes in several major families. The bomber and reconnaissance versions had no guns and the pilot and navigator entered via a belly door. By 1942 the two-stage Merlin 60 and 70 was becoming available, with broad 'paddle-blade' propellers, and cabins began to be pressurised. By 1943 bulged bomb bays were carrying the 4000lb 'cookie' bomb, four times the original planned bombload. The fighters had flat bulletproof windscreens and, because of the four cannon under the floor, the door was moved to the side. The early Mk II with AI.IV radar gave way to later marks in which a bulged nose radar replaced the four machine guns. Most numerous mark of all was the FB.VI fighter-bomber, which had no radar but the full gun armament plus two 500lb bombs in the bomb bay behind the cannon and either two or more under the wings or, alternatively eight rockets or two drop tanks. The T.III trainer was basically a Mk II fighter without radar or armament, and with dual controls.

The Sea Mosquito, built to Admiralty Specification N.15/44 and not properly introduced into service until after the end of the war, was first landed, on the deck of HMS *Indefatigable*, in March 1944 by the redoubtable

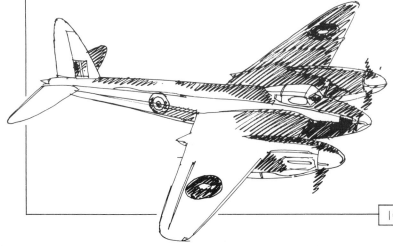

SPECIFICATION

FB.VI

Country of origin: Great Britain.

Manufacturer: de Havilland Aircraft Co Ltd.

Type: Fighter-bomber.

Year: 1941.

Engine: Two 1635hp Rolls-Royce Merlin 25 liquid-cooled V12.

Wingspan: 16.5m (54ft 2in).

Length: 12.35m (40ft 6in).

Height: 4.65m (15ft 3in).

Weight: 10,096kg (22,260lb).

Maximum speed: 612km/h (380mph).

Ceiling: 10,050m (33,000ft).

Range: 2990km (1860 miles).

Armament: Four 20mm Hispano cannon and four 0.303in Browning machine guns, two 500lb bombs in fuselage bay with two 250 or 500lb bombs, or eight rockets, on wing racks. Alternative armament included mines, depth charges and many other stores.

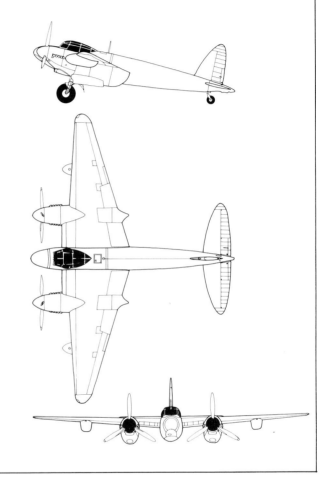

naval test pilot Lieutenant-Commander E. M. Brown. The first production model the torpedo-carrying TR.33, was assigned to 811 Squadron, and a familiarisation programme of 'circuits and bumps' was carried out at Ford naval air station in August 1946.

Remarkable wartime exploits of the 'Mossie' were so numerous and varied it is difficult to choose which of them are most worthy of recording here. One of the many unusual sorties was carried out on the 25th September 1942. British Intelligence sources were advised that the German Gestapo headquarters in Norway's capital, Oslo, housed records of partisans and agents working for the Allied cause. Pinpoint destruction of that particular building would help protect those who were supplying valued secret information. A flight of Mosquitoes undertook the long-range attack, reduced the Gestapo HQ to a heap of blazing rubble and were home, in contemporary parlance 'in plenty of time for tea'.

Another similar high-precision raid, code-named Operation Jericho, was undertaken by no fewer than 18 FB.VIs of 140 wing on 18th February 1944 against the fortress-like prison at Amiens in France. Hundreds of resistance fighters were being held there, facing imminent execution. Two waves of 'Mossies' streaked in fast and low and blasted a gap in the prison walls through which most of the resistance men escaped.

Between its inception and the closing of production at the end of 1950 a total of 7785 Mosquitoes was built, including 1134 in Canada and 212 in Australia. Most were air-combat variants, day- and night-fighters and fighter-bombers. Not a tremendous number, but one thing is quite certain: we shall never see its like again.

2000 hp Pratt & Whitney R-2800 Double Wasp
18 cylinder two-row radial engine driving
a Hamilton constant speed propeller

Two auxiliary fuel tanks
and one long-range fuel
tank-all jettisonable.

F6F-5 in colours of US Navy VF-12, operating
on board the fleet carrier USS Randolph, 1945.

GRUMMAN F6F
HELLCAT

Six 0·5 in
Colt Browning machine
guns mounted
in wings.

Wings could be folded for easy
stowage of aircraft on board carriers.

GRUMMAN F6F HELLCAT

In four months after Pearl Harbor (7 December 1941) the Imperial Japanese Army and Navy swept through the Western Pacific and south-east Asia, conquering an area much greater than any armed force had ever subdued in human history. They were able to do this because they had, unexpectedly, complete mastery of the air. The only significant opposition came from a handful of Grumman F4F Wildcat fighters of the US Navy, and not only were these outnumbered but they were inferior – except in the pilots – to the opposing Navy A6M 'Zero' and Army Ki-43. Something had to be done quickly. Grumman strove to improve the tough but slow F4F and also got out the drawing boards and, under great pressure, designed a new fighter from scratch.

The prototype F6F Hellcat flew on 26 June 1942, with a 1700hp engine. Almost at once it was re-engined with a great Double Wasp of 2000hp, the most powerful available. This made it a real winner, so that despite its great size, strength and weight it could still outfly the lightweight fighters of Japan. Not since the simple days of 1918 did a programme move so fast. The first F6F-3 production Hellcat came off the line on 4 October 1942, despite the fact that the factory was still being built around it! This same factory then proceeded to churn out 12,274 additional F6Fs in just 29 months, every one a nail in the coffin of Japanese hopes. This one type of aircraft absolutely turned the tables on an airpower that a few months before had seemed irresistible, and by the end of 1943 the Rising Sun was beginning to go down with a vengeance.

The F6F put Grumman and the US Navy squarely in the camp that believed in 'big' fighters – in complete contrast to the Soviet designers who made their fighters as small and light as possible. To some extent Leroy Grumman, Bill Schwendler and the other engineers had little choice. The US Navy wanted to fly long distances and carry heavy loads of weapons and equipment, and this demanded a big fighter, and a big engine (which in turn needed still more fuel). The Hellcat's wing was bigger than that of any other mass-produced single-engine fighter of the war, and its bluff squarish shape was often the last thing a Japanese pilot ever saw. It folded about skewed hinges to lie on each side of the rear fuselage, upper surface outward. The main landing gears, attached at the extremities of the horizontal centre section, retracted straight backwards across the wing, the wheels rotating though 90° to lie just in front of the large split flaps.

The 210 gallons of fuel was housed in self-sealing cells under the cockpit, but unlike the Japanese fighters – which often literally ripped apart under the murderous fire from

the Hellcat's six guns – everything was well protected. The pilot and lubricating oil system alone were protected by armour plate weighing 212lb, and Grumman built their aircraft so unbreakable the company was popularly called 'The Grumman Ironworks'. Yet detail finish on every F6F was like a Cadillac, and the exterior was waxed smooth after being given its coat of Midnight Blue paint.

An unusual feature was that the Hellcat designers mounted the wing at an almost zero angle to the fuselage to reduce drag. This, in turn, gave rise to other design problems, and required the Hellcat's 2000hp Pratt & Whitney R-2800 Double Wasp engine to be mounted with a downwards-angled thrustline. It was this design quirk which gave the Hellcat its distinctive tail-down flight characteristic.

However, despite its improvements over the Wildcat, the Hellcat was still less manoeuvrable than most of the Japanese fighters. Where it scored was in its superior diving speed which enabled it to 'get among them'. Also, it had stability which made it an excellent gun platform. But most importantly it had the ability to absorb punishment. Attacked hard, the lighter, less well-armed Zero Sen would fall out of the sky long before the Hellcat. And so by the end of the war the Hellcat had outfought the Zeros to achieve a record kill ratio of no less than 19:1.

The Hellcat was ideally suited to carrier-based operations. Its massive Pratt & Whitney engine would tow it along the deck of the light carriers of the day and into the air without the need of a catapult. Its big, flapped wing would allow it to be flown down through a gap in the clouds and on to the carrier's deck with a minimum of fuss. Many Hellcats were excellent night fighters, equipped with radar.

Few combat aircraft have ever been constructed in such enormous numbers without undergoing prolonged development resulting in visible obvious changes. With the Hellcat only a real expert can tell the first from the last, though of course the radar of the F6F-3N and F6F-5N night-fighter versions did result in a huge pod projecting ahead of the right wing. Apart from these the differences introduced during the manufacture of well over 12,000

SPECIFICATION

F6F-3

Country of origin: USA.

Manufacturer: Grumman Aircraft Engineering
Corporation.

Type: Single-seat naval fighter.

Year: 1942.

Engine: 2000hp Pratt & Whitney R-2800-10 Double
Wasp 18 cylinder two-row radial.

Wingspan: 13.05m (42ft 10in).

Length: 10.23m (33ft 7in).

Height: 3.99m (13ft 1in).

Weight: 6000kg (13,230lb).

Maximum speed: 605km/h (376mph).

Ceiling: 11,430m (37,500ft).

Range: 1755km (1090 miles).

Armament: Six 0.5in Browning machine guns in
wings.

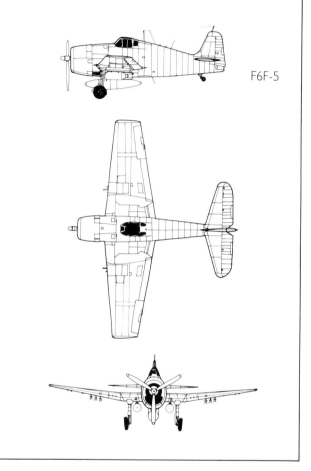

F6F-5

were just a matter of small details. The F6F-5, which with the F6F-3 made up the entire production run, had a windscreen of very slightly changed design, but one had to be in the cockpit to notice. The Dash-5 also had slightly more armour, and under the wings and fuselage it was possible to hang up to 2000lb of bombs or 16 rockets. Some Hellcats in the final production batches had two 20mm cannon in place of the innermost machine guns, and by late 1943 the original R-2800-10 Double Wasp engine had been replaced by the Dash-10W with water injection to increase power for take-off and emergencies to 2200hp. What it boiled down to is that Grumman, despite the frantic haste, got it right first time. Certainly no aircraft did more to win the war against Japan.

The Hellcat saw service with both the British Royal Navy and the Royal New Zealand Air Force, as well as being America's front-line fighter in the Pacific. It is fitting that it last saw active service for the French at Dien Bien Phu as late as 1954. The French who had purchased the G-36 (Wildcat) in 1938 but had fallen to the Germans before their order could be fulfilled, finally got their Grumman fighters a generation later. Despite their advanced age, they gave a magnificent account of themselves.

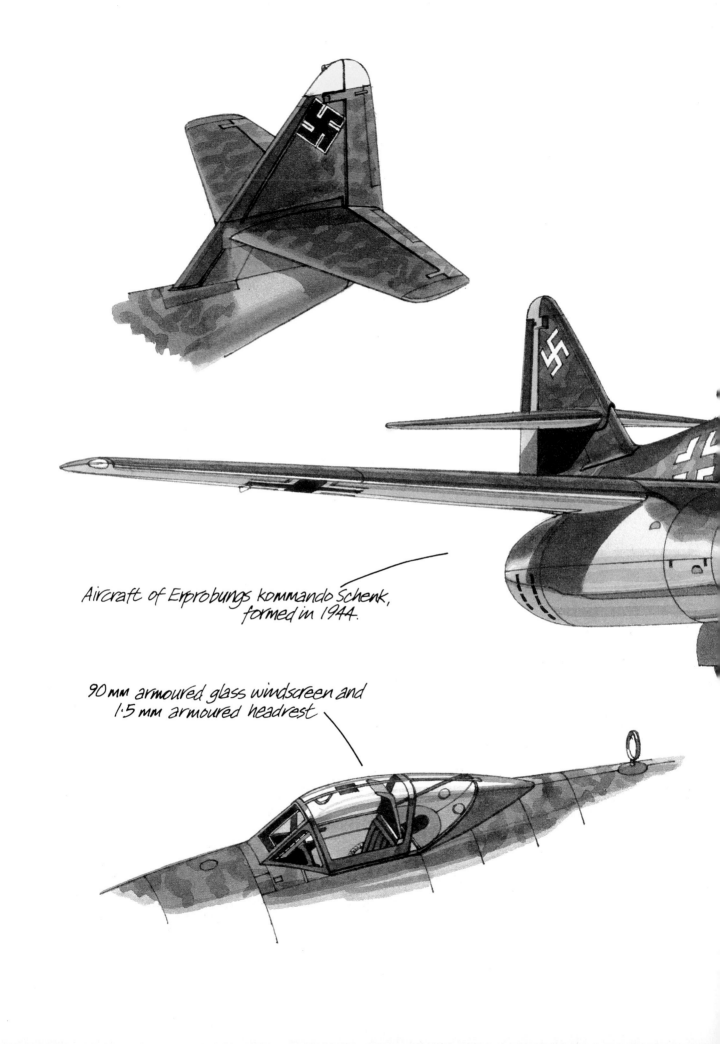

Aircraft of Erprobungs kommando Schenk,
formed in 1944.

90 MM armoured glass windscreen and
1·5 MM armoured headrest

MESSERSCHMITT
Me 262

Four fixed MK 108
30 mm cannon
mounted in nose.

Two Junkers Jumo 004B Axial-flow gas turbines,
each rated at 900 kg thrust. Maximum speed 840 Km/h.

MESSERSCHMITT Me 262

The Me 262 is often described as being the first jet fighter, although other aircraft, including the British Gloster Meteor, are contenders for that title. However, it was certainly one of the first to enter service. Hitler, who always exhibited a strong predilection for aircraft made to drop bombs, insisted that it must be produced primarily as a bomber. This caused some aggravation at Messerschmitt AG, and in the Luftwaffe, but it had no effect on the date when the Me 262 entered service, which was dictated entirely by development of the engines. As it was, the Me 262 was the only jet fighter to see action as a day and night fighter and bomber, and in large numbers.

The first ever jet action was possibly carried out on 18 July 1944, when Hauptmann (Captain) Werner Thierfelder, commander of the EKdo 262 special air unit, crashed after (according to German records) being shot down in combat. On 25 July, an Me 262 made three firing passes at Flt Lt. Wall's reconnaissance Mosquito, all of which Wall managed to evade due to the jet fighter's apparent inability to follow the 'Mossie's' very fast turn – partly because of the jet's higher speed. In any case the radical Jumo 004B engines required very careful handling, and at first only the most skilful pilots were detailed to fly the new jet.

It was in 1938 that Messerschmitt was asked to design a jet fighter. First plans called for the use of two BMW 003 axial turbojets, but BMW was plagued by development problems and so the order was usurped by its rivals Junkers with the Jumo 004. Although there had been many previous German jet engine designs, one of them by Heinkel, airframe development continued by far to outstrip that of engines. Neither of the original 109-003 or -004 models managed to produce adequate thrust with high reliability. So, when the Me 262 first prototype finally took to the air with jet engines on 25 March 1942, it did so with a supplementary Jumo 210 piston engine fitted in the nose. This proved a wise precaution: both BMW 003 turbojets failed in the air, and it was only by the narrowest of margins that the piston engine was able to power the aircraft to a landing.

It was at this stage that the BMWs were replaced by Jumo 004s, and senior Messerschmitt test pilot Fritz Wendel flew the third Me 262 prototype on 18 July 1942, on jets alone. After discovering that he needed to touch the brakes in order to get the tail up (because there was no propeller slipstream), Wendel made a perfect flight.

After further modifications to both engines and airframe, Adolf Galland test-flew the fourth prototype in April 1943 and his enthusiastic report on the aeroplane (soon to be nicknamed *die Schwalbe*, the Swallow) strongly recommended that all fighter production capacity,

except that of the Fw 190, be made over to the Me 262. This was hardly surprising; the 262's handling qualities were superb, and far superior to the mass-produced Bf 109, while performance was of a previously unknown order. Galland's proposal was rejected, but in November 1943 a special committee was formed to oversee and expedite progress of this potential war-winning machine. Even so, and incredibly, Reichsmarschall Goering told Willy Messerschmitt that Hitler insisted that the aircraft must be built to carry bombs.

In the meantime, the Me 262 had been considerably developed with larger fuel tanks and a nosewheel tricycle undercarriage, and with these the fifth prototype was flown in July 1943. Due to the additional airframe weight, and the exceptionally heavy armament of four 30mm cannon, Junkers was asked for even more engine power and this, in spite of concerted effort, was not satisfactorily forthcoming until production of the Jumo 004B-2 began in June 1944. The first batch of Me 262A-1a turbojet fighters, produced in spite of Hitler's constant interference and in fact without his knowledge, was delivered to special unit EKdo 262 only a few weeks later in July 1944.

In most respects, these early operational types offered considerably better performance than any other German machine, but some problems remained. There was a lingering unreliability of the short-life Jumo 004B-2 engine, and aiming and formation-flying difficulties due to the aircraft's tendency to yaw. One of the first A-2a *Sturmvogel* (Stormbird) bomber versions put into service during August 1944 was shot down near Brussels on the 28th of that month by USAAF P-47 Thunderbolts, and two Me 262A-1as of the Kommando Nowotny fell to Urban L. Drew's P-51 in October. Several more of the German jets were beaten in the air by RAF Tempests, and within a matter of only weeks Nowotny himself was shot down and killed. Most of these losses occurred during take-offs or landings.

By this time, of course, the Allies were storming through Europe, and a frantic conversion to different, hastily contrived anti-bomber and ground-attack versions resulted in only about 15 per cent of available Me 262s being left serviceable in the fighter role. Unfortunately for the German command, the A-2a special armament combinations failed to deliver the hoped-for effect, and a few

SPECIFICATION

Me 262A-1a

Country of origin: Germany.

Manufacturer: Messerschmitt AG.

Type: Single-seat fighter.

Year: 1944.

Engine: Two 900kg (1980lb) thrust Junkers Jumo 004B-2 axial turbojets.

Wingspan: 12.5m (41ft).

Length: 10.6m (34ft 9in).

Height: 3.8m (12ft 7in).

Weight: 7131kg (15,720lb).

Maximum speed: 870km/h (540mph).

Ceiling: 11,500m (37,700ft).

Range: 1050km (650 miles).

Armament: Four 30mm MK108 cannon above nose.

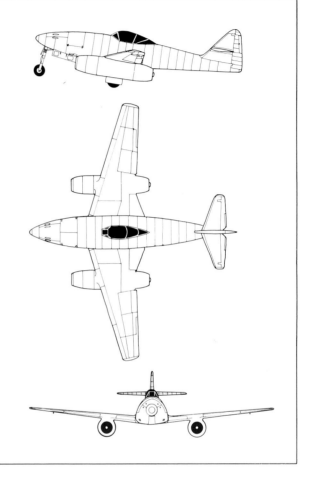

262B-1a night fighters introduced in 1945 arrived too late to be of any real use. Germany was beset by serious shortages, especially of fuel and ammunition and, in spite of the fact that 1433 Me 262s were delivered before VE Day, few became fully operational and erratic deployment of these detracted from their effect.

Nevertheless, this unique and beautiful machine was one of World War II's most advanced aircraft. Reports of Allied aircraft shot down by the jets vary; many state that well over 100 fighters and bombers were destroyed, but no accurate total was ever confirmed. What is quite certain, however, is that the Me 262s were never tested in competition with other turbojet fighters, and that small numbers were shot down by piston-engined aircraft. The 262 could easily outrun any Allied aircraft, and its superb handling and devastating firepower made it a formidable adversary.

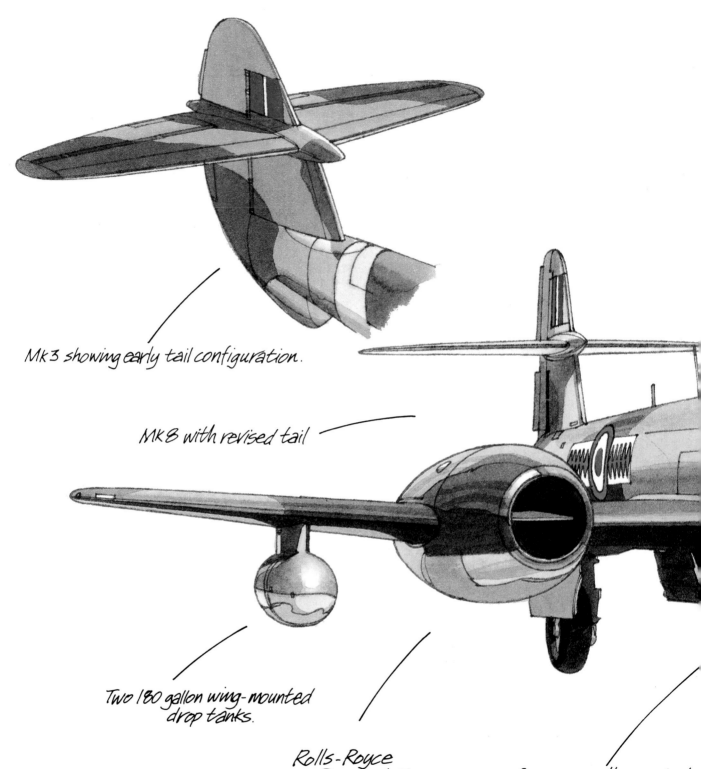

Mk 3 showing early tail configuration.

Mk 8 with revised tail

Two 180 gallon wing-mounted
drop tanks.

Rolls-Royce
Derwent 5
Centrifugal-flow turbo jet.

One 318-gallon central
drop tank.

GLOSTER METEOR

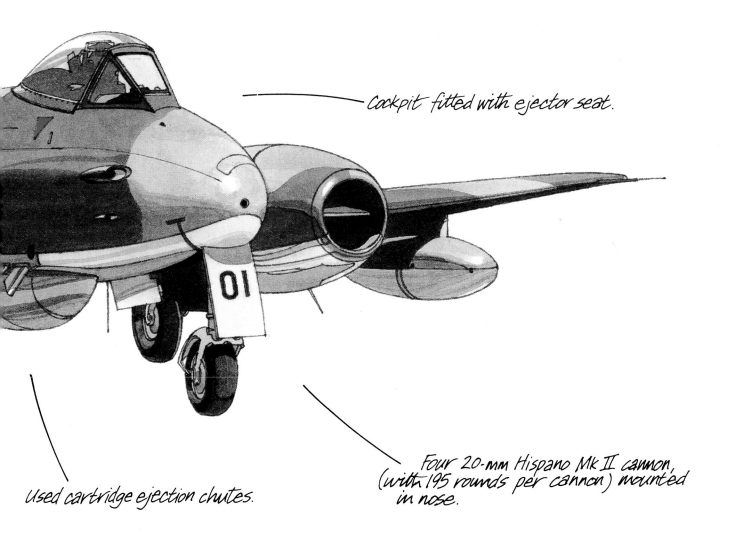

Cockpit fitted with ejector seat.

Used cartridge ejection chutes.

Four 20-mm Hispano Mk II cannon, (with 195 rounds per cannon) mounted in nose.

GLOSTER METEOR

It is intriguing to speculate how the Meteor might have fared had it ever come up against its jet-engined counterpart, the Messerschmitt Me 262. Both were conceived around the same time, in 1940, and both were delivered after a rather long gestation period in July 1944. And, considering their totally separate development, there were striking similarities in basic design, almost as though the huge transitional step from piston to jet could be taken in only one direction. In the event, and although it might easily have been possible, the two were never to meet in anger.

The Gloster twin-jet fighter, to meet specification F.9/40, was designed by a team led by W. G. Carter at Hucclecote and built at a secure works at Bentham. Originally known as the Gloster G41, it was at first named the Thunderbolt, but this name was changed in deference to the American P-47. The original order for twelve unarmed prototypes was reduced to eight, all built before the first one actually took to the air on 5 March 1943.

There was a choice of five types of engine, the first to fly being the Halford H.1 (predecessor of the D. H. Goblin). The first 16 (of 20) Meteor fighters were delivered to the RAF's 616 Squadron at Culmhead from 12 July 1944. The engine chosen was the W.2B/23, built by Rolls-Royce as the Welland, of 1700lb thrust. There was provision for six cannon, but only four were fitted. The Meteor 1 was extremely easy to fly and to maintain, but far slower than the Me 262. At low level it was still the fastest Allied fighter and it did well against V.1 flying bombs.

The first of the 210 Meteor Mark 3s, powered by 2000lb Rolls-Royce Derwent 1s, was flown in September 1944. This had numerous improvements including a sliding canopy. Later, the airframe was strengthened to take the very powerful Rolls-Royce Derwent 5, and versions of this transformed Meteor 4 began to enter service in 1946, the wings later being clipped in order to enhance the rate of roll. The tail of the Mk 4's successor, the Mk 8, was redesigned to give small improvement in buffet threshold. The engine inlets were then enlarged, giving a little more speed. The Mk 8 entered service in 1949, well in time for the Korean War. All told, the Meteor remained in RAF service for 17 years and, including those sold for export (to 12 countries not including German target tugs), 3875 were built. This is more than ten times the total for Britain's first supersonic fighter, the Lightning.

To the men who first flew it, the Meteor came as a stunning revelation. Pilots previously subjected to the vibrating din and clatter of large piston engines marvelled at the Meteor's smooth and silent performance, especially on take-off and landing. There were no fussy propeller-pitch, mixture, carb-air or radiator controls, though the engines took longer to 'spool up' to full thrust. When landing, there was no need for Meteor pilots to worry about crashing nose-over through a too-harsh application of the brakes. With the exception of top-speed flying at high altitudes, the aircraft handled beautifully, though the airframe and its handling were not as good as the Me 262. The engines, however, were of a totally different order of reliability and responsiveness. One immediate first-sight impression was of unprecedented all-round view from the cockpit far ahead of the wing, though this was impeded on the Mk 1 by the rather clumsy canopy.

On the debit side, like all early turbojet aircraft, the Meteor had an enormous thirst, and pilots needed to learn very quickly how to minimise pre-flight checks and take-off time. The Derwents burned up 40 gallons of fuel just to lift the aeroplanes safely off the ground and this, together with the amount required to be held as a safety margin, made considerable inroads on actual operational endurance. Fuel consumption continued high even at cruising speed although this, it must be remembered, was well above that of the Meteor's piston-engined contemporaries. The Mk 1 had a top speed of 410mph but at sea level its speed of about 405mph was very exceptional. Later types went on to create many records, most noted of which was an absolute world speed record, on 7 November 1945, of 606.26mph.

One of the reasons why Meteors were not sent out to face the Me 262 until January 1945 was a wish to prevent any falling into unauthorised hands. There was an urgent need in summer 1944 to intercept V.1 flying bombs. Perhaps not the best of performers at high altitudes, the Meteor 1 was capable of superb acrobatics at low levels, at which the V-bombs were flown, and 616 Squadron destroyed two of the pilotless missiles the first time they were met, on 4 August 1944. The guns had hardly ever been fired in the air and, with the first bomb, the circuits failed. Resourceful Flying Officer Dean manoeuvred alongside the bomb and tumbled it over with the tip of his own wing, a feat best appreciated by those who are aware that *any* mid-air collision, let alone with a V.1, is normally disastrous.

Although designed purely as a fighter, it was recognised early on that with minor adaptations the Meteor would make an excellent ground-attack aircraft. Gloster did

SPECIFICATION

Mk I

Country of origin: Great Britain.

Manufacturer: Gloster Aircraft Co Ltd.

Type: Single-seat fighter.

Year: 1944.

Engine: Two 771kg (1700lb) Rolls-Royce Welland W.2B/23 turbojets.

Wingspan: 13.1m (43ft).

Length: 12.6m (41ft 4in).

Height: 4m (13ft).

Weight: 6259kg (13,800lb).

Maximum speed: 660km/h (410mph).

Ceiling: 12,200m (40,000ft).

Range: 1600km (1000 miles).

Armament: Four 20mm Hispano cannon in nose.

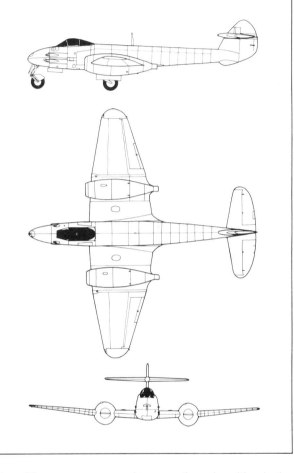

some tests at their own expense, but this line of development was never required by the RAF. The only major variations to basic shape were various tandem two-seat versions introduced after the end of World War II. The first, the T.7, trainer, was instantly identifiable by its long side-hinged framed canopy.

The second two-seater was again designed and built in the absence of any agreed requirement for a two-seat twin-jet all-weather day and night fighter to supersede the Mosquito. Gloster were developing the Javelin, but this ran so late that a modified Meteor had to be bought as a stop-gap. The contract for the Meteor NF.11 went to sister-firm Armstrong Whitworth who were already involved in Meteor production. The Armstrong Whitworth aircraft that was finally accepted was a much-modified version of the Mk 8, with the canopy of the T.7, a nose extension to accommodate the radar, and with the four 20mm cannon moved to an outboard position in the wings. The prototype flew on 31 May 1950. Delivery began soon afterwards. The NF.11 was followed by three further NF marks, by far the best being the NF.14 with new radar, updated avionics, larger fin and a sliding clear-vision canopy. The NF.14 remained in front-line service until No 60 Squadron, RAF, switched to Javelins in 1961. Meteors of all types saw service in many parts of the world and were the only British jet fighters to operate in the Korean War, flown in the ground attack role by 77 Squadron Royal Australian Air Force.

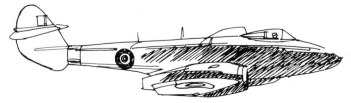

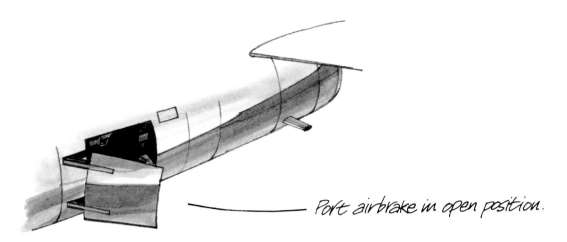

Port airbrake in open position.

Six 0·5 in Colt Browning machine guns.

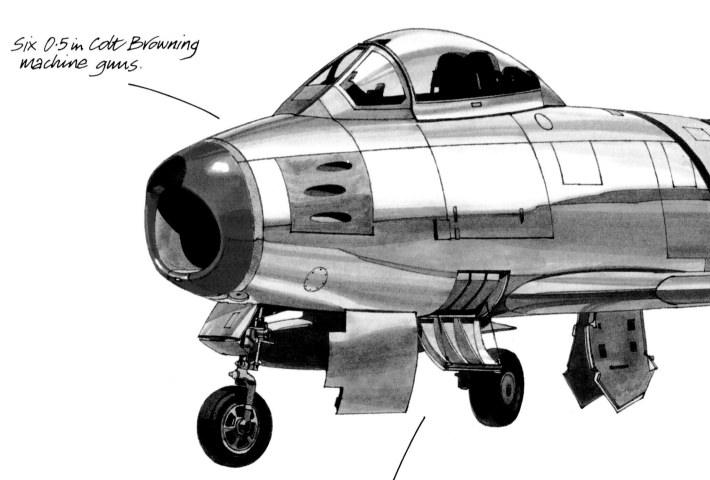

Open ammunition bay door, used as a step.

NORTH AMERICAN F-86 SABRE

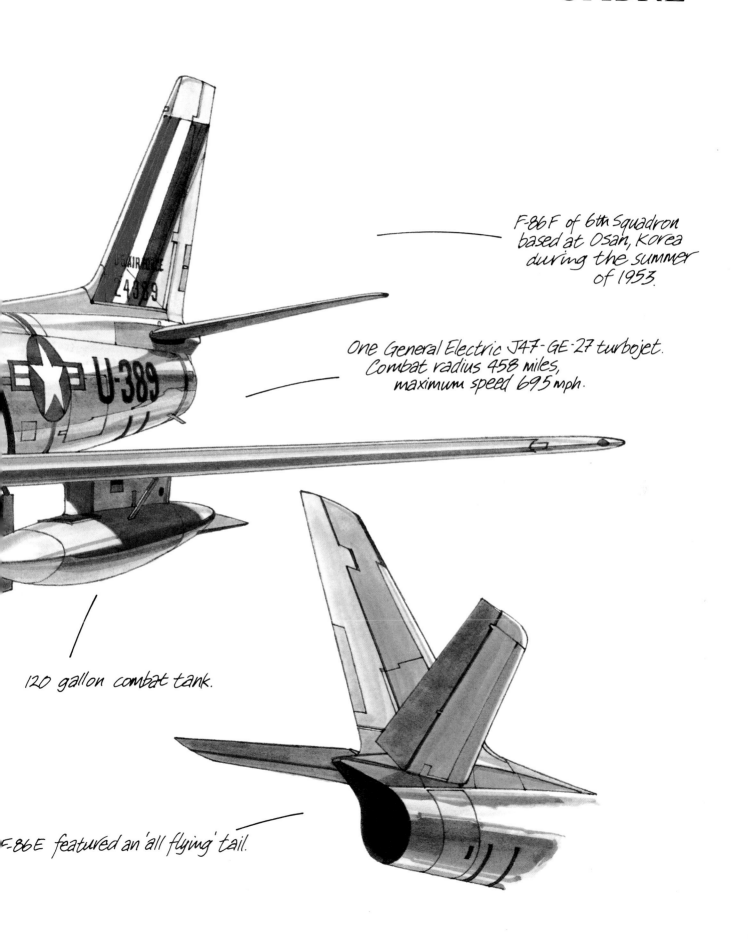

F-86F of 6th Squadron based at Osan, Korea during the summer of 1953.

One General Electric J47-GE-27 turbojet. Combat radius 458 miles, maximum speed 695 mph.

120 gallon combat tank.

F-86E featured an 'all flying' tail.

NORTH AMERICAN F-86 SABRE

North American Aviation, riding high on the late-model P-51s at the end of World War II, was well-placed to grab a major share of the market for first-generation jet fighters. Instead, like Boeing with the B-47 bomber, it had the courage to delay its programme a year while it cranked in all the new aerodynamic knowledge gained from defeated Germany. In particular, it replanned the XP-86 fighter with wings and tail swept back like an arrowhead at 35°.

The result was the best fighter of its age – apart from an unexpected rival, the Soviet MiG-15. The two met over Korea in large numbers and, had the F-86 (as the XP-86 became) been built in its original form the Allies would have had nothing in the class of the MiG-15 at all. As it was, the F-86 Sabre became not only the fastest and most glamorous fighter of the post-war era, but it ushered in a new era with speedbrakes, powered controls, 'all flying' tailplanes, pressurised cockpits (yet with enormous gold-fish-bowl canopies) and 'bonedome' helmets and partial-pressure survival suits that completely changed the image of the combat pilot. So outstanding an aircraft was bound to have a long career, with many versions, and at all times the Sabre was loved and respected as a fighter that almost never malfunctioned (despite amazing new complexity) and seemed to obey its pilot's commands before they were issued!

Historically, the F-86 Sabre and the MiG-15 are fixed in parentheses, and it is difficult to write of one without referring to the other. Quite contrasting in appearance, there were also many important internal differences, one of them being in the armament. Whereas the MiG design allowed for the mounting of an integrated package of heavy cannon, the Sabre was designed to perpetuate the P-51 armament of six 0.5in guns, three on either side of the nose. Early Sabres were equipped to carry two 1000lb bombs, but these could only be accommodated at the expense of drop tanks, so reducing the operative radius to 50 miles. With drop tanks replacing the bombs, the radius of action was stretched to 250 miles.

Unlike the MiG-15, the F-86 was an instant success and was especially popular with the men who flew it. It had a good rate of climb and could dive so fast that the only early limitation was the pilot's capacity to absorb 'g'. It was by far the most important air-combat weapon of the Allies throughout the Korean war, and for five years (1949-54) it remained the only fighter in the world even remotely competent to take on the MiG-15, although the fact that it did so with such devastating effect was due very largely to the greater skill of its pilots.

The Sabre was subject to a programme of constant design improvements, some of them resulting directly from Korean experience. The F-86E was fitted with an 'all-flying tail', the tailplane becoming the primary control surface in the pitching plane. The F-86F replaced the leading-edge slats by a 'hard' leading edge extended forwards by 6in at the root and 3in at the tip. These important developments increased operating Mach limit to 0.92, improved control and manoeuvrability especially at high altitudes, and delayed the onset of air-compressibility effects at near the speed of sound. But curiously not all modifications were introduced by the designers. During the Korean war there existed a body of Sabre pilots known as the 'chuck-it-out brigade', most notable of its members being Major Vermont Garrison of the famous 4th Fighter Wing. Garrison and his cohorts exercised no scruple in stripping their Sabres of any component they considered to be superfluous, in their eagerness to reduce weight and outperform the MiG-15. Garrison himself even advocated removal of the APG-30 radar gunsight, stating that he would just as soon aim his guns using 'a gumsight' – a lump of chewing gum stuck on the windscreen.

One of the Sabre pilots' greatest irritations was the apparent reluctance of their North Korean opposite numbers to engage in dogfights. All along the Yalu river, MiG-15s could and did take evasive action by zooming across the border into airspace over 'neutral' Manchuria. In November 1951, however, two Sabre pilots of USAF No 336 Squadron, Captain Ken Chandler and Lieutenant Dayton Ragland, spotted 12 MiG-15s parked on the ground at Uiju, definitely inside North Korean territory. Chandler and Ragland swooped in and strafed, destroying four MiGs and damaging several others.

Only two days later, 31 Sabres of No 4 Fighter Wing on a sweep along the Yalu encountered 12 Tupolev Tu-2 piston-engined bombers escorted by 16 Lavochkin piston-engined fighters and a further high cover with 16 MiG-15s. Minutes later, the Sabres had destroyed eight of the Tupolevs, three of the Lavochkins and one of the MiGs.

Due without doubt to the very heavy Sabre-inflicted losses, the beginning of 1952 saw a change in Chinese tactics. They began to send up several flights at medium altitude, with others flying top-cover several thousand feet above. The Sabre squadrons caught on quickly, using their

SPECIFICATION

F-86A

Country of origin: USA.

Manufacturer: North American Aviation, Inc.

Type: Single-seat fighter-bomber.

Year: 1948.

Engine: 2200kg (4850lb) General Electric J47-1 axial turbojet.

Wingspan: 11.31m (37ft 1in).

Length: 11.43m (37ft 6in).

Height: 4.47m (14ft 9in).

Weight: 7359kg (16,223lb).

Maximum speed: 1086km/h (675mph).

Ceiling: 15,240m (50,000ft).

Range: 1368km (850 miles).

Armament: Six 0.5in Colt Browning M-3 guns plus two underwing hardpoints carrying 1000lb each, alternatively eight rockets.

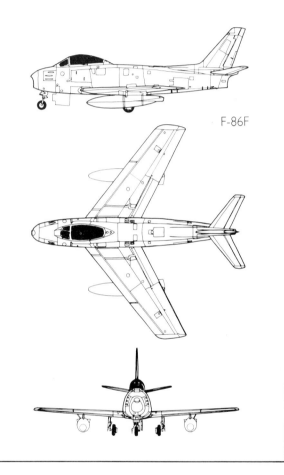

F-86F

high-flying F-86Es to engage the upper echelons, while other F-86s hit those at lower levels. This way, Sabres destroyed eight MiGs in January; the Chinese switched tactics again, changing from large formations to flights of just two or four, and flying at 40,000ft. Thus they were able to penetrate further south before dropping down to 20,000ft in attempts to stop attacks on their ground forces by American fighter-bombers, mainly F-84 Thunderjets. This greatly reduced air contact by Sabres.

The most numerous version of all (2504 built) was an extremely complex radar-equipped all-weather interceptor, the F-86D. Distinguished by its chin inlet under the radome, the 'Dogship' version had no guns but a retractable box of rockets, aimed and fired automatically under computer control.

Other versions of the Sabre went on long after Korea to form the fighter backbones of a score of air forces all over the world. Many expert pilots thought the Orenda-engined Canadair Sabre 6 the best version of all. Sabres were assembled in Italy by Fiat and in Japan by Mitsubishi. The final variation, the F-86K, a simplified version of the 86D with guns instead of rockets, was built primarily for European NATO air forces, most being assembled by Fiat in Italy.

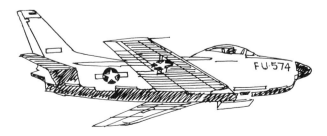

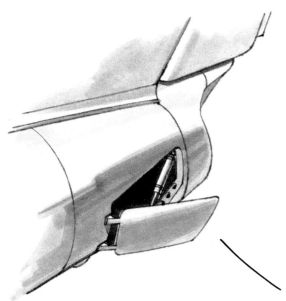

Port side airbrake open.

Two Nudelmann - Suranov 23 mm Cannon mounted on left-side of the nose. One Nudelmann cannon of 37 mm mounted on right side of the nose.

MIKOYAN-GURYEVICH
MiG-15

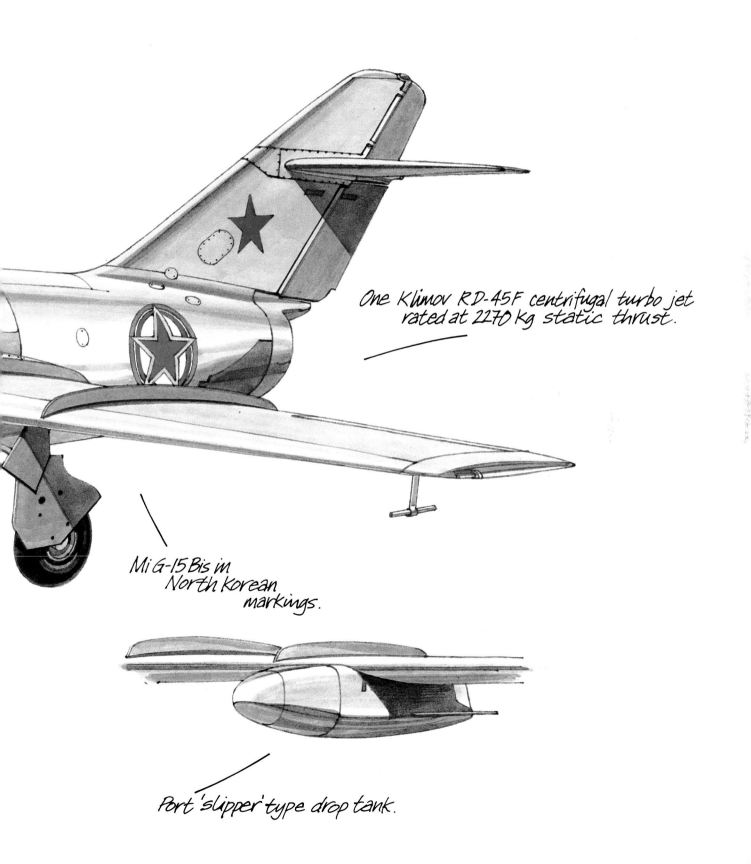

One Klimov RD-45F centrifugal turbo jet
rated at 2270 kg static thrust.

MiG-15 Bis in
North Korean
markings.

Port 'slipper' type drop tank.

MIKOYAN-GURYEVICH MiG-15

The MiG-15 and its American contemporary the NAA F-86 Sabre were the first aircraft to show the true potential of the jet as a superlative fighting aircraft. They were in a league of their own.

The MiG-15 was a masterpiece of simple yet advanced design, although most ironically, and as with its contemporary the Yak-23 and the Il-28 bomber, its construction was only made possible by the amazing decision of the British to send to Moscow their newest jet engine, the Rolls-Royce Nene. Even stranger, Britain did little with this world-beating engine itself and produced no rival to the MiG-15 until seven years later.

The designers at the Mikoyan-Guryevich (MiG) bureau were working to a brief for a single-seat jet fighter with a speed of Mach 0.9, a very fast rate of climb to a ceiling greater than 10,000m and, carrying heavy armaments, to have an endurance of at least one hour. The design team easily fulfilled these requirements once the Nene was available. The prototype, called Aircraft S, or the I-310, flew on 30 December 1947. It was an outstanding aircraft, dived to a Mach number of 0.92 (92 per cent of the speed of sound) and with unrivalled manoeuvrability, marred only by a tendency to stall/spin in very tight turns. After being fitted with rear-fuselage airbrakes which opened automatically at over Mach 0.9, the MiG-15 was put into service in October 1948, fully six years ahead of any British swept-wing aeroplane which might reasonably be termed its counterpart. Standard armament, fitted to all MiG-15s including the prototype, comprised a vast NS-37 with 40 rounds and two NS-23s with 80 rounds each. In 1949, the MiG-15bis introduced the improved VK-1 engine, a refined airframe and pylon attachments for drop-tanks, rockets or bombs. Most had the NS-23 guns replaced by new NR-23s.

By the time the Korean War started in June 1950, the Russian MiG pilots (though not the Chinese or Korean fliers) had plenty of experience and knew very well how to make best use of their fearsome machine. Western pilots were given their first shock sighting of the sleek silver menace on 1 November, when a flight of four American P-51 Mustangs was flying along the Yalu river. Wisely, the Mustang pilots opted to turn tail and run, and it was not until late the following month, when USAF F-86 Sabres arrived on the scene, that the Russian jet fighter met with any real opposition. The first-ever full-scale battle of these giants took place on 22 December, when eight F-86s took on 15 MiG-15s and claimed six of the enemy while sustaining no casualties of their own. Nine days later the Sabre's claims had risen to eight MiGs destroyed and two 'probables' against a Sabre loss of just one.

This should by no means be taken to suggest, however, that the MiG-15 was outclassed by the Sabre, because it certainly was not. The Russian jet had a much higher (near-vertical) rate of climb, was able to dive equally fast and had at least as good, if not better, manoeuvrability. Also, MiGs were considerably faster at 8000m the height at which most dogfights were carried out. It would follow, therefore, that these early Sabre victories might be credited to pilot superiority – Americans versus Chinese and Koreans, not Russians – rather than MiG deficiency. Nevertheless, by 20 May 1951, Sabre pilot Captain James A. Jabara had become the world's first jet 'ace' with a total of six MiG kills, and it is doubtful if any Korean or Chinese pilot matched that score before the end of hostilities in 1953. The official USAF totting-up of final figures suggests total MiG claims during the conflict were 807 against the American total of only 101 jets, though these figures are highly uncertain. Jabara was credited with 15 of the MiGs. The MiG-15 turned over to the USAF near the end of the war by its defecting pilot, Lieutenant No Kum Suk, was not included in the 807.

Inevitably, there are many Sabre versus MiG stories and naturally, as almost all familiar in the 'West' were told by that side, they tend to favour the F-86. But the superior performance of which the Russian aircraft was capable is well illustrated by the fact that, in a desperate effort to match its speed when in pursuit, some F-86s were briefly fitted with an under-fuselage pod housing special booster rockets.

Summing up on Korea, it would appear perfectly obvious that the MiG-15 was never employed to anything even approaching its maximum operational potential. One striking instance: on 23 June 1952, a massive American attack was launched on the huge hydro-electric complex just across the river from Manchuria and this, said to have been the biggest single air raid since World War II, was carried out with impunity. *Not one* of the 200 or so MiGs known to be based within 80km of the area rose to meet the attack; most were seen to take off and fly north, in the

SPECIFICATION

MiG-15 bis

Country of origin: Soviet Union.

Design Bureau: Mikoyan-Guryevich OKB.

Type: Single-seat fighter.

Year: 1948.

Engine: 2700kg (5952lb) thrust VK-1 turbojet.

Wingspan: 10.1m (33ft 1in).

Length: 10.86m (35ft 7in).

Height: 3.4m (11ft 2in).

Weight: 6045kg (13,327lb).

Maximum speed: 1075km/h (668mph).

Ceiling: 15,545m (51,000ft).

Range: 1424km (885 miles).

Armament: One 37mm NS-37 cannon under right side of nose and two 23mm NR-23 cannon under left side.

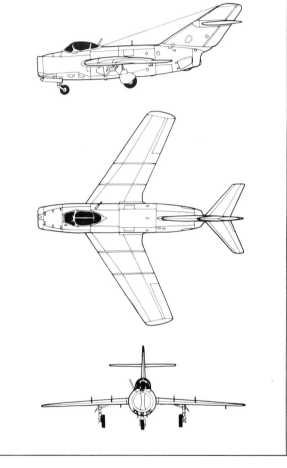

belief, it later emerged, that the USAF raiding force was on its way to hit industrial targets inland in Manchuria. So, with no fewer than 208 American fighter-bombers and 108 F-86 escorts in the air, what could have been the mightiest aerial battle of the war simply never took place.

However, at least 5000 MiG-15s were built, and the aircraft continued in service long after the end of that war. Poland built versions called LIM-1 and -2, the Czechs built the S-102 and -103, and the two-seater trainer was built in large numbers as the MiG-15UTI. Even today many hundreds of trainers are still in use around the world.

MiG-15 variants went on to be flown by the air forces of more than a score of countries, including large numbers in China. In 1955 the United Arab Emirates bought MiG-15s from Czechoslovakia, and others were sold to places as far afield as Cuba, Tanzania and Cambodia.

One Rolls-Royce Avon 207 axial-flow turbojet

Four 30 mm Aden Cannon.
100 rounds for each gun.

Ammunition link collector box
and cartridge case ejector barrels.

HAWKER HUNTER

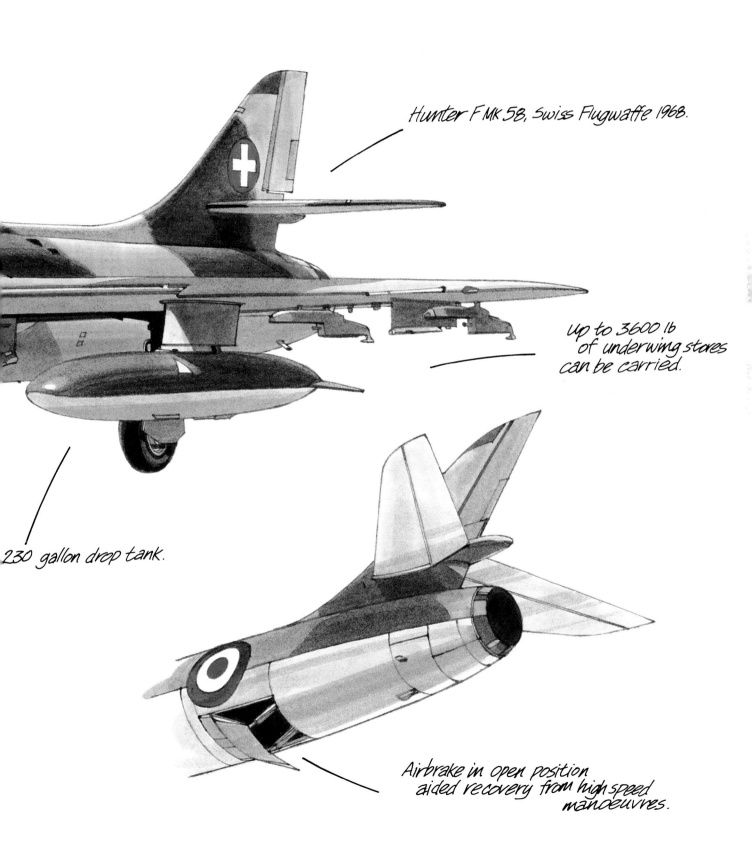

Hunter F Mk 58, Swiss Flugwaffe 1968.

Up to 3600 lb
of underwing stores
can be carried.

230 gallon drop tank.

Airbrake in open position
aided recovery from high speed
manoeuvres.

HAWKER HUNTER

Britain's Royal Air Force waited a long time for its first native transonic aircraft, but patience – or rather impatience – was finally well rewarded. The Hawker Hunter is generally acknowledged to be the best single-seat fighter of the mid-1950s. But the birth of this beautiful baby was not an easy one. The first test flight, on 21 July 1951, revealed many serious problems, some of which had not been remedied even after the RAF took delivery of the first production models in July 1954. There was difficulty in fitting an airbrake (as an afterthought); then this was damaged by spent shellcases, which had to be collected in huge bulged containers; there was pitch-up and then pitch-down, and engine surge when the guns were fired; and difficulty at high speeds with longitudinal control. All of these faults were eventually remedied, but the big problem fundamental to most jet fighter aircraft, that of inadequate internal fuel capacity, remained.

However, the F.Mk 4, flown on 20 October 1954, had additional wing fuel tanks and also attachments for drop tanks, and the Hunter promptly went on from there to become, worldwide, the best loved 'pilot's aeroplane' of its age. It could tolerate almost any abuse, it was close to perfection in handling, it had no flight limitations, it was virtually unbreakable and it had excellent engines. These and numerous other outstanding qualities endowed the Hunter with a reputation that was second to none. It was very handsome in appearance, and a marvellous aeroplane to fly.

The Hunter design, embarked upon as early as 1948 by a team led by Hawker's Sir Sydney Camm, introduced several new features in its cockpit arrangement, being the first-ever British layout to provide from the start of design for the fitting of an ejection seat. All instruments and controls fell readily in sight or to hand, an invaluable aid to pilot efficiency, especially when manoeuvring at high speeds. Later Hunters were capable of level flight at Mach 0.95, and supersonic speed was easily reached in all versions by putting the aeroplane into a 30° dive from

heights above 30,000ft. Recovering was equally simple: the pilot merely needed to throttle back as he eased out of the dive and, if necessary, use the airbrake. The Hunter was remarkably steady as a gun platform and, once the problem of disposal of empty shell cases was resolved, the aircraft made full use of its devastating armament of four 30mm Aden guns (each much more powerful than the MK 108 guns of the Me 262), installed in a quick-demountable pack complete with ammunition magazines, winched up as a single unit. Later versions were able to carry a wide variety of underwing armaments, including rockets and bombs. It was indeed in its ground-attack role that the Hunter, in its latter years, was most employed.

In 1953 the next stage was to be a Hunter with an afterburner, but Camm did not like this. He preferred to use a more powerful basic engine, and Rolls-Royce had produced one: the 10,000 lb thrust Avon 203. The result was the Hunter F.6, and it had an all-flying tailplane, and wings with a dogtooth leading edge (retrofitted to earlier versions). It was different from its predecessors not so much in appearance as in performance. So much so, in fact, that it was adopted by the famous Black Arrow aerobatic display team of the RAF's No 111 Squadron, and also by the rival Blue Diamonds team of No 92 Squadron. In its more practical application, the F.6 as a fighting machine was fitted to carry a formidable array of weapons – two 1000 lb bombs and two 100-gallon tanks, *or* 2in rocket batteries on the underwing inner pylons and 3in batteries on the outers, or various retarded bombs and other stores. Each of these variations was additional to the removable pack of four 30mm Adens.

This assortment of devastating firepower was developed further in the FGA.9 (fighter, ground attack), with a strengthened airframe for sustained high-weight operations carrying increased underwing loads, and with a braking parachute above the jetpipe. This reached the RAF in October 1959, with No 8 Squadron based at Khormaksar, Aden. When in April 1968 Fighter Command effectively became Strike Command, Britain's tactical support and strike force was mainly represented by two FAG.9 squadrons, Nos 1 and 54. The last of this type was flown by No 8 Squadron, disbanded on its return from the Far East at the end of 1971. A few went on for use as trainers at RAF Valley, and with the Tactical Weapons Unit at Chivenor and Brawdy.

Fighter and attack Hunters served with over a dozen air forces scattered all over the world. In its final form for export, the Hunter could carry eight 1000lb bombs and two Sidewinders. The Hunter was such a wonderfully 'easy' aircraft that, even in the hands of an inexperienced

SPECIFICATION

F.1

Country of origin: Great Britain.

Manufacturer: Hawker Aircraft Ltd.

Type: Single-seat fighter-bomber.

Year: 1953.

Engine: 2948kg (6500lb) Rolls-Royce Avon 100 turbojet.

Wingspan: 10.26m (33ft 8in).

Length: 13.98m (45ft 10in).

Height: 4.26m (13ft 2in).

Weight: 7347kg (16,200lb) (without external load).

Maximum speed: 1144km/h (710mph).

Ceiling: 15,240m (50,000ft).

Range: 689km (490 miles) without drop tanks.

Armament: Four 30mm Aden cannon below cockpit, plus underwing pylons for two 1000lb bombs and 24 3in rockets.

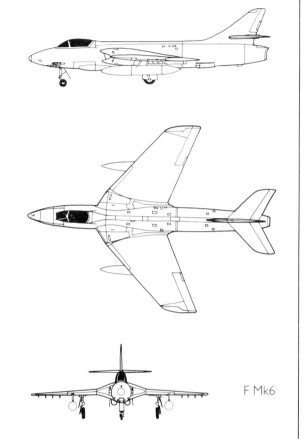

F Mk6

pilot, it could be flown at near-optimum performance. Piloted by an expert, it was one of the most deadly aerial weapons of its day, and it is fortunate that its full operational capacity was seldom exercised. RAF Hunters based in Cyprus and Malta were engaged in limited operations during the Suez crisis of 1956, and Hunters later saw some action in Aden. Basically, however, this most potent of Britain's fighting aircraft of the pre-1970 period was never deployed in anger. Some foreign air forces, though, made intensive use of its potential in both air/air and air/surface roles, notably during the wars between India and Pakistan, and with Jordan in the Middle East – but most of the Hunters then flying the world over were effective only as an ominous deterrent. During the past 15 years, the biggest fleet has been that of Switzerland.

Perhaps the most astonishing feature of this thorough-bred aeroplane is the fact that total production of Hunters, including those built under licence in Belgium and Holland, did not even reach 2000. However, the 1972 that *were* manufactured remained in worldwide service over a period of very many years, being sold over and over, refurbished and sold yet again. Demand remained insatiable well into the 1970s and British Aerospace Kingston bitterly regretted that many had foolishly been scrapped. The Royal Navy was still using the FAG.11 as a ground-attack trainer when this was written in 1985, as well as the special two-seat T.8M to train pilots on the Sea Harrier's Blue Fox radar.

It would seem that Hawker's decision to terminate production in 1966 was more than a trifle premature. Indeed, the company has profited considerably more from the overhaul and refurbishing of Hunters than it ever did from original sales.

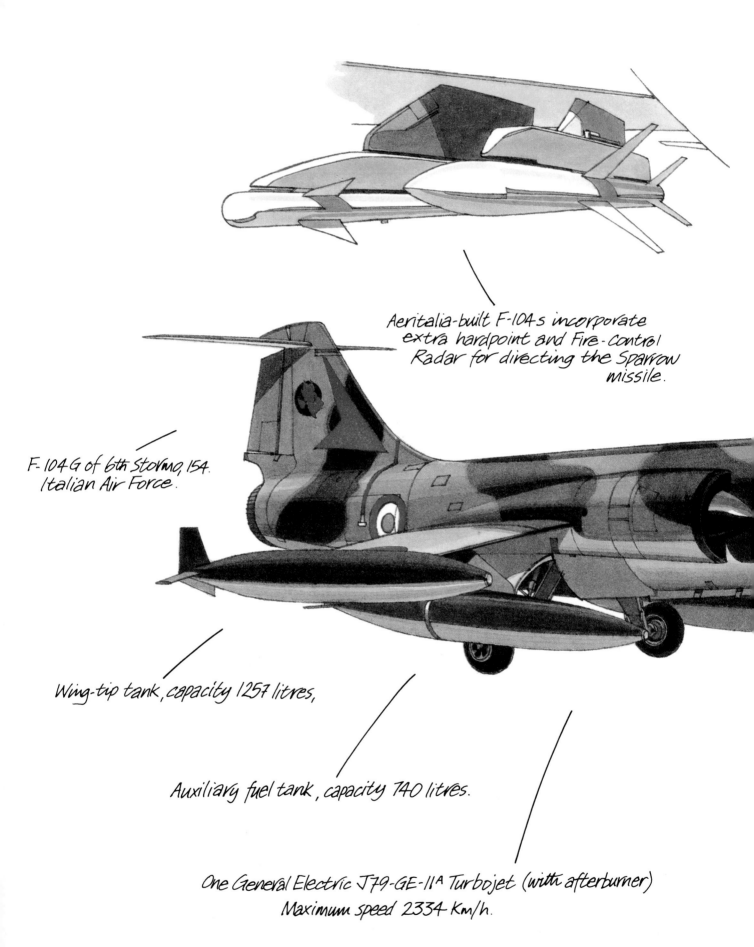

Aeritalia-built F-104s incorporate extra hardpoint and Fire-control Radar for directing the Sparrow missile.

F-104 G of 6th Stormo, 154. Italian Air Force.

Wing-tip tank, capacity 1257 litres,

Auxiliary fuel tank, capacity 740 litres.

One General Electric J79-GE-11ᴬ Turbojet (with afterburner) Maximum speed 2334 Km/h.

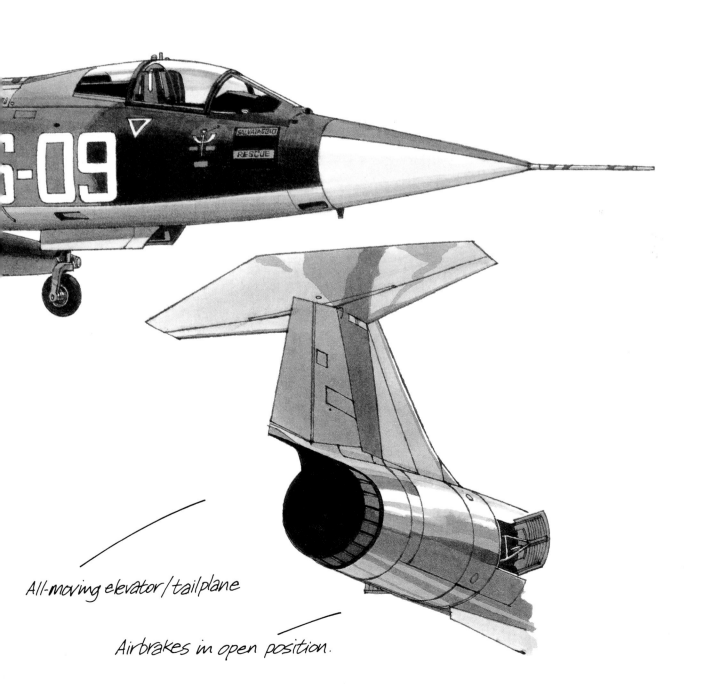

All-moving elevator/tailplane

Airbrakes in open position.

LOCKHEED F-104 STARFIGHTER

The Starfighter might paradoxically be regarded as a very successful failure. It was brought into being in response to urgent calls from USAF pilots engaged in trying to beat the MiG-15 in the Korean War of 1950-53 for a completely new and dominant kind of fighter aircraft. They wanted much more speed, higher combat altitudes, and far greater manoeuvrability in dogfights, even at the expense of range, weapons or equipment. The F-104 did much to satisfy the first two of these requirements, but was somewhat lacking in the third.

Conceived in 1951 by the famous Lockheed designer Clarence L. 'Kelly' Johnson as a successor to his F-80 Shooting Star, the F-104 certainly *looked* very different. It was barely spared from having the appearance of a pilotless rocket by thin and extremely short wings set very far back on the long fuselage, and a comparatively enormous tailplane carried almost at the top of an equally-large fin. (One less-apparent peculiarity was an ejection seat which shot the pilot out downwards from under the fuselage). The very first test pilot might have wondered if the aircraft would even be capable of getting off the ground.

But it did, and when the prototype XF-104 took to the air on 7 February 1954, it flew beautifully. The engine was a Wright J65 US version of the British Sapphire turbojet. The F-104A flew almost exactly two years later, its performance vastly improved by the more-powerful General Electric J79. So much more powerful indeed that, thanks to efficient supersonic inlets and variable nozzle, the aircraft achieved a speed well in excess of Mach 2, and this at a time when some other Western fighters were hard-pressed to pass Mach 1. The engine of this exceedingly fast F-104 was fitted into a well-designed supersonic housing, the engine inlets being arranged on either side of the fuselage positioned well ahead of the tiny wing.

The F-104 was the first aircraft designed from the start to have blown flaps, blasted by compressed air from the J79. Initial armament comprised a Sidewinder AAM at the tip of each wing, and one M61 gun, the amazing new six-barrel cannon from General Electric. Lockheed manufactured 153 of this type, but it had a rather difficult and sometimes dangerous development history, and in any case was extremely unforgiving of any but the most skilled and precise pilot.

This early version of the F-104 was a disappointment in too many respects, including range, agility, and armament capacity, and only around half of this number was accepted, in 1958, for service with the USAF Tactical Air Command. The rest went to Pakistan and Jordan. Other variants, the F-104B two-seat trainer and the F-104C fighter/bomber were also produced in small numbers. The F-104D was a two-seat version of the F-104C, and like the C could be fitted with a rather clumsy non-retractable inflight-refuelling probe.

Lockheed rescued the F-104 from disaster by a further development programme, using private company funds, to meet expected foreign markets. This calculated risk resulted eventually in the introduction of the F-104G, also called the Super Starfighter. The G first flew on 5 October 1960, and proved itself an instant success. Differing little in outward appearance from the previous 104s, it was in fact a very different aeroplane.

It had a reinforced airframe and many other refinements, not least in avionics. These included Nasarr radar and, for the first time in a service aircraft, pure inertial navigation. The Germans ordered no fewer than 750 for its Luftwaffe and Marineflieger forces, and a multi-national manufacturing programme was instituted. At that time, the Starfighter was born anew as the only low-level strike and reconnaissance aircraft capable of flying all-weather electronically guided missions at supersonic speed in the manner then required. It sold not only to Germany but to Italy, Belgium, the Netherlands, Norway, Denmark, Greece and, later, many other nations.

Canada built a version called the CF-104, and Japan went into production with the F-104J based on the old F-104C. Various two-seat TF-104G, RF-104G and RTF-104G versions appeared for training, reconnaissance and electronic warfare. Later in 1966, a new interceptor variant was designed and developed in conjunction with Aeritalia. This F-104S had a better J79 engine and represented a return to the aeroplane's original role as a fighter, but with powerful radar and large Sparrow radar-guided missiles. Aeritalia built 205, of which 40 were sold to Turkey.

In their early years in the 1960s, the F-104Gs ran into very serious trouble. The Luftwaffe and Marineflieger suffered an appalling level of casualties – due almost entirely to the fact that F-104s were being flown by inexperienced pilots. An intensive programme of modifications did little to restore public confidence in the aircraft, though switching to the British Martin-Baker seat had an immediate beneficial effect on the number of pilots killed.

Other air forces suffered no such problem as these, because they picked only experienced pilots who never let the Starfighter 'bite them'.

The fact remains that the Lockheed F-104 Starfighter recovered like the Phoenix from the ashes of an early

SPECIFICATION

F-104G

Country of origin: USA.

Manufacturer: Lockheed-California Co.

Type: Single-seat low-level strike fighter.

Year: 1960.

Engine: 7167kg (15,800lb) General Electric J79-11A turbojet with afterburning.

Wingspan: 6.68m (21ft 11in).

Length: 16.69m (54ft 9in).

Height: 4.11m (13ft 6in).

Weight: 13,054kg (28,779lb).

Maximum speed: 2334km/h (1450mph).

Ceiling: 16,765m (55,000ft).

Range: 2220km (1380 miles) (with drop tanks).

Armament: One 20mm M61A-1 cannon (requiring reduced fuel load), two Sidewinder air-to-air missiles plus one 2000lb bomb below fuselage and two 454kg (1000lb) stores under wings.

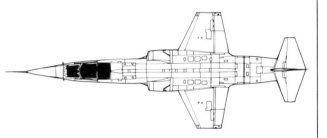

death, and went on from there to enjoy a remarkable rejuvenation. It was adopted in its several variations by the air forces of many countries – Pakistan was the only one of these to employ the aircraft in actual combat, the results being somewhat mixed, but including several clear air-combat victories over opposing fighters. Curiously Japan's F-104Js served only in the air-defence role, while the Canadian CF-104 was originally configured for the opposite end of the tactical mission spectrum: strike and reconnaissance, the gun being replaced by extra fuel. Later the Canadians tasked their aircraft for a wide range of duties including combat at all heights. Other countries which purchased secondhand aircraft, included Taiwan and Spain.

The total number of Starfighters exceeded 2500, a very far cry from the 153 with which, after initial failures, production might have terminated.

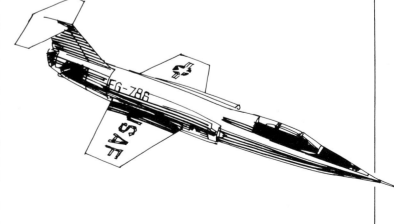

A-4E of VA-55 operating from USS Hancock
during Vietnam war.

Dorsal 'hump' houses avionics systems.

A-4C showing steam catapult
launch gear.

Two 20mm Mk12 guns
in wing roots.

513

RESCUE

306

McDONNELL DOUGLAS A-4 SKYHAWK

Fin-tip ECM fairing.

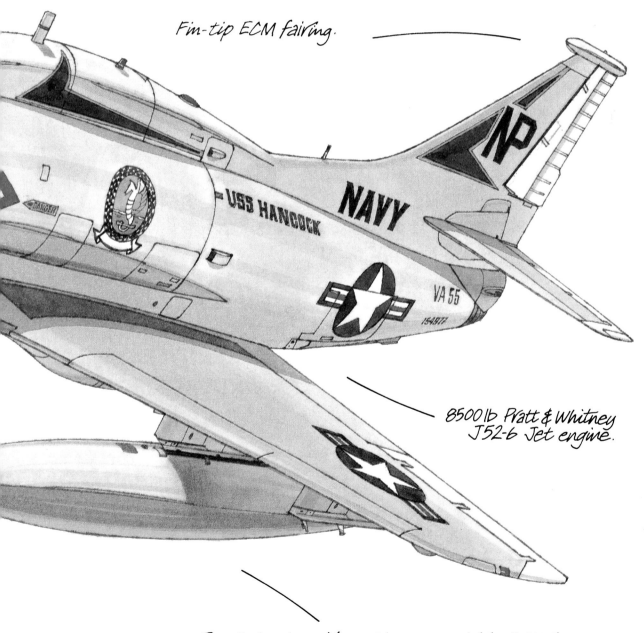

8500 lb Pratt & Whitney
J52-6 Jet engine.

The Skyhawk could carry its own weight, 12,000 lb
in underwing stores – though a typical load could
be two wing-mounted fuel tanks and 10 x 500 lb bombs.

McDONNELL DOUGLAS A-4 SKYHAWK

This marvellous little aeroplane might or might not be the finest ever built, but in its ability to beat the customer's specification it has no equal. Its designer, Ed Heinemann, went to work in 1952 on a US Navy specification calling for a carrier-based attack bomber capable of carrying heavy loads. The aircraft was to have a maximum weight of 30,000lb and be capable of speeds up to 495mph. When Heinemann, who was then chief engineer of the Douglas factory at El Segundo in California, came up with his design for an aircraft capable of fulfilling all of the Navy's requirements yet weighing *less than half* the specified maximum weight – only 11,200lb – nobody believed him, because it just wasn't possible.

But it was. Heinemann had designed an astonishingly small aeroplane with wide but very short wings, so short indeed that folding for stowage below decks was unnecessary. This in turn made it easier to design the whole mainplane from wing-tip to wing-tip with one-piece skins enclosing integral fuel tanks occupying almost the whole interior. During the planning stages, these and many other radical innovations aroused serious doubts in the US Navy hierarchy, but the sceptics were in for a tremendous surprise. When the prototype XA4D-1 took to the air on 22 June 1954, it not only achieved the asked-for speed, but far exceeded the requirement, and the aircraft went on, not much later, to set a new world record for circuit-flying of 695mph, a speed which *bettered* the original specification by an incredible 200mph. The engine was the Wright J65, the British AS Sapphire built under licence.

Once over their shock, the Navy chiefs hastily up-rated their performance requirements and delivery to squadrons of the much-revised Skyhawk A4D-1 production model began in October 1956. Known to its design team and test pilots as 'Heinemann's Hot Rod', the aeroplane now acquired another appellation: US Navy and Marine flyers called their new aircraft the 'Scooter'. They loved it. It behaved so well in the air, with instruments and controls all so readily to hand that one pilot new to the Skyhawk said 'It was like making the transition from driving the station wagon to driving a sports car...and when you started to do rolls and other aerobatics, it was almost as if you were outside of the airplane and doing it all yourself.' The Skyhawk was especially good for carrier touchdowns at sea. Its instant responsiveness was a great advantage and, once altitude and airspeed were under control, the aircraft would fly at a constant rate of descent all the way down onto the carrier's deck.

Later versions were hardly deserving of the affectionate name 'Scooter', because Navy demands for more and heavier armaments, and an ever-increasing range, necessitated the addition of a flight-refuelling probe and strengthening of the airframe to absorb the thrust from Pratt & Whitney's more powerful J52 engine, to enable gross weight to be increased to almost the originally specified 30,000lb. But the ratio of aircraft empty weight to carrying capacity remained near-constant, and these later Skyhawks were able to carry approximately double the burden originally required. Modifications carried out in the late 1950s increased the weapon load to 9155lb, almost equal to the weight of the aircraft when 'clean'.

From 1962 the A4D designation became A-4 and soon the A-4F introduced a 'camel hump' on the fuselage aft of the cockpit to house extra avionics, which at first included guidance for Bullpup missiles. The A-4F was the last Skyhawk attack version designed and built especially for the US Navy. It had better pilot protection from ground fire, a more advanced ejector seat, and lift spoilers for a shorter landing run. Most subsequent single-seat variations were built primarily for delivery to the US Marines, though the lightweight TA-4J two-seater remains the Navy's main air-combat trainer.

Coming far too late for use in the Korean War, introduction of the A-4Es and A-4Fs was nevertheless fortuitous. The conflict in South East Asia was rapidly gathering momentum, and these improved Skyhawks served alongside the A-6 and A-7 as the most important attack aircraft flown by the US Navy and Marines. Operating from carriers and from land bases, they flew many thousands of ground-attack missions destroying a wide variety of targets including the SA-2 (SAM) missile sites.

By the mid-1960s the A-4Fs and A-4Cs had been endowed with a fearsome collection of weapons. In view of all this, it came as a great disappointment to Douglas Aircraft when in 1964 the US Navy decided to switch from Skyhawks to a newer aircraft, bought with great urgency, which materialised as the larger A-7 Corsair. However, the US Marines remained loyal and, when they declined to follow the Navy's lead, the A-4M

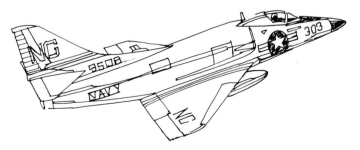

SPECIFICATION

A-4C

Country of origin: USA.

Manufacturer: Douglas Aircraft Co. (from 1966 McDonnell Douglas Corporation).

Type: Single-seat attack aircraft.

Year: 1959.

Engine: 3493kg (7700lb) Wright J65-16A turbojet.

Wingspan: 8.38m (27ft 6in).

Length: 12.29m (40ft 4in).

Height: 4.57m (15ft).

Weight: 12,437kg (27,420lb).

Maximum speed: 1102km/h (685mph).

Ceiling: 14,935m (49,000ft).

Range: 1480km (920 miles).

Armament: Two 20mm Mk 12 cannon. Pylons for total weapon load of 2268kg (5000lb) (later versions 4152kg (9155lb)).

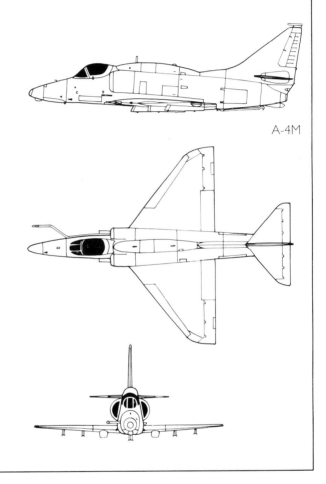

A-4M

Skyhawk II was specially developed to cater for the Marine Corps' particular requirement, and provided an important advance in the Skyhawk's performance. The new J52-P-408 engine generated 20 per cent more thrust and managed at the same time almost to eliminate the tell-tale smoke trail left by the previous J52-powered A-4 versions. The aircraft has gone on to serve the Marines well, and has plenty of life left yet.

The first Skyhawks delivered to Israel – and put immediately into active service – were slight variations of the A-4E. Re-designated the A-4H (H for Hebrew), the aircraft introduced small changes in configuration, most notably a larger-area square-tipped fin. The aeroplane was fitted with powerful twin 30mm DEFA cannon instead of the normal US Navy 20mm weapons, and some of these aircraft were modified in 1970 with the 'camel hump'

avionics fairing which was first seen in the A-4F.

So, the Skyhawk has remained extremely popular with the pilots of many other air forces including, among others, Indonesia, Brazil, Kuwait, New Zealand, Malaysia and Singapore (whose trainers have two bubble canopies). Not least, as far as Britain is concerned, came Argentina. In the 1982 conflict over the Falkland Islands – 30 years after the aircraft was first designed – the Argentine Air Force and Navy used Skyhawks to sink British ships.

Even today Heinemann's 'bantam bomber' is a potent weapon. Originally its production was planned to last from 1954 to 1958 or 1959. Nobody thought that the original Douglas line, moved to Long Beach, would go on turning out new Skyhawks until 1980! Nor that IAI, Grumman and other firms would enjoy a lucrative business in refurbished A-4s into the second half of the 1980s.

Two 375 gallon drop tanks, six centrally mounted M117 750 lb HE bombs and two wing tip mounted M117's with extended anti-personn fuses.

Petal type airbrakes in closed position.

75779

One Pratt & Whitney J75-P-19W turbojet, maximum speed 1254 mph.

REPUBLIC F-105 THUNDERCHIEF

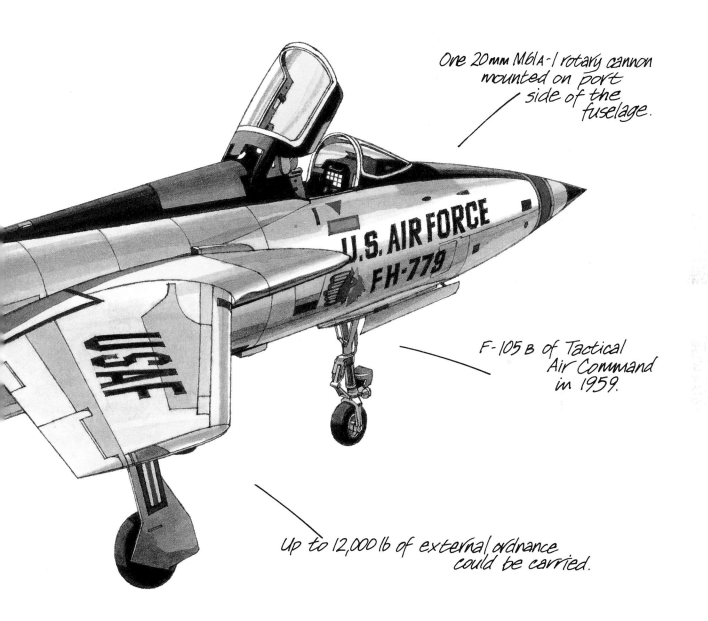

One 20mm M61A-1 rotary cannon mounted on port side of the fuselage.

F-105 B of Tactical Air Command in 1959.

Up to 12,000 lb of external ordnance could be carried.

REPUBLIC F-105 THUNDERCHIEF

Hard upon the heels of the Super Sabre came the rest of the so-called 'Century' series of USAF fighters. Of these, which included the big twin-engined F-101 Voodoo, the pioneer F-102 Delta Dagger interceptor, the rapier-like F-104 Starfighter and the 'second generation' F-106 Delta Dart, the most impressive of all was the F-105 Thunderchief. Known variously by the men who flew it as 'the Lead-sled', 'the Thud', and 'the Ultra Hog' (all terms affectionate rather than pejorative) the Thunderchief was a huge great beast of an aircraft, the biggest and most powerful of its type at that time, and a true 'one-man air force'. At the same time it looked more like a fighter than any of the current bombers, though it surpassed some of the bombers in weight. It was almost 65ft long, about 20ft tall, and had a wingspan of 35ft. An average pilot could walk under the bomb-bay doors without ducking, and was barely able to reach up and touch the edge of the extraordinary reverse-shape engine inlets. It looked at first glance as though it ought to have a crew of two or three, but it was in fact initially designed and operated as a single-seat nuclear-bomb deliverer with a capacity for fighter-interceptor duties. Republic did later construct some 150 stretched-fuselage two-seaters, as explained later.

The Thunderchief began life as project AP-63 at Republic Aviation on Long Island, New York, which designed the aircraft as a private venture. Intended as a successor to the F-84, this new aircraft was to be capable of delivering either conventional or nuclear weapons, demanding very high speed and long range, even at low altitudes. Its first flight on 22 October 1955 was powered by a Pratt & Whitney J57 engine, the same as the F-100 and much less powerful than the planned J75, but nevertheless achieved a performance in excess of the speed of sound. Republic then carried out an almost complete redesign. The giant afterburning J75 was fitted, and fed by unique sharp-lipped inlets in the wing roots which sloped forwards from the roots, giving a strange shape in plan-view. The huge fuselage was area-ruled, being made narrower past the wings and larger at front and rear. The tail end was formed by a mighty engine nozzle with surrounding 'petal flaps' that could be opened to form four enormous airbrakes.

First production of this improved F-105B began in May 1956, for delivery to the USAF Tactical Air Command. The aircraft embodied such a mass of advanced technology that pilots were of necessity subjected to weeks of special training before they were able fully to master the various new skills essential for maximum operation.

Although it was the biggest single-seat, single-engined combat aircraft ever built, the F-105, despite its odd forward-swept engine inlets and large internal bomb bay, was a very well-mannered fighter-type aeroplane and a true delight to fly. Republic built only around 70 of the B model, but of the main version, the F-105D, some 600 were delivered. Equipped with the General Electric radar fire control, doppler navigation, and complex computers to calculate air data and exact aiming parameters for toss-bombing with nuclear bombs (in which the attack at treetop height tosses the bomb high in the air, so that the aircraft can get well clear before the bomb falls back on to its target), as well as an integrated autopilot, the F-105D was the very first aircraft of any type with a capacity for both air-to-air fighting and air-to-ground semi-automatic weapons delivery using avionic systems as complex as those fitted to modern multi-role fighters. Among these advanced capabilities were radar models for air search, contour mapping, terrain following and automatic tracking of air or ground targets, even in blind conditions. All of these, together with a capability to attack at speeds in excess of Mach 1 – 'clean' yet carrying a heavy bombload –, indelibly stamped the Thunderchief as an aeroplane which in many respects was ahead of its time.

The F-105 was offered almost ideal conditions and opportunity to demonstrate its awesome powers by the outbreak of the war in Vietnam, where it rapidly became known as the 'one-man air force'. Fitted with complete equipment for multi-role low-level operations in all weathers (although of course the nuclear toss-bombing capability was not used), it was also capable of extremely impressive performance at high altitudes. This, together with very adequate dog-fighting qualities, formed an exceptional and most formidable combination. Supersonic aircraft require vast engine thrust to overcome drag at full speed, but the F-105's mighty engine delivered enough power and more, and its excess thrust at lower speeds allowed for very tight and sustained turns without any falling-off of speed. So important was the Thunderchief considered in its multiplicity of roles (not least of which being that of radar-bombing through Vietnam's omnipre-

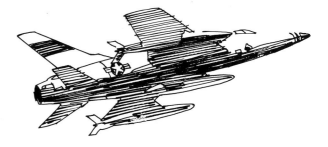

SPECIFICATION

F-105B

Country of origin: USA.

Manufacturer: Republic Aviation Corporation.

Type: Single-seat all-weather fighter-bomber.

Year: 1956.

Engine: 12,020kg (26,500lb) Pratt & Whitney J75-P-19W turbojet with afterburning.

Wingspan: 10.65m (34ft 11in).

Length: 19.58m (64ft 3in).

Height: 5.99m (19ft 8in).

Weight: 18,144kg (40,000lb) (clean).

Maximum speed: 2018km/h (1254mph).

Ceiling: 15,850m (52,000ft).

Range: 3846km (2390 miles).

Armament: One 20mm M61 cannon, internal bay for 3629kg (8000lb) bombs plus five pylons for 2722kg (6000lb).

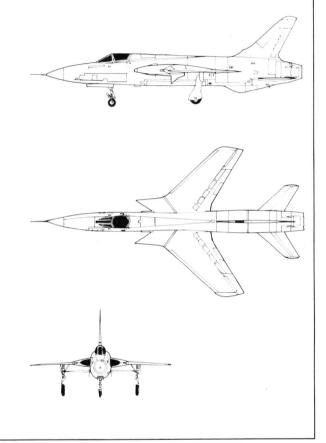

sent low cloud) that throughout the first five years of that Far East conflict, F-105s carried out an amazing 75 per cent of all USAF attack missions. From March 1963, a wing of F-105s was also based in Thailand.

Unlike most aircraft in Vietnam, the great 'Thuds' exceeded the speed of sound on almost every mission. Often carrying Paveway 'smart bombs', they made many precision attacks. They played a key role in dropping spans of the great Paul Doumer bridge.

F-105Ds continued in service for more than a decade after final deliveries were made in 1965. There were numerous updates and conversions, by far the most notable of these being the one which incorporated Thunderstick II all-weather weapon-delivery avionics, a type readily identified by a prominent saddleback fairing which stretched from cockpit to fin.

The F-105F tandem-seater was originally bought as a combat-capable conversion and weapons trainer. In Vietnam, it provided the ideal basis for an aircraft to suppress hostile anti-aircraft defences, in the Wild Weasel programme. Many were rebuilt as F-105Gs, with special passive receivers to detect and locate enemy ground radars, and carrying various ECM (electronic counter-measures) jammer pods, some conformally scabbed on the side of the fuselage. New weapons for the mission comprised Shrike and Standard ARM anti-radiation missiles, carried on wing pylons.

The Thunderchief was not an aeroplane to promote that throat-filling sense of aesthetic beauty inspired by some others of its day, but it was a very impressive aircraft created at a most opportune time. It bore the brunt of the attack burden in Vietnam, when vitally needed, and it faithfully satisfied many requirements beyond those for which it was designed.

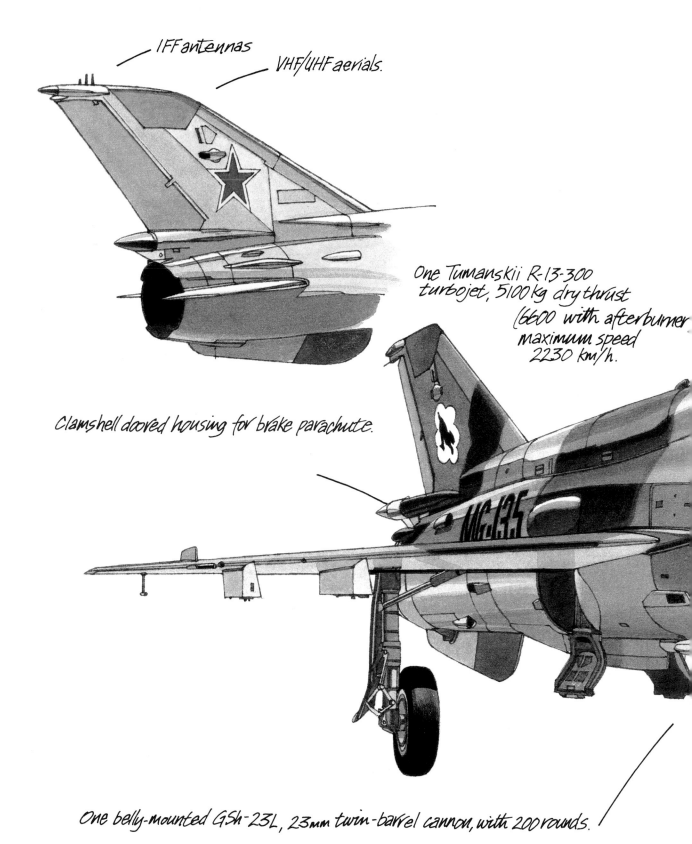

IFF antennas

VHF/UHF aerials.

One Tumanskii R-13-300 turbojet, 5100kg dry thrust (6600 with afterburner maximum speed 2230 km/h.

Clamshell doored housing for brake parachute.

One belly-mounted GSh-23L, 23mm twin-barrel cannon, with 200 rounds.

MIKOYAN-GURYEVICH
MiG-21

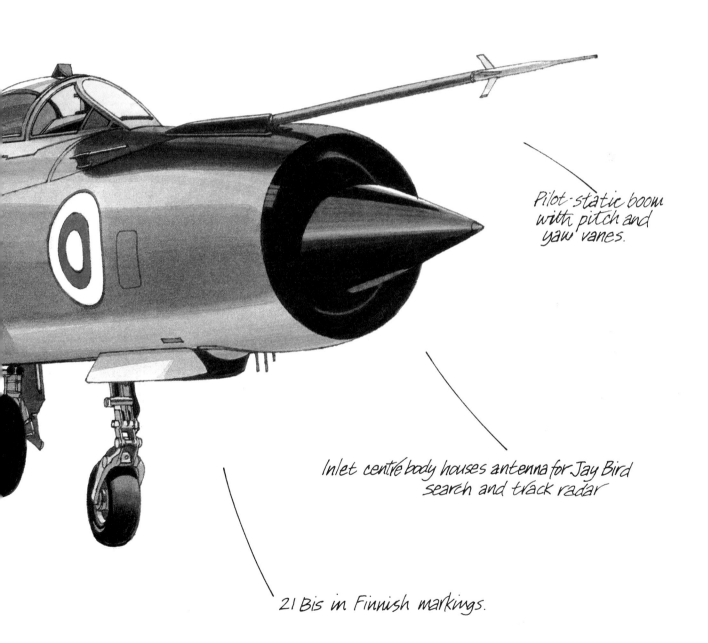

Pilot-static boom
with pitch and
yaw vanes.

Inlet centre body houses antenna for Jay Bird
search and track radar

21 Bis in Finnish markings.

MIKOYAN-GURYEVICH MiG-21

On 16 June 1956, an attractive but unremarkable little delta-wing aircraft made its first flight. Few would have believed, even the rapidly growing Mikoyan-Guryevich OKB, its designers, that 30 years and far more than 10,000 aircraft later, the MiG-21 would still be in production.

Back in the mid '50s, Russian aviation technology was based firmly on their experience of the Korean War. The TsAGI, the Soviet aerodynamic research agency, had formed the opinion that the best configuration for a lightweight fighter should be a delta wing with a conventional tailplane.

The MiG bureau were one of those charged with putting this theory into practice. Eventually the designers succeeded, probably beyond their wildest dreams. Yet the first aircraft, while they flew well and were relatively inexpensive to produce, were outclassed by the US fighters they were designed to combat. For a start they were underarmed; the first had just two 30mm guns mounted in the wing roots, but to save weight this was changed to a single gun. Internal fuel load was a mere 2340 litres.

The first pre-production MiG-21s reached the VVS – the Soviet Air Force – in late 1958. By 1959 a K-13A ('AA-2 Atoll') air-to-air missile had been added to the MiG-21's extremely basic armament. This missile had a range of approximately 6.5km with a 6kg warhead, and an infra-red seeker head driving canard control fins, and was almost certainly based on the early American Sidewinder. But to carry this modest weapon the left-hand gun was usually removed to save weight.

None of this stopped other Warsaw Pact countries from ordering the MiG-21, once the Soviet Union gave them permission. Like the VVS, they were impressed with its manoeuvrability and its economics, and small numbers of MiG-21Fs were made in Czechoslovakia. The same early version has been made in China as the J-7 (F-7 is the export version). The Indians, who were building up their own aircraft industry, began to make the MiG-21 them-

selves, in preference to any Western fighter. India traditionally would have chosen British, but Britain was insisting that fighters were obsolete and hardly trying to export any. This linked Hindustan Aeronautics with MiG fighters, and today the Indian Air Force has followed with the MiG-27M and MiG-29.

One of the most marked changes in appearance came in 1960 when the addition of search radar in a much larger nosecone resulted in the whole forward fuselage being enlarged in the MiG-21PF. The fin was made wider (later it became wider still) and the revised canopy led into a saddle fairing housing additional fuel.

The non-stop development of the MiG-21 for 25 years rested on Tumanskii's bureau producing a succession of new engines. The MiG-21F (F=boosted) had the R-11F engine, and in 1961 the SPS (blown flaps) development replaced the track-mounted Fowler flaps by plain flaps blown with compressed air from the revised R-11F2S engine.

Early MiG-21s had a unique canopy, without a separate windscreen, moulded from a single giant sheet of plastic and hinged at the back. When the pilot ejected, the canopy was pulled away to serve as a windshield in front of the pilot. But the MiG-21PFMA of 1963 changed to a side-hinged canopy, separate fixed windscreen and a new ejection seat. Still more power was forthcoming from the R-11-300 engine. At this time an extra pair of wing pylons were added, a zero/zero seat (giving sea-level, zero-speed ejection capability) and the new GSh-23L twin-barrel guns mounted in a pack in the bottom of the fuselage.

As Soviet avionics technology improved, it was fed into the MiG-21. By 1967, the MiG-21MF, with the new R-13 engine, was a totally different aircraft from the one that had first flown eleven years before. The blown flaps were perhaps just as important as the progressive power increases and the improved weapons. They had a dramatic effect on reducing landing speed, and enabled the MiG-21 to operate off much smaller airfields. The rival Mirage III, being tailless, could not have any flaps and landed at a much higher speed.

But the MiG-21 designers believed they could extract still more from this already prolific aeroplane. They virtually started again and designed a wholly new fighter with the same shape but a new airframe with none of the compromises caused by 20 years of piecemeal changes. Called the MiG-21bis, the latest version also has the R-25, a much more powerful yet lighter and more economical engine. Jay Bird radar, which is capable of guiding the semi-active versions of the AA-2-2 Advanced Atoll and the AA-8 Aphid air-to-air missiles, has been fitted ever

SPECIFICATION

21MF

Country of origin: Soviet Union.

Design Bureau: Mikoyan-Guryevich OKB.

Type: Single-seat multi-role fighter.

Year: 1958.

Engine: 6600kg (14,550lb) thrust Tumanskii R-13-300 afterburning turbojet.

Wingspan: 7.15m (23ft 5in).

Length: 13.46m (44ft 2in), not including probe.

Height: 4.5m (14ft 9in).

Weight: 9400kg (20,723lb).

Maximum speed: 2230km/h (1386mph) at high altitudes.

Ceiling: 18,000m (59,000ft).

Range: 1100km (683 miles).

Armament: One twin-barrel 23mm GSh-23L cannon plus up to 1500kg (3307lb) of bombs, rockets or missiles.

21SMT

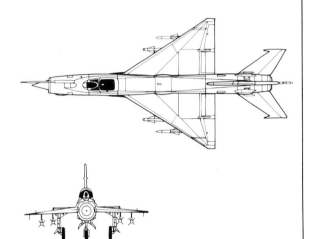

since the MiG-21PFMA. The Aphid – aptly code-named by NATO, though its real designation is R-60 – is one of the smallest if not the smallest AAM ever built. It is also believed, probably because of its small size, to be the most manoeuvrable of all AAMs up to its estimated range of 5.5 kilometres.

Large numbers of MiG-21s are reconnaissance or EW (electronic-warfare) versions or tandem-seat trainers. Of the total number of MiG-21s in service, more than 1600 are with countries outside the Warsaw Pact. These include Afghanistan, Algeria, Angola, Bangladesh, China, Cuba, Egypt, Ethiopia, Finland, India, Iraq, Laos, Mozambique, Nigeria, North Korea, Somalia, South Yemen, Sudan, Syria, Tanzania, Uganda and Vietnam. The USA and Israel even have aircraft for evaluation, the former having a whole 'squadron' used to assist fighter tactics and training.

With such a large number of aircraft in front line service

all over the world, it is highly likely that this likeable little fighter will be with us into the next century. Western equipment suppliers hope to find good business updating the newer MiG-21s for several air forces, notably China, Egypt and India.

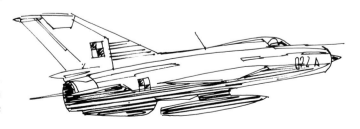

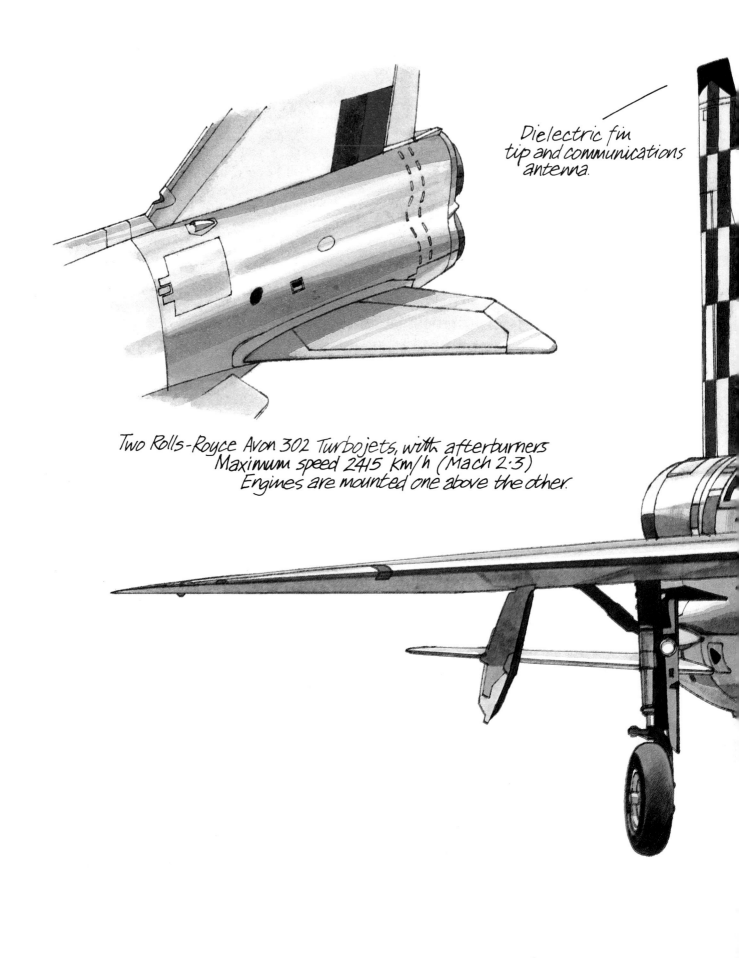

Dielectric fin
tip and communications
antenna.

Two Rolls-Royce Avon 302 Turbojets, with afterburners
Maximum speed 2415 km/h (Mach 2·3)
Engines are mounted one above the other.

BAC LIGHTNING

Aircraft of Nº56 Squadron.
RAF Wattisham.

Intake bullet
fairing houses Ferranti
Airpass Radar.

Red Top IR-homing AAM missile - two carried.

BAC LIGHTNING

Bearing in mind an only half-hearted interest by the Royal Air Force and a positive antipathy to the project by politicians, it is something of a mystery why W.E.W. (Teddy) Petter of the English Electric company was ever given sight of a study project for a supersonic aeroplane, let alone given permission to proceed with the work. But design of the first-ever British-developed military supersonic research aircraft did indeed proceed, and a prototype with the designation P.1, was flown in August 1954. Powered by a pair of Sapphire engines mounted one above the other, and with sharply swept but untapered wings and a low tailplane, it achieved the desired Mach 1 with ease. It was from these early beginnings, when the sole objective was to fly beyond Mach 1, that the aeroplane later known as the Lightning was eventually to emerge.

Only very gradually did the RAF accept the need for a supersonic fighter. Then the P.1 was completely redesigned into the prototype P.1B, flown in April 1957, and on 25 November 1958 the first officially designated Lightning was flown. It had a brand new fuselage, and its Rolls-Royce Avon afterburning engines powered the aeroplane to a speed of Mach 2. Further progress was made with the building of 20 pre-production machines, and service use of the BAC Lightning F.1 began in June 1960, with 74 Squadron at RAF Coltishall.

The F.1 showed early promise as an extremely agile and very popular home-defence interceptor, but its range – it had a radius of only 150 miles – was drastically limited by a moderate internal wing-tank fuel capacity and very high fuel consumption. Fuel capacity was later increased, but the problem was never really overcome. Within its limits however, the F.1's superb handling and manoeuvrability

enabled it to outfly virtually all of its contemporary opposition, and it had the then rare capability of achieving and even slightly exceeding Mach 1 in 'cold' thrust, without using the afterburners.

In spite of the fact that some RAF chiefs were at last beginning to recognise what might be exciting potential, further development of the Lightning continued to be absolutely crippled by a belief in Government circles that the days of manned aircraft were over. On the very day the P.1B first flew, Mr Duncan Sandys, Minister for Defence, published a White Paper in which it was explained that the RAF would be 'unlikely to require' any more fighters or bombers. Such aircraft were clearly obsolete, and would be 'replaced' as fast as possible by missiles. All new aircraft were therefore being cancelled; but the Lightning 'unfortunately has already proceeded too far to cancel'. It was thus reluctantly being allowed to continue, on the strict understanding that no money was spent on developing it further.

Moreover, the aircraft's detractors pointed perhaps unfairly to its most obvious faults: a short combat radius, limited weapons, and a comparatively poor serviceability record leading to a low flying rate. Nevertheless, the F.1 was not only Britain's first but also its only all-weather supersonic interceptor. After prolonged arguments, reluctant permission was given to proceed with the Lightning F.2, with small improvements. A prototype was flown on 11 July 1961, and the aircraft entered service with the RAF's 19 and 22 Squadrons in the summer of 1963.

After yet more dissent from bureaucratic doubters, the Lightning F.3 was produced. Among its many other refinements, such as more powerful engines, this version had a modified wing plan with extended outer sections designed to increase the aircraft's range by reducing subsonic drag. It also had an enlarged ventral fuel tank which served the same purpose, as well as an enlarged square-topped fin. The new variant quickly established itelf as an even more exhilarating performer. No one, and especially not its pilots, was ever able to accuse, the Lightning of being less than impressive and delightful to fly. Against the inevitable old arguments, those determined few who supported the aircraft laboured doggedly on. Curiously the T.4 and T.5 dual-control trainer versions were given a side-by-side cockpit, most unusual for a Mach 2 fighter!

The amazing obstacle course which resulted eventually in a design for the final and definitive Lightning F.6 might well have led lesser design teams to give up in despair. Petter had gone to Folland in 1953 and Freddy Page (now Sir Frederick Page) headed the team. Government

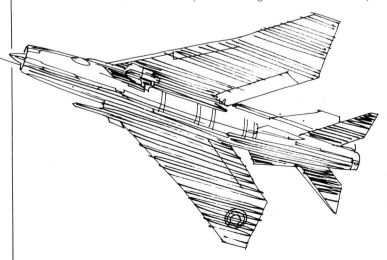

SPECIFICATION

F.6

Country of origin: Great Britain.

Manufacturer: British Aircraft Corporation.

Type: Single-seat interceptor.

Year: 1964.

Engine: Two 7112kg (15,680lb) Rolls-Royce Avon 302 turbojets, with afterburning.

Wingspan: 10.6m (34ft 10in).

Length: 16.25m (53ft 3in).

Height: 5.95m (19ft 7in).

Weight: 22,680kg (50,000lb).

Maximum speed: 2415km/h (1500mph).

Ceiling: Over 18,290m (60,000ft).

Range: 1290km (800 miles).

Armament: Either two Red Top or two Firestreak missiles, plus optionally two 30mm Aden cannon.

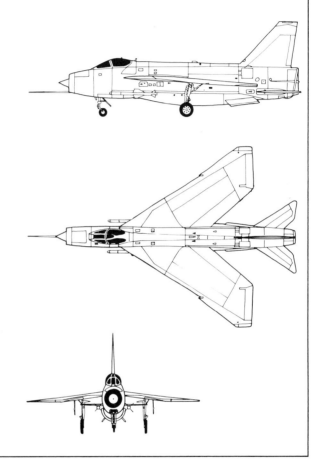

hindrance was ceaseless, and the company had to pay for almost all the improvements. At last the prototype F.6 was flown in April 1964. The first models off the production line were delivered to RAF No 5 Squadron at the end of 1965.

This new Lightning, whose two Rolls-Royce Avon 301-series turbojets each produce over 11,000lb of thrust, rising to 16,300lb with full afterburner, remains a sparkling performer to this day. Interchangeable armament packages include pairs of Red Top or Firestreak guided missiles, an option of two 30mm cannon, and, in export versions, up to 6000lb of assorted bombs, rockets or other stores mounted above or below the wings. The F.6 is even today a formidable fighting machine in close air combat.

Yet, in spite of its popularity among those best qualified to know, total production of all Lightning types was only 338. Some saw service in Germany, but Lightnings were sold for export to only two countries, Kuwait and Saudi Arabia. Had Britain been motivated like France, with the Government actually helping, the story would have been very different and the production total might have been at least doubled.

With hindsight, there is not the slightest doubt that the BAC Lightning was a most underrated aeroplane. Had development been permitted to follow a reasonable course, the F.6 would certainly have evolved much earlier, and probably in an improved form. As it was, belated recognition of the aircraft's superb qualities is marked by the fact that it remained in front-line service with the RAF Fighter/Strike Command long after F-4 Phantoms began gradual replacement in 1974. In 1980 British Aerospace carried out fatigue tests on an F.6 in order to validate the aircraft for continued service with RAF Nos 5 and 11 Squadrons for several years to come.

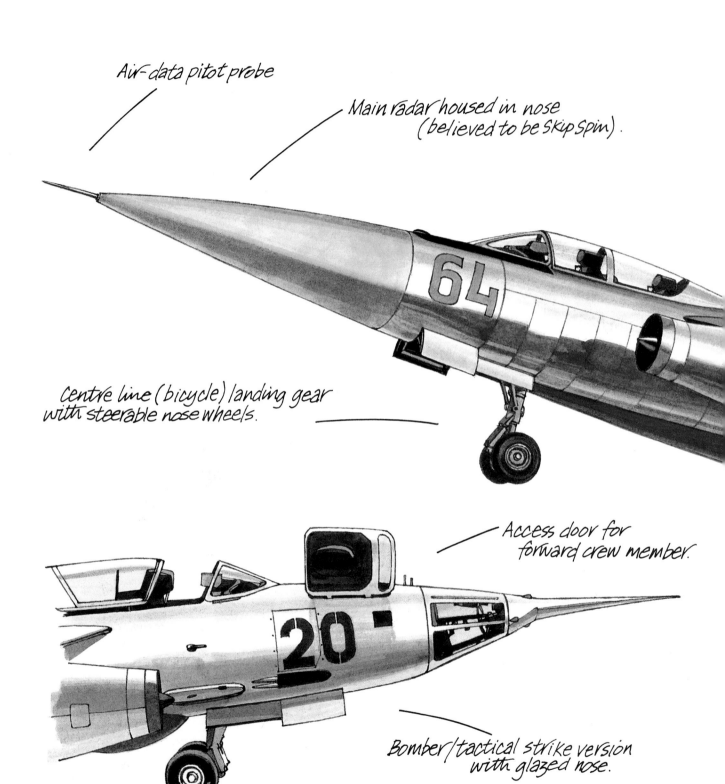

Air-data pitot probe

Main radar housed in nose
(believed to be Skip Spin).

64

Centre line (bicycle) landing gear
with steerable nose wheels.

Access door for
forward crew member.

20

Bomber/tactical strike version
with glazed nose.

Two Tumanskii R-11 turbojets with afterburner
maximum speed 2000 Km/h.

Rearward radar and ILS aerials.

YAK-25 to YAK-28

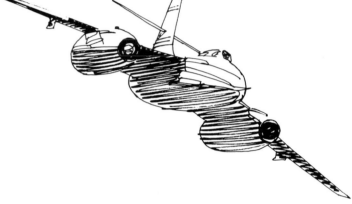

Yakovlev's achievements in the field of aeronautical design spanned an active career of over half a century. His military involvement began in 1938, with the hugely successful Yak-1 and its successors, and he went on from there to work on every important Russian development including many types and sizes of jets, helicopters and VTO (veritical take-off) designs. Apart from A.N. Tupolev, no other single individual ever made such a great and lasting contribution to his country's aircraft technology, and when in November 1951 the Kremlin asked for a new all-weather day-and-night jet fighter, Yakovlev rose to the challenge. His Yak-25 beat the competing La-200B and MiG I-320R hands-down and so became the forerunner of that large and diverse series that culminated in the Yak-28s.

Perhaps the most surprising feature of the Yak-25 is that the original design was ever accepted at all. The Kremlin chiefs, seldom before known to look with favour upon radical innovation, approved Yakovlev's proposal for a completely new concept in design and development. The Yak-25 was to have its two jet engines slung low beneath non-tapering swept wings, a tailplane set high on a swept fin, and tandem landing gears with most of the aircraft's weight borne by a main unit only slightly aft of the centre of gravity, and stabilised by wing-tip outrigger wheels. A technically challenging arrangement, Yakovlev had already used this landing gear on the single-jet Yak-50. A decade later, independently, it was used on Britain's Harrier.

Pilot and observer sat in tandem ejector seats behind a nose made heavy by the very large radar installation known to NATO as Scan Three. The aircraft was armed with two big NS-37 guns under the fuselage, and a retractable battery of rockets. This first version had a top speed of 1015km/h.

Types developed from the Yak-25 early on included the Yak-25R for reconnaissance duties, the dual-trainer Yak-25U, and a type known as the Yak-RV. This last was a single-seater with a short-fuselage and long-span unswept wing. It was used, as was the American U-2, for ultra high-altitude reconnaissance.

Few post-war aircraft have gone through more variants, and the biggest step forward came in 1958 with the designing of a wholly new and very different family, the larger and heavier Yak-28s. A prototype flew in 1960, and the series went into service during 1963-64. They had completely new airframes, widely spaced twin-wheel landing gears, a bigger fuel capacity, updated radar systems, and a comprehensive range of armament including, in some versions, air-to-air missiles. Aerodynamic improvements incorporated a redesigned wing for supersonic flight, and the structure was strengthened to match the power delivered by the new afterburning Tumanskii R-11 engines.

The Yak-28 was developed along two lines: the 'Brewer' (NATO code-name) bomber and reconnaissance models, and the 'Firebar' interceptors. These types and their variants had their wings raised closer to the top of the fuselage in order to allow for a large internal load capacity for bombs, cameras and other sensors, and receivers and jammers for EW (electronic warfare). Most of the Brewer range have a sliding canopy for the pilot and a glazed nose for the navigator/observer. The less numerous Yak-28U trainer, which has stepped cockpits for instructor (in front, under a hinged canopy) and pupil, was given the NATO code-name 'Maestro'. This has no weapons, and lower-powered engines.

Like the British Buccaneer, the Soviet Yak Brewer was a most capable tactical aircraft which achieved few sales to foreign buyers. But, and again like the Buccaneer, the Brewer was one of those aeroplanes which governments are most reluctant to sell. It had multi-role capability, was a bumper bundle of futuristic design and equipment, and had massive powers of destruction. Possibly potential foreign sales were politically blocked.

The Yak-28P Firebar – the P suffix denotes *perekh-vatchik* or interceptor – was the first supersonic all-weather two-seat fighter to enter service with the IA-PVO, the Soviet air-defence organisation. It differed from the Brewer in having a dielectric nosecone housing an air-intercept radar (NATO code-name 'Skip Spin') thought to be effective over a range of some 40km – probably an under-estimate. Firebars dispensed with the internal weapons bay in favour of enhanced fuel tankage. Most carry two 'AA-3 Anab' missiles, one guided by an infra-red homing head and the other by radar, and can

SPECIFICATION

Yak-28P

Country of origin: Soviet Union.

Design Bureau: Yakovlev OKB.

Type: Two-seat interceptor.

Year: 1962.

Engine: Two 5950kg (13,120lb) Tumanskii R-11 turbojets with afterburning.

Wingspan: 12.95m (42ft 6in).

Length: 21.65m (71ft).

Height: 3.95m (12ft 11in).

Weight: 20,000kg (44,100lb).

Maximum speed: 2000km/h (1240mph).

Ceiling: 16,764m (55,000ft).

Range: 2575km (1600 miles).

Armament: Two Anab air-to-air missiles (infra-red and radar), with provision for two additional close-range K-13A or R-60 missiles.

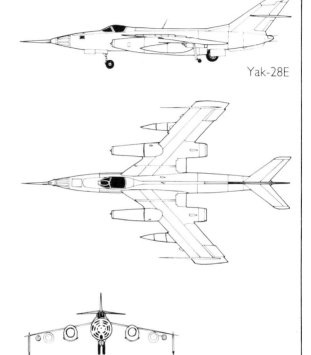

Yak-28E

supplement these by a pair of K-13A ('AA-2 Atoll') close-range missiles. A distinctive feature of the Yak-28P – apart from its long and very pointed nose, which in 1974 was lengthened – was the tail-warning radar system, also thought to have a range of some 40km. Production of the Yak-28P, believed to number around 300, was discontinued well before 1970, but some of these, and also many Brewers, are still in service in several parts of the Soviet Union.

Many figures concerning the Yak-25s and Yak-28s are somewhat vague, because the Russians have always been reluctant to release hard data and the West is compelled to rely on estimates. However, Western sources agree that the total number manufactured of all variants is between 2000 and 3000. Not an enormous total, but there is no doubt that the aircraft represented a significant advance in Soviet aeronautical technology.

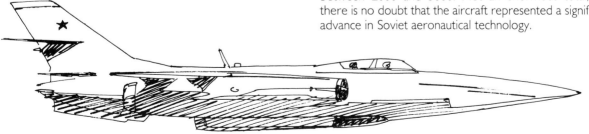

Aircraft flown by Randy Cunningham and Willie Driscoll, who accounted for 38 MiG fighters in Vietnam.

F-4J

F-4G

Fully variable exhaust nozzles.

McDONNELL DOUGLAS F-4 PHANTOM II

4B

The nose landing gear could be extended by the pilot to raise the nose and increase the angle-of-attack for take-off and landing.

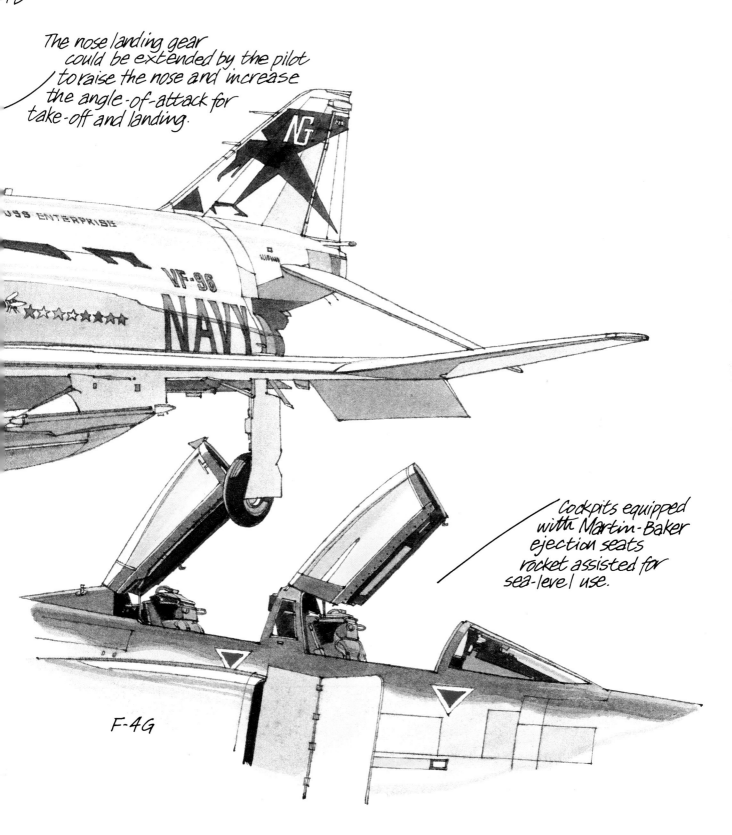

Cockpits equipped with Martin-Baker ejection seats rocket assisted for sea-level use.

F-4G

McDONNELL DOUGLAS F-4 PHANTOM II

The world's most successful post-war fighter almost never happened. In May 1953, the McDonnell Aircraft Company tendered for the award of a lucrative US Navy contract to provide a supersonic carrier-based fighter with four 20mm guns, and lost.

Undeterred, and with what can only be considered blind faith in their design team, they pressed on to produce a twin-engined fighter aircraft that has rightly claimed the most important place in modern combat-aviation history.

The F-4 Phantom II has seen service with 12 different countries, flying with equal facility off airfields and carriers. It has served with distinction in almost every combat theatre from Vietnam to the present time, and has been produced in numbers that rival the massive production schedules common during World War II.

It would be foolish to pretend that the Phantom is a beautiful aeroplane. Yet its unusual upward-swept outer wing panels and sharply anhedral tail surface give it a distinction of its own. This combination of unswept wing and downswept tail is what gives the Phantom its stability as a gun missile firing platform. Even at speeds near Mach 2, it remains as steady as a rock.

Back in the mid-1950s, things were looking black for the Phantom. The US Navy decided to award their contract for a supersonic fighter to McDonnell's rivals, Vought, for their F-8 Crusader. But fighter design was proceeding at such a pace that requirements were likely to change dramatically overnight.

McDonnell's revised proposals, submitted only a few months later, met with qualified approval by the US Navy. The proposed Phantom – named after its successful early post-war predecessor, the Phantom I – passed through a phase as an attack aircraft with 11 external stores pylons and finally settled as a single-seat all-weather tactical fighter with a full complement of missiles. Nine months later, in 1957, the US Navy Bureau of Aeronautics discovered that

it could well need an aircraft of this type and gave McDonnell the opportunity it was looking for: a development contract.

As is so often the case, the aeroplane itself had the last word. As soon as the Phantom took to the air on 27 May 1958, it began to prove itself to all those who had derided it. Its role was to be as a carrier-based first-line defence for the US Navy. Armament was simple indeed: four air-to-air Sparrow missiles, radar-guided and controlled from the rear seat that had by then become essential to accommodate the second crew member needed to handle all the avionics. It was up against an excellent rival in Vought's F8U-3 Crusader III, but beat it on almost every count. Almost from day one, the Phantom began to pick up world records for its performance.

The 45/F-4A pre-production models were used by the Navy for development and evaluation purposes only. The first major variant, the F-4B, went into service both with the Navy and the Marine Corps in December 1960; 637 were built, and a large number of these saw action in the skies over Vietnam.

The F-4B was immediately distinguished by its bigger nose housing Westinghouse APQ-72 radar, and with an infra-red detector in a separate fairing under the nose. Another visible change was to raise the rear cockpit above the top line of the fuselage.

At the time, most observers believed that aerial warfare of the future would be a matter of being roughly in the right part of the sky at the right time, pushing a button and leaving the missiles to do the rest. The Phantom was an ideal platform for this kind of warfare.

Amazingly, reports began to come in of Phantom pilots engaging in World War I-style dogfights – and winning (though the absence of a gun was a drawback). The world and particularly the US Air Force began to sit up and take notice. Within months and after minor modifications, such as dual controls and larger breaks, inertial navigation and improved weapon-aiming systems, the Air Force began to take delivery of 583 F-4C Phantoms.

Delighted, the Air Force followed the 825 F-4Ds. These looked identical, but had completely revised weapon systems more suited to land-based warfare. Further variants followed. Best and last of all, the F-4E developed more power, carried more fuel, a heavier bombload, and had slatted wings to improve manoeuvrability. Not surprisingly, the E model at last featured an internal gun, under the nose. Britain's Royal Navy and Royal Air Force ordered special variants with Rolls-Royce Spey engines.

The floodgates were open and 5195 Phantom F-4s were built in just over 20 years. Phantoms are still in

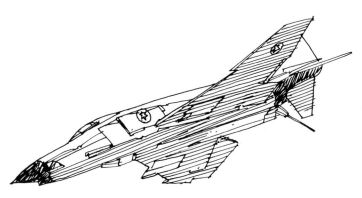

SPECIFICATION

F-4E

Country of origin: USA.

Manufacturer: McDonnell Douglas Corporation.

Type: Two-seat multi-role fighter.

Year: 1967.

Engine: Two 8120kg (17,900lb) General Electric J79-GE-17 turbojets with afterburning.

Wingspan: 11.68m (38ft 4in).

Length: 19.2m (63ft).

Height: 14.96m (16ft 3in).

Weight: 27,380kg (60,360lb).

Maximum speed: 2414km/h (1500mph).

Ceiling: 18,970m (62,250ft).

Range: 4184km (2600 miles).

Armament: One 20mm M61A-1 multi-barrel rotary cannon, four Sparrow air-to-air missiles and four Sidewinder close-range missiles, or up to 7258kg (16,000lb) of external ordnance in many hundreds of combinations.

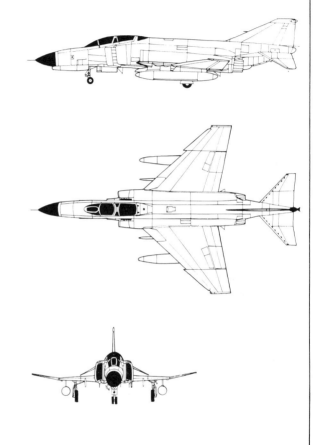

front-line duty for the USA, Britain, Japan, West Germany, Israel, Turkey, Greece and South Korea.

As Commander 'Duke' Cunningham said: 'The F-4 is one of the most honest airplanes in the world. She will almost talk to a pilot. She will tell you every move she is going to make.'

Part of the Phantom's success over Vietnam had to be due to the advanced combat training its pilots were given. Instead of flying against other Phantoms, pilots were matched against different aircraft types that more closely reproduced the different performance levels of their North Vietnamese opponents, the MiG-17s, -19s and -21s. It's worth remembering that although the MiG-17 was much older, it was more manoeuvrable and therefore much better suited to dogfighting. Completely new techniques had to be developed to fight it. These included

practice dogfights against Douglas Skyhawks which could be asked to behave much like the agile MiGs.

The last Phantom F-4 came off the production line in May 1981, exactly 28 years after the Phantom project was born. Such successful fighting aircraft appear only once in a generation.

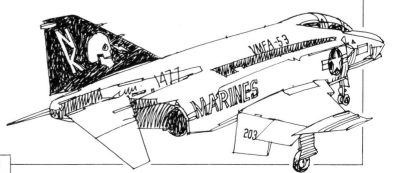

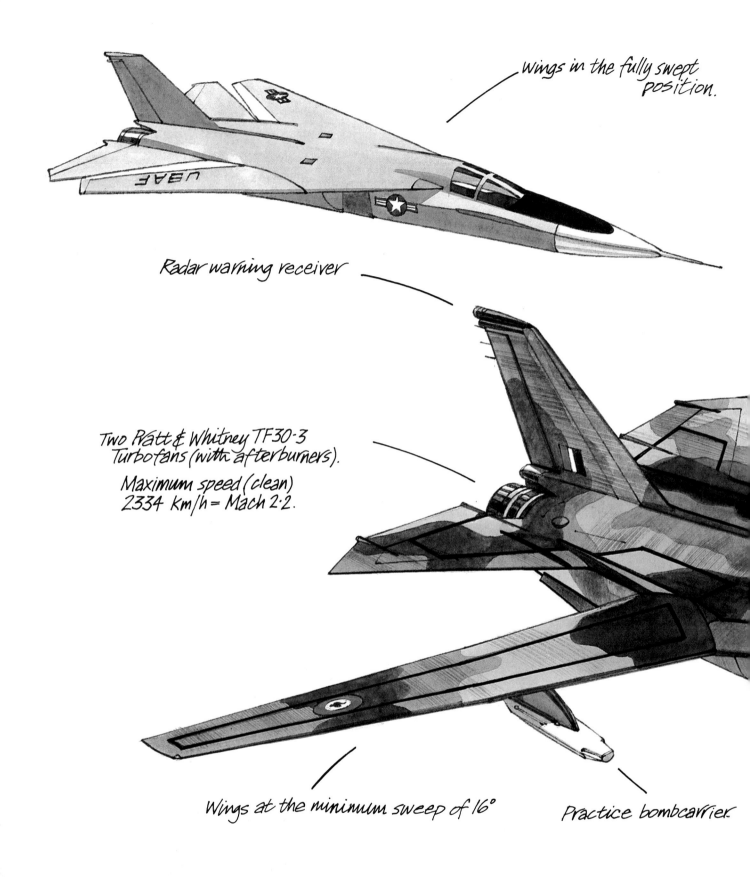

wings in the fully swept
position.

Radar warning receiver

Two Pratt & Whitney TF30-3
Turbofans (with afterburners).

Maximum speed (clean)
2334 km/h = Mach 2·2.

USAF

Wings at the minimum sweep of 16°

Practice bombcarrier.

GENERAL DYNAMICS F-111

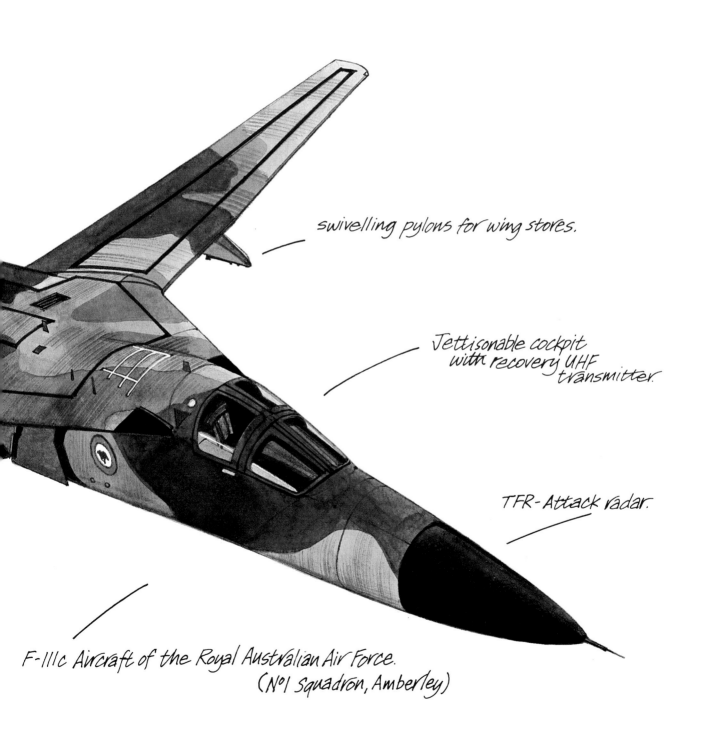

swivelling pylons for wing stores.

Jettisonable cockpit with recovery UHF transmitter.

TFR-Attack radar.

F-IIIc Aircraft of the Royal Australian Air Force.
(Nº1 Squadron, Amberley)

GENERAL DYNAMICS F-111

In 1947 a British designer, Sir Barnes Wallis, began work on a revolutionary new concept in aerodynamics. Wallis is famous for designing the R.100 airship, the Wellington bomber, the bouncing cylindrical bomb used by the Dambusters and the 10-ton 'Earthquake' bomb. After the war, he returned to aircraft design and came up with the idea of the variable-geometry wing. The basic idea had been suggested in Germany in 1944, but no-one had worked out a way of turning theory into practice.

Wallis' 'swing-wing', as it was later called, was not followed up by the British aircraft industry, because the government said combat aircraft were no longer wanted. It was therefore left, as was so often the case in the post-war years, to the United States to develop to a practical level of aerodynamics and engineering. NASA (US National Aeronautics and Space Administration) played the central role, though Wallis' company (Vickers-Armstrongs) was required to hand over all its research documents to the US government.

In 1959 the USAF Tactical Air Command began looking for a replacement for the F-100, F-105 and other fighter/bombers. Almost from the word go, things went sadly wrong. A new Secretary for Defense, excited by the options available through variable geometry, high performance afterburning turbofans, new materials such as titanium, and a veritable revolution in aircraft electronics, decided that the new aircraft should be designed to fulfil two differing roles by combining the USAF tactical fighter/bomber requirement with a separate naval fleet-defence interceptor version.

To make matters worse, TAC revised their specification, demanding mission radius and ferry range fantastic by previous standards, to a point where it became virtually impossible to achieve a cost-effective solution. But eventually, on 24 November 1962, General Dynamics, Fort Worth, was awarded the contract. (This also caused enormous political arguments.) The first YF-111A, unique in that it was the first swing-wing aircraft other than

experimental or research prototypes, flew just over two years later on 21 December 1964.

The aeroplane was already plagued with problems. Its Pratt & Whitney TF30 turbofans could not (as yet) develop the kind of thrust the designers were looking for. Structural problems arose with the airframe, and these were exacerbated by financial and political difficulties. All these were magnified to a point where, instead of being considered as one of the Western world's leading fighters, to be built and sold in its thousands, it was being spoken about openly as a scandalous failure.

Only one type of F-111 did prove a failure. Helped by Grumman, General Dynamics pressed on and developed the F-111B for the US Navy. Flying for the first time on 18 May 1965, it proved very disappointing in performance and grossly overweight. It was eventually cancelled in favour of the Grumman F-14 Tomcat, subject of a later entry in this book. Meanwhile, the plant in Fort Worth eventually delivered 141 F-111As to the USAF.

Obvious deficiencies in these aircraft had prompted rapid development work, and further variants quickly followed. Twenty-four F-111Cs with wings of increased span and stronger landing gear went – *ten* years late – to the Royal Australian Air Force. Chronologically, these were preceded by the slightly more powerful F.111E. Next in line came the F-111D with a fractionally more powerful engine and with completely revised avionics. The problem was that this aircraft, due mainly to the enormous cost of its radar and other electronic equipment, was built at almost prohibitive expense. Finally, GD produced the ultimate variant, the F-111F. This has much more powerful engines and its avionics have capability comparable to the D, but achieved at a more realistic price.

In its attack role the F-111, fitted with a giant Pave Tack sensor pod, can out-perform all other aircraft, with the exception of the Soviet SU-24 'Fencer' and the redoubtable Anglo/German/Italian Panavia Tornado (which knocked F-111s for six in a 1982 navigation/bombing contest). These two apart, the F-111 is the only aircraft able to fly long distances at extremely low level, and then deliver a tactical nuclear or conventional payload in a single pass over a target, all the time employing effective electronic countermeasures.

Weapons include the GBU-15 glide bomb, the B43 nuclear bomb and many other stores, plus up to 29,000 lb of conventional bombs or dispenser pods for small bomblets. It is possible to instal a 20mm M61 gun with no less than 1084 rounds, and all versions can carry Sidewinder self-defence missiles. But it has long been obvious that the F-111 is a bomber rather than a 'fighter'.

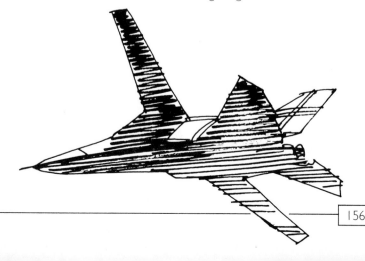

SPECIFICATION

F-111E

Country of origin: USA.

Manufacturer: General Dynamics Corporation.

Type: Two-seat all-weather attack aircraft.

Year: 1970.

Engine: Two 8390kg (18,500lb) Pratt & Whitney TF30-3 augmented turbofans.

Wingspan: 19.2m (63ft) (unswept).

Length: 22.4m (73ft 6in).

Height: 5.22m (17ft 1in).

Weight: 44,905kg (99,000lb).

Maximum speed: 2334km/h (1450mph).

Ceiling: 13,720m (45,000ft).

Range: 3747km (2328 miles).

Armament: Internal bomb bay: normally occupied by fuel or other devices but can carry two nuclear weapons or two 2000lb bombs, or 20mm M61A-1 gun. Eight underwing pylons can carry a total of 14,290kg (31,500lb) external stores including bombs and drop tanks.

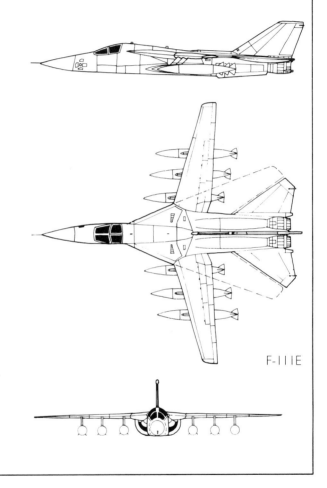

F-111E

As a belated attempt to counter the Soviet Union's pre-eminence in the early 1970s in electronic air warfare, it was decided to rebuild F-111As into a specialist high-power ECM (electronic countermeasures) platform. This job was given to Grumman, partly as a result of their work in this field, but also because they had been the associate contractor on the F-111B programme and already knew the aeroplane.

The first EF-111A Raven, as it is called, flew on 10 March 1977. No extra crew member is required; the entire jamming system is managed by the Electronic Warfare Officer (usually a second pilot) from the right-hand seat. Forty-two of these aircraft have been converted, and these are certain to feature in any future major air conflict, trying to clear a path through hostile defences for NATO aircraft – which could well be F-111s.

Thus, apart from the Raven, the F-111 turned out to be a bomber. Had this been realised 20 years ago, the F-111 would have achieved much wider recognition as the superb aircraft that it undoubtedly is. This fact has certainly been appreciated by the USAF, which is due to spend over $1 billion updating the avionics of all 381 F-111s in service.

ARI.18223
Radar warning receiver.

Aircraft of 801 squadron, painted in post-Falklands low visibility colours.

ROYAL NAVY

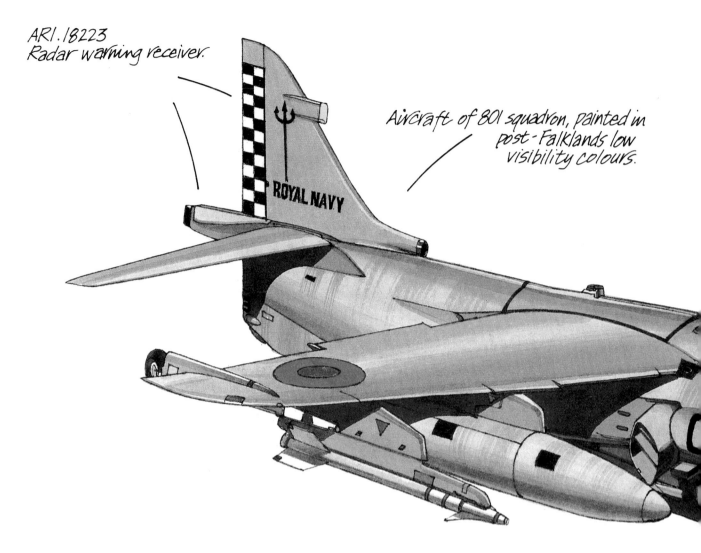

AIM-9L Sidewinder missiles, four are commonly carried.

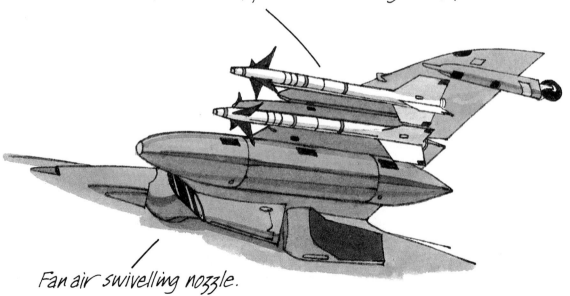

Fan air swivelling nozzle.

BRITISH AEROSPACE HARRIER

One Rolls-Royce Pegasus 104 vectored-
thrust turbofan rated at 9752 kg.

Maximum speed 1191 km/h.

Blue Fox radar.

BRITISH AEROSPACE HARRIER

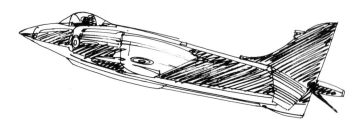

Not long after the jet engine had been invented, aircraft designers began to look for new ways to harness its thrust. The unprecedented combination of high power and light weight opened the way to VTOL (vertical take-off and landing) aircraft.

The concept of vectoring the thrust downwards dates from the late 1940s. By the late 1950s a spate of V/STOL (vertical or short take-off and landing) aircraft, many of them prop-driven were being test flown on both sides of the Atlantic.

Most of the early V/STOL schemes were ungainly and complex, some having batteries of special vertical turbojets used only at take-off and landing. A French engineer, Michel Wibault, proposed a VTOL scheme in which an engine drove giant air compressors delivering through pipes which could be vectored downwards, to lift the machine off the ground, or to the rear, for forward flight. At Bristol Dr Stanley Hooker and his engine designers simplified this into a much neater and more compact solution which eventually became the Bristol (now Rolls-Royce) Pegasus engine. A turbofan, it delivers fan air to left and right front nozzles and hot jet gas to left and right rear nozzles, all four nozzles rotating in unison. At Hawker Aircraft Sir Sydney Camm's designers created the P.1127 around this unique engine.

The prototype Hawker P.1127 hovered for the first time on 21 October 1960. Five months later, it made its first proper flight. From this stemmed first a squadron of aircraft called Kestrels and then, from early 1969, regular RAF service by the production Harrier, a fully developed combat aircraft. Although these aroused considerable interest, much of this seemed to be idle curiosity rather than serious interest in the aircraft's potential for military use. This amused tolerance by the world's air forces and aircraft makers continued for over 20 years.

Then, unexpectedly, the Harrier startled the world. In May, 1982 pilots of the British Royal Navy and RAF showed the world, and in particular the Argentinian air force and navy, just what a deadly weapon the Harrier can be. Helicopters apart, the Harrier was the *only* aircraft that Britain could deploy in its bid to liberate the Falkland Islands and their inhabitants. Its ability to take off from the tiny decks of Britain's two small carriers, HMS *Hermes* and *Invincible*, with no catapult or arrester gear, was of course fundamental. But what shocked the pilots of the Skyhawks, Mirages and Super Etendards was the little aeroplane's staggering manoeuvrability.

To return to the pioneer P.1127, it was obvious that considerably more power was needed if the aircraft was to have a useful combat potential. Initially rated at 11,000lb

thrust, the Pegasus was next uprated to 15,000lb and supplied for the Kestrel, an intermediate development aircraft formed into a single British/American/German squadron for NATO evaluation purposes. Britain's own government and RAF had been prohibited from showing any interest, because it was official policy to believe that there was no longer any need for manned combat aircraft. A truly revolutionary new idea was just what was needed to overcome this nonsensical belief, and in 1962 plans for a much bigger, highly supersonic development, the P.1154, went ahead. In 1965 this was suddenly scrapped by the British government. However, permission was given for the development of the smaller subsonic Harrier, which was first supplied to the RAF with a 19,000lb thrust Pegasus engine in January 1969.

Today there are several versions of the Harrier in service. The GR.3 close-support attack and reconnaissance model has the Pegasus 103, of 21,500lb thrust. Four squadrons of these are serving with the Royal Air Force. They carry two 30mm Aden cannon in detachable pods and five pylons can carry up to 5000lb of bombs, rocket pods and Sidewinder self-defence missiles. The GR.3's avionics include a laser nose, inertial navigation and a HUD (head-up display).

Another main variant is the Sea Harrier. Basically the same as a GR.3, the Sea Harrier has a redesigned front end with the pilot placed at a higher level to allow room for further avionics and additional cockpit interfaces and controls. This also improves all-round visibility. In the nose is a Blue Fox radar, arranged to fold through 180° to reduce length to fit small ship lifts and hangars. It was this aircraft, still hardly settled down in service, that was so spectacularly successful in the South Atlantic: it scored 23 air-combat victories, plus three probables, over assorted Argentinian aircraft without suffering a single loss. Six Sea Harriers *were* lost, but these were either destroyed by ground fire (2) or lost in accidents (4), the latter all being caused by appalling weather conditions.

Although the Sea Harrier is perfectly capable of vertical take-off, it normally uses a 'ski-jump' take-off ramp to increase mission capability. On take-off the engine nozzles are all vectored rearwards at the beginning of the short

SPECIFICATION

GR.3

Country of origin: Great Britain.

Manufacturer: British Aerospace Aircraft Group (previously Hawker Siddeley Aviation).

Type: Single-seat V/STOL close-support aircraft.

Year: 1967.

Engine: 9752kg (21,500lb) Rolls-Royce Pegasus 103 vectored-thrust turbofan.

Wingspan: 7.7m (25ft 3in).

Length: 14.27m (46ft 10in).

Height: 3.43m (11ft 3in).

Weight: 11,793kg (26,000lb) (not VTOL).

Maximum speed: 1186km/h (737mph).

Ceiling: 15,240m (50,000ft).

Range: 3300km (2070 miles) (with drop tanks).

Armament: Four underwing pylons and one pylon under the fuselage can carry maximum operational external load of 2270kg (5000lb). Two under-fuselage strakes can be replaced by 30mm Aden gun pods. Assorted stores carried can include AIM-9L Sidewinder AAMs.

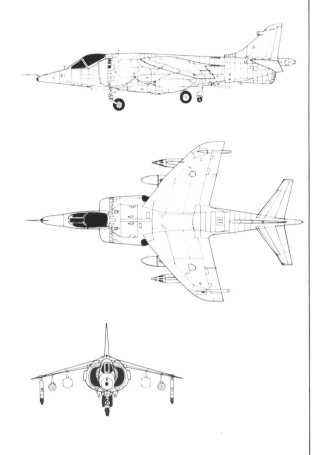

but exciting run. As the Harrier reaches the end of the ramp, sloping at 7° to 15° (depending on the installation), the nozzles are suddenly vectored 50° downwards, hurling the aircraft into the sky while still accelerating it horizontally. Weapon or fuel loads can be greatly increased, and safety on engine failure is also far better.

In 1982, a fascinating new shipborne launching method was announced, the Skyhook. Developed by BAe as a private venture, it would enable even small frigates and destroyers to carry a complement of Harriers without a traditional flight deck. Cranes on each side of the ship lift two aircraft into the air, then swing them outboard. At this point the engine is started; as soon as it is supporting the aircraft, the special 'grabs' release it. At the end of its

mission, the Sea Harrier hovers alongside the ship. The Skyhook, which has an inbuilt sensor, is automatically positioned so that the 'grab' can clasp the aircraft. Then the crane swings it inboard and on to the deck or straight into the hold. As with the ski ramp, it takes a long time for navies to understand and accept new ideas.

Harriers are in service with Britain, the US Marines and the navies of India and Spain. Although not yet produced in anything like the numbers that its designers had every right to hope for, the Harrier has proved beyond doubt and in the most conclusive way possible that it is no gimmick. With incredible slowness the penny is gradually dropping: future combat aircraft dare not require airfields. The Harrier was simply the first of the warplanes of the future.

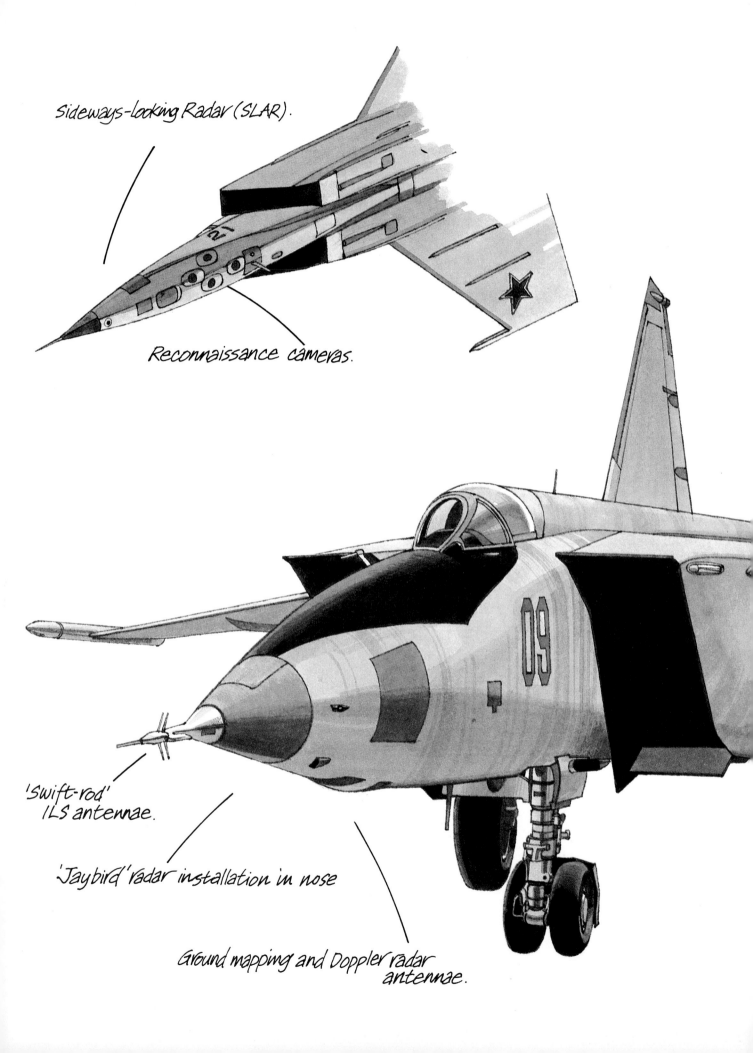

Sideways-looking Radar (SLAR).

Reconnaissance cameras.

'Swift-rod' ILS antennae.

'Jaybird' radar installation in nose

Ground mapping and Doppler radar antennae.

MIKOYAN-GURYEVICH
MiG-25

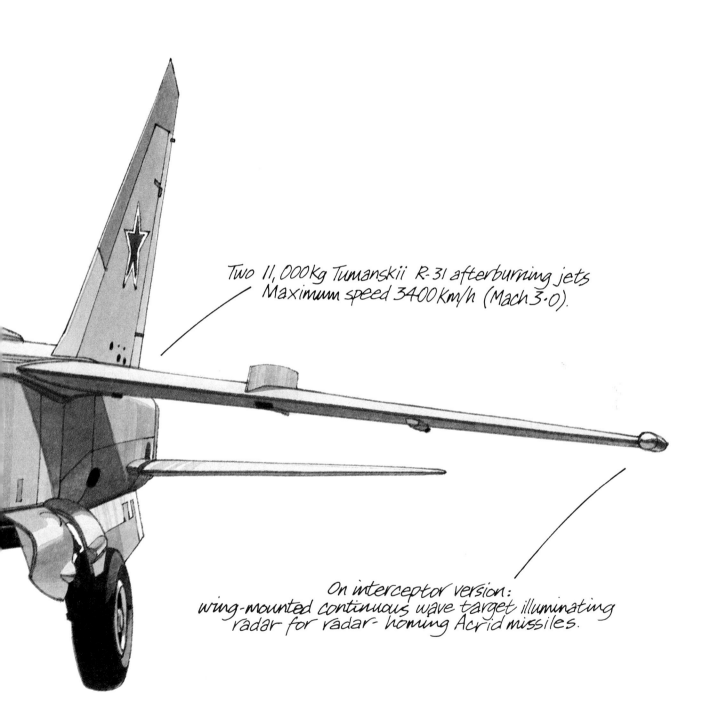

Two 11,000 kg Tumanskii R-31 afterburning jets
Maximum speed 3400 Km/h (Mach 3.0).

On interceptor version:
wing-mounted continuous wave target illuminating
radar for radar- homing Acrid missiles.

MIKOYAN-GURYEVICH MiG-25

Apart from the USAF SR-71 reconnaissance aircraft, the MiG-25 is the fastest combat aircraft in service in the world. It was designed by the MiG Bureau to counter a threat that never became a reality. In 1958, the Bureau was asked to develop an ultra-fast high-altitude interceptor specifically to shoot down the USAF's B-70 – then projected as the fastest bomber in the world. Despite the fact that the B-70 was cancelled, the MiG-25 went into production. It was designed for one thing only: speed. This is demonstrated by the fact that when the MiG-25 is travelling at speeds approaching Mach 3, its turning circle has a radius of tens of miles.

The MiG-25, code-named 'Foxbat' by NATO, uses an ultra-thin unswept wing, with a thickness/chord ratio of just four per cent, the leading edge being sharply tapered. Enormous ducts supply air from sloping inlets to the Tumanskii R-31 turbojets, which at high speeds act more like ramjets. These engines are rated at 11,100kg each, with afterburner.

They are, naturally, very thirsty. No less than 17,900 litres of specially developed fuel is housed in nine welded steel tanks in the fuselage and in addition one cunningly designed box tank is welded into the basic structure of each wing.

The Foxbat has limited control surfaces compared with many modern combat aircraft. This is understandable as its role is restricted to high-speed stand-off interception. Movable surfaces consist of powered inboard ailerons, all flying tailplanes, twin rudders and unblown plain flaps. Twin braking parachutes can be deployed from the dorsal spine above the fully variable exhaust nozzles. That these parachutes are necessary is further evidence of the Foxbat's designers' dedication to a single high-speed concept; it needs a very long runway for both take-off and landing! Steel has been used for the main airframe construction, with the exception of the razor-thin wing leading edges, which are made of titanium.

The Foxbat entered service in 1970 after a first test flight by the Ye-266 some six years earlier. The original radar, designed in 1960, may be primitive and use thermionic valves (vacuum tubes), but it is extremely effective, relying on 600 kilowatts to blast through enemy electronic countermeasures. Since 1970, at least 300 of these interceptors have been delivered.

Early in its career, it became apparent that the MiG-25 would be ideal for the high-altitude photo-reconnaissance role. Reconnaissance versions are distinguishable by their slightly smaller wingspan with straight leading edge. The nose is more tapered, the big interception radar being replaced by a small forward-looking radar, five very powerful cameras and either of two types of SLAR (side-looking airborne radar). It is estimated that over 200 of these MiG-25Rs are in service.

Until 1976, the MiG-25 was little known outside the Soviet Union. But on 6 September of that year, Lieutenant Viktor Belyenko dropped into Hakodate airport, Japan, with a request for political asylum and bearing a small gift for the West: a perfect example of a MiG-25 interceptor.

Western analysts took the aircraft apart and ran the engines before sending it back. The gaff was blown, and so the Soviet Union felt able to supply MiG-25s to several interested countries. Users include Algeria, India, Libya and Syria. In fact it was a MiG-25 belonging to the Syrians that was shot down amid much acclaim on 29 July 1980 by an Israeli F-15 Eagle.

Few Western visitors have had the chance to chat with the pilots of No 106 Squadron, Indian Air Force, who had been flying Canberras until 1981, when the unit took delivery of eight MiG-25R reconnaissance versions. It was rather like climbing out of a wheelchair and into a Formula One racing car. The squadron converted without difficulty and has been well pleased with the performance and indeed everything except generally high level of costs, especially on fuel.

As has been normal Soviet practice, a two-seat trainer was developed at an early stage in the MiG-25 programme, but the MiG-25U version (christened Foxbat-C by NATO) did not enter service until 1973. As in the Yak-28U, the second (instructor) cockpit is placed in front of the original, where it replaces the radar. The student, of course, sits in the 'normal' cockpit.

The MiG-25 was designed to carry four of the biggest known air-to-air missiles (NATO 'AA-6 Acrid'), one pair with IR homing and the other with semi-active radar homing. Often only two are carried, and even today MiG-25s sometimes fly with the widely used 'AA-3

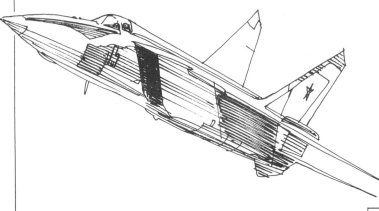

SPECIFICATION

Country of origin: Soviet Union.

Design Bureau: Mikoyan-Guryevich OKB.

Type: Long-range all-weather interceptor.

Year: 1968.

Engine: Two 11,000kg (24,250lb) Tumanskii R-31 turbojets with afterburning.

Wingspan: 13.95m (45ft 9in).

Length: 23.82m (78ft 2in).

Height: 6.1m (20ft).

Weight: 36,200kg (79,800lb).

Maximum speed: 3400km/h (2115mph).

Ceiling: 24,400m (80,000ft).

Range: 3000km (1860 miles).

Armament: Four underwing pylons carrying AA-6 Acrid (radar and infra-red), or possibly AA-X-9 air-to-air missiles.

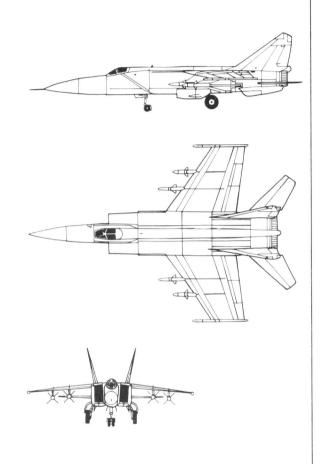

Anab'. Carried by no other aircraft, the 'Acrid' has a warhead with at least 60kg of high explosive. The semi-active radar version is capable of a range of up to 80km.

The MiG-25 has yet to have a head-on confrontation with Israeli F-15s, which were produced for the USAF specifically to counter the MiG-25. Over the years the F-15 has been updated, and so has the MiG-25. The MiG-25M, called 'Foxbat-E' by NATO. has a new radar giving partial 'look-down, shoot-down' capability for destroying hedge-hopping intruders. It also has more powerful R-31F engines. Today the completely new MiG-31 ('Foxhound') has replaced the MiG-25 in production. A much more manoeuvrable two-seater, it has eight of the new X-9 missiles and many other new features.

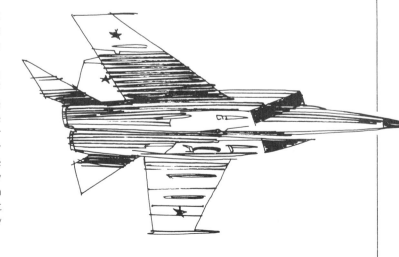

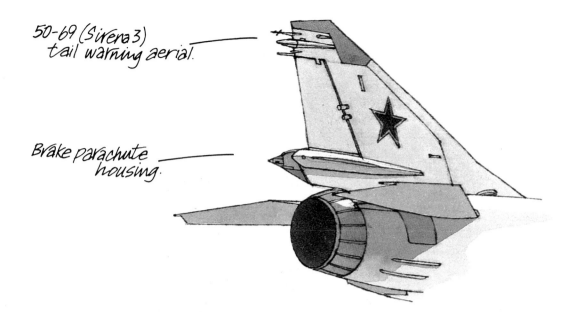

50-69 (Sirena 3)
tail warning aerial.

Brake parachute
housing.

'High Lark'
Radar.

36

One internally-mounted
23mm GSh-23L twin-barrelled cannon.

Laser range finder.

MIKOYAN-GURYEVICH
MiG-23

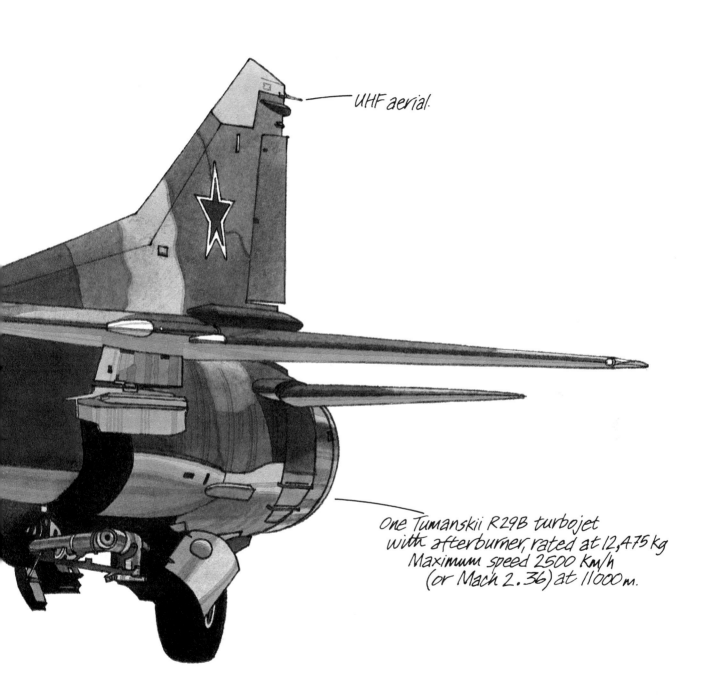

UHF aerial.

One Tumanskii R29B turbojet
with afterburner, rated at 12,475 kg
Maximum speed 2500 Km/h
(or Mach 2.36) at 11000 m.

MIKOYAN-GURYEVICH MiG-23 & -27

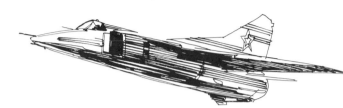

The MiG-23 followed the smaller MiG-21 as the most common interceptor of Soviet Frontal Aviation. While each version is not truly a multi-role aircraft, the desire to combine high-speed interception with the ability to take off and loiter with a heavy load of both fuel and missiles led the design team to adopt a variable geometry layout.

Initial perfection of the new aerodynamic shape was carried out at TsAGI, the national aerodynamic centre. The method of pivoting the wing near the leading edge to a small fixed wing-triangle, known as a glove, was developed initially in the United Kingdom. The same shape, but larger, resulted in the formidable Su-24.

The first flight of the MiG-23 prototype from Col-Gen Artem I. Mikoyan's Design Bureau was probably towards the end of 1966. It is thought that the prototype, the Ye-231, was powered by a Lyul'ka AL-7F-1 turbojet. It featured a shoulder-mounted wing, a large fin and a folding ventral fin, and F-4 Phantom-style variable inlets. The large single main wheels folded into the fuselage much like the F-111.

As is common practice in the USSR, a small number of these aircraft entered service in 1970 for evaluation by Frontal Aviation. Considerable redesign then followed. The switch to the Tumanskii R-27 engine enabled the wings to be moved forward and the rear fuselage to be made shorter, ending in front of – instead of far behind – the tail. At the same time giant dogtooth discontinuities (visible when the wings are swept back) were added at the inboard end of the extended leading edges of the wings. These cause a powerful vortex of the airflow when the aircraft is making a tight turn to help keep the upper-surface flow attached. Further revision was made to the trailing-edge flaps, extended in three sections (slotted but not blown) along the entire outer wingspan. In 1973 the MiG-23 was ready for large-scale production, and an average of 300 have been delivered each year. NATO calls it the 'Flogger'.

The basic air-combat version, the MiG-23MF has one twin-barrel 23mm GSh-23L cannon, two air-to-air missiles on pylons mounted on the inlet ducts and one or two air-to-air missiles on pylons mounted below each wing glove. Combat radar is the type known in the West as High Lark. It is also able to carry air-to-surface missiles, and is very well equipped with electronic countermeasures. Export variants and the predictable tandem two-seat trainer, the MiG-23U, have a smaller radar called the Jay Bird.

In 1977, MiG-23s (apart from the trainers) began to be fitted with the more powerful Tumanskii R-29B which develops 11,500kg afterburning thrust. This engine has

been fitted from the start in an attack version of this highly successful aeroplane. In many obvious respects the attack version is so different that the Russians gave it an entirely different designation, the MiG-27. This is tailored to low fuel consumption at subsonic speeds at low level, and current versions have an R-29 uprated to 12,475kg thrust.

The MiG-27 has fixed inlets, a simple engine nozzle and a new nose to give improved downward view (called 'ducknose' by Russian pilots). It also has extra cockpit armour, a new six-barrel 23mm gun, drop tanks which can only be used when the wings are at the minimum sweep position and, of course, enhanced air-to-surface missile carrying capability. This includes the AS-7 Kerry, with a 100kg conventional warhead and a range of some 11km. A further refinement is the provision of low-pressure tyres for operation from rough airstrips.

Yet another MiG from the same family and one that has found much favour with other nations is the MiG-23BN. This has the pointed attack nose of the MiG-27, but the variable aperture inlets of the interceptor. It is further evidence of the adaptability of the most numerous Soviet frontline fighter.

The MiG-23 and -27 have been bought by Algeria, Bulgaria, Cuba, Czechoslovakia, East Germany, Egypt, Ethiopia, Hungary, India, Iraq, Libya, Poland, Romania, Sudan, Syria and Vietnam.

A carrier-based version has been predicted for many years, and many have been used for training on a dummy carrier marked out on a Crimean airfield, but it is unlikely that the MiG-23 will be chosen for the carrier now approaching completion, except in the training role.

The IA-PVO air defence force has about 500 MiG-23s, while some 2000 attack versions form the backbone of Frontal Aviation. Several hundred have been exported, and the MiG-27M is in licence production by Hindustan Aeronautics in India.

It is now becoming understood that, though of course designers cannot disobey the rigid rules of aerodynamics and structures, a great deal of fighter design is concerned with mere fashion. In the early 1960s everyone was excited at jet-lift V/STOL (vertical/short take-off and landing); today it is out of fashion, though airfields would be

SPECIFICATION

23MF

Country of origin: Soviet Union.

Design Bureau: Mikoyan-Guryevich OKB.

Type: Single-seat air-combat fighter.

Year: Approx 1970.

Engine: 12,475kg (27,500lb) Tumanskii R-29 turbojet with afterburning.

Wingspan: 14.25 (46ft 9in) (unswept).

Length: 16.8m (55ft 1in).

Height: 4.35m (14ft 4in).

Weight: 18,900kg (41,670lb).

Maximum speed: 2500km/h (1553mph).

Ceiling: 18,600m (61,000ft).

Range: 3220km (2000 miles).

Armament: One 23mm GSh-23L twin-barrel cannon, plus four pylons carrying 3628kg (8000lb) external load, including two AA-7 Apex medium-range missiles and up to eight AA-8 Aphid air-to-air missiles.

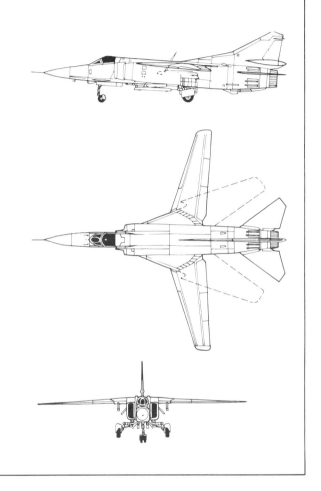

the first places destroyed in any future war. In the same way, in the 1960s everyone understood how the variable-geometry 'swing wing' can almost make one aircraft do the work of two, reshaping itself for each part of the mission; today this valuable technique is out of fashion. Current American analysts tend to sneer at the 'Flogger' family because they have pivoted wings. A 1980 assessment says: 'the MiG-23 is an aberration in Soviet planning; it looks as if they deliberately traded range for manoeuvrability'. Today we may have learned what every single aircraft put into production in the Soviet Union tells us: the Russians only buy what is best for their purpose. The fact that each year since 1973 at least 300 'Floggers' of various kinds have poured off the production lines ought to tell us that, if we in the West sneer at this type, perhaps the fault lies in our own assessment. Of course, we could always ask the Indians, who expect to keep their own production line going at least through the year 1990.

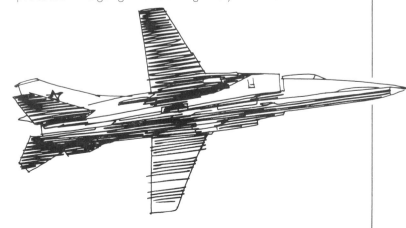

F1. A2 ground attack aircraft of the 1st squadron (Waterkloof) South African Air Force.

VHF 1.

Radar warning receiver. (RWR)

Matra 155 Rocket launcher
(4 carried).

RWR

Brake parachute
housing.

237

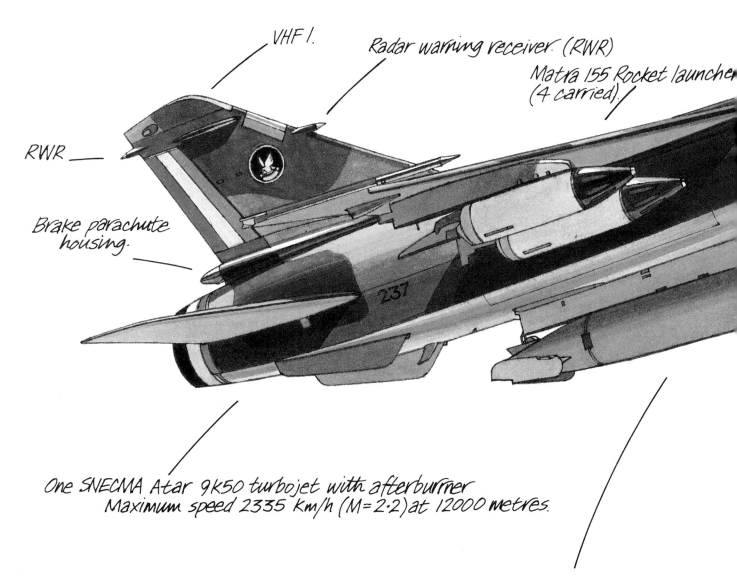

One SNECMA Atar 9K50 turbojet with afterburner
Maximum speed 2335 km/h (M=2·2) at 12000 metres.

1700 litre auxiliary fuel tanks.

DASSAULT-BREGUET
MIRAGE F1

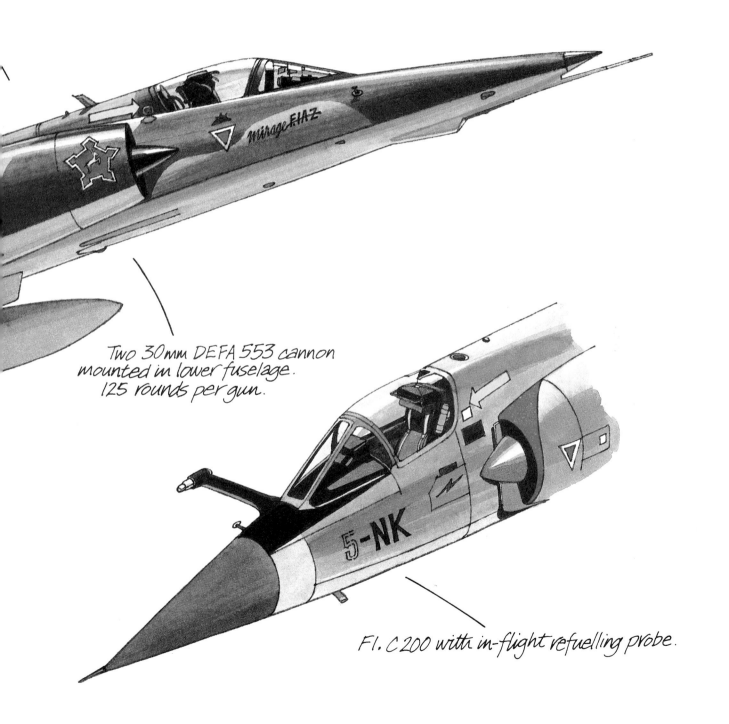

Two 30mm DEFA 553 cannon
mounted in lower fuselage.
125 rounds per gun.

F1. C 200 with in-flight refuelling probe.

DASSAULT-BREGUET MIRAGE F1

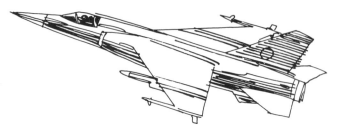

Trying to find a successor to the Delta Mirage III, Avions Marcel Dassault began a study in the early sixties of all existing configurations. As a result, the tailless delta shape was abandoned, and the Mirage F1 was born. It featured a return to the traditional layout of stubby swept-back wings stabilised by a conventional tail. Marcel Dassault himself insisted on retaining the name 'Mirage', in spite of the fact that this new F1 aeroplane bore no resemblance what-soever to its predecessors, or to the big 'Mirage 4A' strategic bomber!

The first Mirage F1 prototype was flown on 23 December 1966, and although the mainplane area was only about 70 per cent that of its delta-wing namesake, it provided sufficient lift to fly at increased weights, with the approach speed and landing run reduced by 20 and 30 per cent respectively. Increased thrust from the latest Atar 9K50 engine helped, but the main advance was the addition of powerful leading- and trailing-edge flaps. The F1 proved much more agile at both subsonic and supersonic speeds. There was a slight loss in wing fuel capacity, but this was more than overcome by adopting integral fuselage tankage, thus retaining overall mission flexibility impaired by a need for drop tanks. Indeed, with a smaller airframe than the deltas, the Mirage F1 has internal stowage for 40 per cent more fuel.

Production of the F1-C began in 1973, after the first flight of this version in February of that year. Primary consideration was for air defence, although it was also well fitted for the attack role. In 1979 the F1-C-200 began to enter service with operating radius extended by the addition of an air-to-air refuelling probe, though this cannot be retracted. This improvement gave rise in 1983 to the Mirage F1-CR, a completely re-equipped variant designed for long-range tactical reconnaissance.

In the interim, there were many refinements. As far back as 1967, the French engine-makers, SNECMA, embarked upon the design of a more modern engine for the Mirage. Flight-testing of this M53 engine, which now powers the Mirage 2000, took place in a Mirage F1, but Dassault failed to sell this in a contest against the F-16 and the old Atar remains the Mirage F1's engine to this day.

At the same time, in the pure interception role, with Cyrano IVM radar and Matra Super 530 missiles, the F1 remains competitive. The Cyrano IVM is not in the same class as modern multimode look-down, shoot-down radar systems, nor does the F1 have a modern multifunction-display cockpit, but it can still do an excellent job with a competent pilot, and is one of the most popular types in France's Armée de l'Air.

Several overseas customers, notably including South

Africa, selected the F1.A, a simplified day attack model corresponding to the delta Mirage 5 and distinguished by its slender conical nose. At the other end of the scale is the F1.E all-weather attack version with an inertial navigation system, improved HUD (head-up display) and nav/attack computer.

Almost incidental to its catalogue of other refinements, very fast scrambling of the F1-C was made possible by a ground conditioning truck which cools the IR missile-seekers, radar and cockpit, and heats the navigation and other parts the radar. Another interesting feature of the F1 is that, unlike most other Mirages, production was shared by companies abroad. SABCA and Sonaca of Belgium built the rear fuselage, and a licence to manufac-ture is held by the Armaments Development and Production Corporation of South Africa, though so far as is known complete Mirage F1s have not yet been manufactured in that country. Another major export customer was Spain, whose national aircraft manufacturing company, CASA, makes major fuselage sections for all F1s ordered.

It is unusual for a company with a sustained 'track record' of fighter aircraft building, to switch from one configuration (the tailless delta) to a totally different one (the tailed high wing) and then back again to the tailless delta in three successive generations. At the same time there is no doubt that in almost all respects the Mirage F1 is superior to any of the first-generation Mirage IIIs and 5s, and fitting in over 690 Mirage F1s into Dassault-Breguet's other production programmes has had a tremendous beneficial effect in assisting the entire French supporting industry to develop new types of equipment for the Mirage 2000 and for the Dassault-Breguet Rafale (ACX).

Armed with its Matra Super 530 missiles, its Matra Magic dogfight weapons, and two built-in 30mm cannon, the F1-C was a fighting machine of the first rank, and foreign sales naturally followed, especially to countries in the Middle East. The Greek Air Force equipped two squadrons with F1-CGs for service out of Tanagra, and also acquired F1-BH tandem-cockpit trainers. Kuwait took 18 F1-CK fighters and two F1-BK trainers for its main air

SPECIFICATION

F1.C

Country of origin: France.

Manufacturer: Avions Marcel Dassault-Breguet Aviation.

Type: Single-seat fighter and attack aircraft.

Year: 1973.

Engine: 7200kg (15,873lb) SNECMA Atar 9K-50 turbojet with afterburning.

Wingspan: 8.4m (27ft 7in).

Length: 15m (49ft 2in).

Height: 4.5m (14ft 9in).

Weight: 16,200kg (35,715lb).

Maximum speed: 2335km/h (1450mph).

Ceiling: 20,000m (65,600ft).

Range: 900km (560 miles).

Armament: Two 30mm DEFA 553 cannon; centreline and underwing pylons for 4000kg (8820lb) assorted stores. Missile loads include Super 530, Magic and Sidewinder air-to-air missiles and AS.30, AS.37, LGB 'smart bomb' and Durandal or Beluga attack weapons.

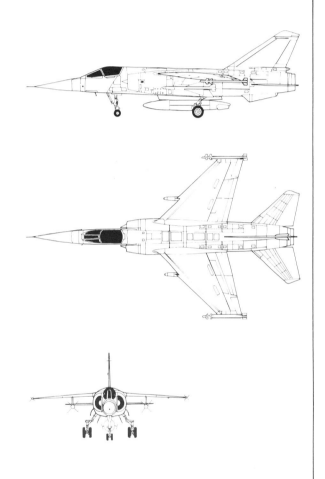

force base at Kuwait City.

Other foreign users include Ecuador, Morocco, Libya, Iraq, Jordan, Qatar, South Africa and Spain. Israel might have been a good customer, but after an earlier refusal by the French Government to allow delivery of Mirage 5 deltas specially developed for Israel and already paid for, the two countries were not on the best of terms. There was also the fact that, following this incident, Israel Aircraft Industries produced their own, improved, Mirage, the J79-engined Kfir.

Dassault's privately funded gamble with the Mirage F1 resulted in an excellent aircraft. Since 1975 it has far out-sold the delta Mirage III and 5, and in 1985 the sales total was over 700.

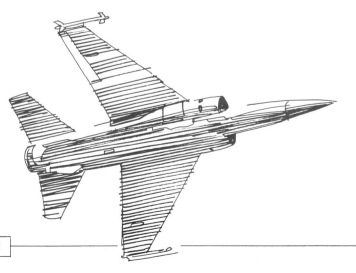

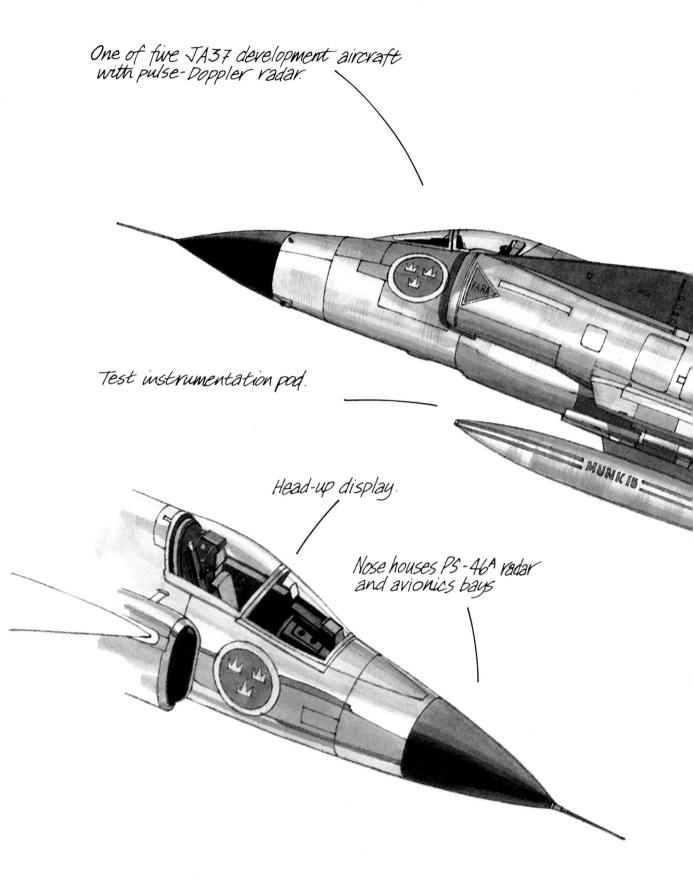

One of five JA37 development aircraft
with pulse-Doppler radar.

Test instrumentation pod.

Head-up display.

Nose houses PS-46ᴬ radar
and avionics bays

SAAB VIGGEN

One Volvo Flygmotor RM 8B turbofan with afterburner.
Maximum speed 2135 Km/h (Mach 2).

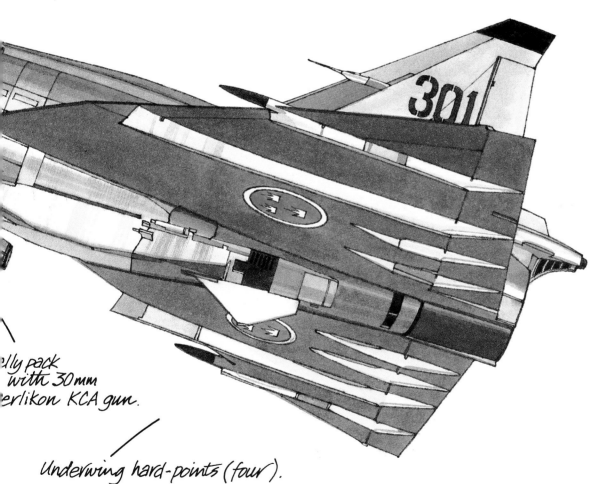

...lly pack
...with 30mm
...erlikon KCA gun.

Underwing hard-points (four).

SAAB VIGGEN

Sweden is a country with a large land mass, a relatively low population and a small super-efficient aircraft industry. So when in 1958, the forward-looking Royal Swedish Air Board asked Saab (now Saab-Scania) to start thinking about a replacement for the Draken, the company planned not just a single aeroplane, but a whole family. System 37 embodied a primary group of three aircraft each of which, although deriving from a common basic premise, was separately designed from the start to perform its own specific task. Among those several requirements common to all was an ability to take off and land using very short – 500m – and narrow strips of ordinary roads or highways. This single capacity was to make all types of the aeroplanes survivable in any future war, in the sharpest contrast to the airfield-tied aircraft of the NATO air forces.

Working to this brief, Saab produced an aeroplane which blazed a spectacular trail in Western aircraft design, an aircraft so far ahead of its contemporaries as to be virtually out of sight. The System 37 prototype had a unique configuration, with such large canard foreplanes that its head-on appearance was similar to that of a bi-plane. Not so apparent to the observer was an airframe made light yet very strong by the use of honeycomb primary structure, every small cavity of the space thus saved being utilised in some way. The weight saving also permitted a larger internal fuel capacity. Another major innovation was the departure by Saab from the company's normal practice of using a Rolls-Royce engine. It wanted to use the British Medway, but the British government cancelled this engine in 1964; instead, Saab had to choose the American Pratt & Whitney JT8D civil turbofan. This, after near-total redesign in Sweden, became the military RM8, with an afterburner designed by Svenska Flygmotor.

The first-generation members of the System 37 group were the single-seat AJ37 attack aircraft (which formed the bulk of initial production), two reconnaissance models and the SK37 tandem dual-control trainer, as described later.

The superb Viggen (Thunderbolt), flown in prototype form on 8 February 1967 and delivered for service as the AJ37 in June 1971, is a truly remarkable flying machine in just about every respect. It has no internal armament, all weapons of defence and attack being carried on pylons – three beneath the fuselage and a further two under each wing. These can accommodate an extremely wide range of stores up to a total of 6000kg including RB04 and RB05 missiles for attack, and RB24 or RB28 missiles for defence. All of this plus a tactical radius with all external stores, but *without* drop tanks, of around 1000km. The large delta

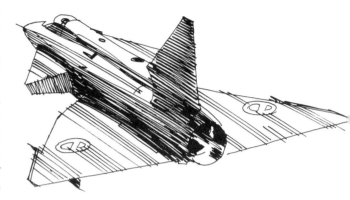

wing and flapped canard foreplanes provide tremendous high lift, and also enable the aircraft to perform, with full afterburner, extremely tight turns even at low speeds. Altogether the JA37 Viggen was in the 1970s widely recognised as the most formidable fighter-attack aircraft then in service in Europe, if not in the world.

The SF37 and SH37 were employed for overland and oversea reconnaissance respectively. Both have long-range fuel capacities. The former has its slender, pointed nose filled with cameras, and carries night-illumination equipment plus Red Baron multisensor pods. The SH37's equipment is similar, but it has a nose radar for air/surface use, its display being recorded by its own camera.

The SK37 trainer was fitted with an extended swept-back fin tip giving greater area, also used to house a VHF aerial. As with all Viggens, the entire vertical tail can be folded down sideways to fit inside low-ceilinged operational shelters and underground pens. The rear cockpit is raised above that for the pupil, but is still provided with a periscope to give the instructor a good view for landing.

The later JA37 variant is a total redesign, purely for all-weather interception. Fitted with a very powerful 30mm Oerlikon KCA gun, and usually armed with two RB71 Sky Flash and four RB24 Sidewinder missiles, it also has avionics at the very forefront of technology, at least the equal of those in use by any other contemporary aircraft in the world. They include the Ericsson UAP-1023 pulse doppler radar which affords outstanding look-down shoot-down capability, even in the presence of intensive hostile ECM. Other equipment includes an advanced Marconi Avionics HUD (head-up display), Singer-Kearfott main digital computer, and ILS and EW systems compared to which those of other NATO tactical aircraft (except the F-15) seem miserably inefficient. And the JA37's flying performance is both versatile and magnificent. The big afterburning engine, more powerful than that of the AJ37,

SPECIFICATION

AJ 37

Country of origin: Sweden.

Manufacturer: Saab-Scania AB.

Type: Single-seat all-weather attack aircraft.

Year: 1971.

Engine: 11,790kg (25,970lb) Volvo Flygmotor RM8A (licence-built Pratt & Whitney) turbofan with afterburning.

Wingspan: 10.6m (34ft 9in).

Length: 16.3m (53ft 6in).

Height: 5.6m (18ft 5in).

Weight: 20,500kg (45,195lb).

Maximum speed: 2125km/h (1320mph).

Ceiling: 18,300m (60,000ft).

Range: 2414km (1500 miles).

Armament: Seven pylons carrying 6000kg (13,230lb) of stores: RB04E and RB05A attack missiles plus RB24 Sidewinder or RB28 Falcon air-to-air missiles. Can carry RB75 Maverick precision-attack missiles, plus gun or rocket pods and 16 bombs.

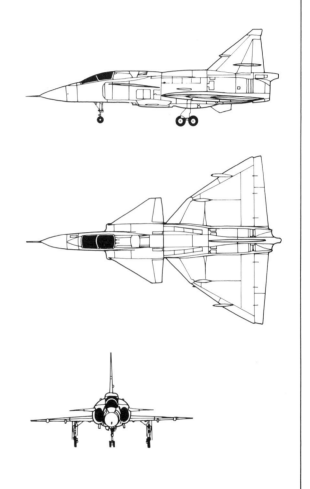

provides very high thrust for superb acceleration, fast climb and good manoeuvrability at all altitudes.

Looking ahead, the Saab-39 JAS Gripen (Gryphon), due to fly in 1986 and to enter service with the Swedish Flygvapen in 1990, will be smaller and much less fuel-greedy than its older brothers, and so is confidently expected to outdo them in every respect.

But it still might reasonably be said that, apart from its undeniable qualities as a powerful deterrent, the Saab-37 Viggen series has run true to Swedish form in not bringing a profitable return. The aircraft's enormous potential as a war machine remains unexploited, and the huge investment in human and financial resources has never produced anything but the original aim: the defence of Sweden. The total number produced is unlikely to rise beyond the present 329 on order (180 being early AJ, SF, SH and SK37s), export of the aircraft having been severely restricted due to the strict neutrality of the Swedish government. The US State Department vetoed a possible sale to India, on the grounds that the Viggen's RM8 engine was a derivative of the American P&W JT8D, a sanction which might well have influenced the decision in 1975 of four NATO nations to buy the F-16 instead, and Austria's ill-fated plans to buy the Viggen as a replacement for its Saab 105ös. Altogether any prospect of foreign sales was scotched. Nevertheless, Sweden's first ranking in the field of fighter-attack aircraft design was established with the Viggen, for the fifth time in succession.

Single seat Jaguar 'A' French Air Force
EC 4/11 'Jura' based at Bordeaux.

VHF/UHF Aerial.

Two Rolls-Royce Turboméca Adour
two shaft augmented turbofans.
Maximum speed 1699 km/h.

Airbrake

SEPECAT JAGUAR

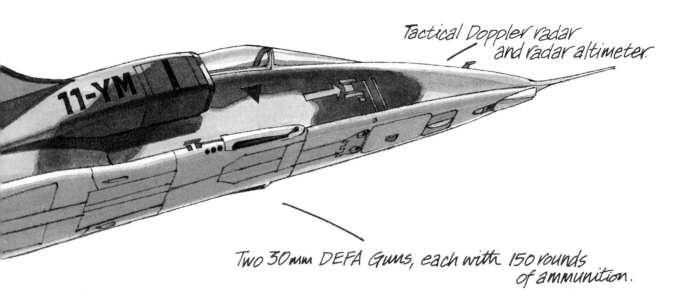

Tactical Doppler radar and radar altimeter.

Two 30mm DEFA Guns, each with 150 rounds of ammunition.

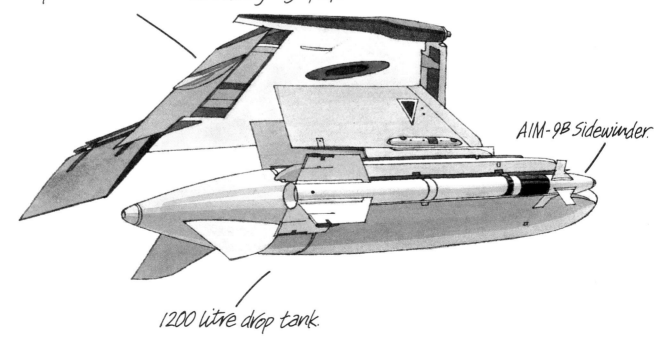

Two-piece double-slotted trailing edge flaps.

AIM-9B Sidewinder.

1200 litre drop tank.

SEPECAT JAGUAR

In 1965 Britain's defence chiefs identified the need – later shown not to exist – for a supersonic trainer; at the same time France was looking for a similar aircraft with some light strike capability. The two countries decided to pool their resources, and their industries formed the SEPECAT Group, out of Breguet (soon to be merged with Dassault) and the British Aircraft Corporation (later to become part of British Aerospace).

The result of this co-operation was the Jaguar, one of the most effective front-line strike aircraft of modern times. France received a supersonic attack aircraft with a far better performance than they ever expected (or could have afforded) had they 'gone it alone'. And Britain was not slow in realising that the Jaguar would be wasted purely as a trainer. This was especially as the astronomic rise in fuel prices from 1973 made training at supersonic speeds a luxury that few, if any, nations could afford.

The Jaguar has proved highly suitable for export development, but as the Breguet-Dassault merger made it strictly competitive with Dassault's own Mirage series, the nationalistic French company has bitterly contested export sales of the Jaguar – even though in many cases it shares Mirage manufacture in the same way with other companies. Thus, most of the development and marketing effort has been made by Britain; indeed, in 1980 all development work was formally taken over by British Aerospace.

With a top speed of Mach 1.6, the Jaguar has performance similar to the latest combat aircraft, and much faster than most attack types such as the A-7 and Super Etendard. Moreover, its designers also went for manoeuvrability, and the ability to operate from rough airstrips. In this latter respect it is outstanding. The Jaguar has demonstrated operation from a British motorway carrying a heavy bomb load, and it can also use unpaved surfaces; amazingly however, the user squadrons do not follow the example of the Warsaw Pact air forces and practise the capability as routine.

The Jaguar uses an efficient high-mounted wing with full-span flaps, spoilers, and tailerons. Although it is twin-engined the engines are relatively very small, being Rolls-Royce Turboméca Adour augmented turbofans delivering between 3313kg and 3810kg of thrust depending on the variant.

The first Jaguar (E) flew in France on 8 September 1968, followed just over a year later by the maiden flight of the first British built Jaguar (GR.1). A marine version was planned for the French Aéronavale and demonstrated complete compliance with the requirements, but on this occasion Dassault managed to get it cancelled in favour of the less advanced but all-French Super Etendard.

RAF Jaguars have a full and recently updated inertial navigation system, with head-up display, projected map display and a laser ranger and marked-target seeker in a stylish 'chisel nose'. The RAF received 203 Jaguar GR.1s and dual-control T.2s. From the start they had a radar warning system, with receiver aerials on the fin, but ECM (electronic countermeasures) protection was confined to the time-honoured principle of flying fast and low.

At last in 1983 a stop-gap measure was added, consisting of six jammer, flare or chaff cartridges housed beneath the braking parachute bay. These will be replaced in due course by a new radar warning receiver, jammer pod and Phimat chaff dispenser. All RAF Jaguar attack aircraft have a neat retractable inflight-refuelling probe.

The French Jaguar A has much simpler avionics, but of the 200 delivered to the Armée de l'Air, the last 30 are equipped with a laser pod to guide the AS30L laser-homing ground attack missile. The Jaguar E is the French trainer version, most of the trainers (of all customers) having only one gun.

The most advanced Jaguar variant of all was ordered by the Indian Air Force. Forty were supplied complete from British Aerospace, and a further 76 are being assembled by Hindustan Aeronautics, the first of which flew in March 1982. These aircraft, known as Jaguar Internationals, are fitted with more powerful engines and overwing missile pylons. The Indian Jaguars have in the attack mode a head-up display similar to RAF models and a weapons guidance system as sophisticated as that fitted into the Sea Harriers. Some of these Jaguars are planned to carry AM39 Exocet anti-ship missiles, together with Thomson CSF Agave radar as fitted to the Super Etendard.

One further Jaguar is worth a mention. In order to

SPECIFICATION

Country of origin: Britain/France.

Manufacturer: SEPECAT (BAe and Dassault-Breguet).

Type: Single-seat attack and reconnaissance.

Year: 1971.

Engine: Two 3313kg (7305lb) to 3810kg (8400lb) thrust Rolls-Royce Turboméca Adour afterburning turbofans.

Wingspan: 8.7m (28ft 6in).

Length: 15.5m (50ft 1in).

Height: 4.9m (16ft 1in).

Weight: 15,700kg (34,612lb).

Maximum speed: 1699km/h (1056mph).

Ceiling: 15,240m (50,000ft).

Range: Ferry range 3524km (2190 miles).

Armament: Two 30mm DEFA 553 or Aden cannon plus five pylons carrying up to 4536kg (10,000lb) of external weapons (4763kg [10,500lb] using extra overwing AAM pylons).

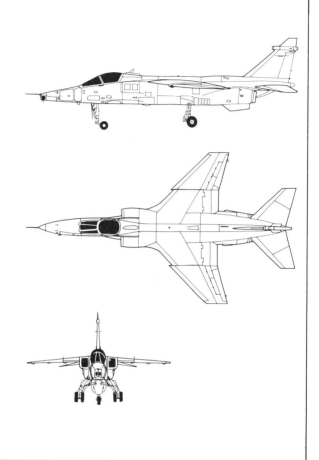

support the design of next-generation combat aircraft, British Aerospace has made a Jaguar deliberately unstable by adding large leading edge strakes, having previously flown with neutral stability caused by weights near the tail. The ACT (active-controls technology) Jaguar is the most unstable and advanced aircraft of its type today, with a quadruplex FBW (fly by wire) control system without manual reversion, to control a totally unstable aircraft which could not be flown by the pilot alone even for a split second!

For an aeroplane that was planned to become a training aircraft with some attack capability, the Jaguar has instead for 15 years been a major part of NATO's front-line attack and reconnaissance force. Export customers – Ecuador, Oman and Nigeria as well as India – have repeatedly returned with more orders.

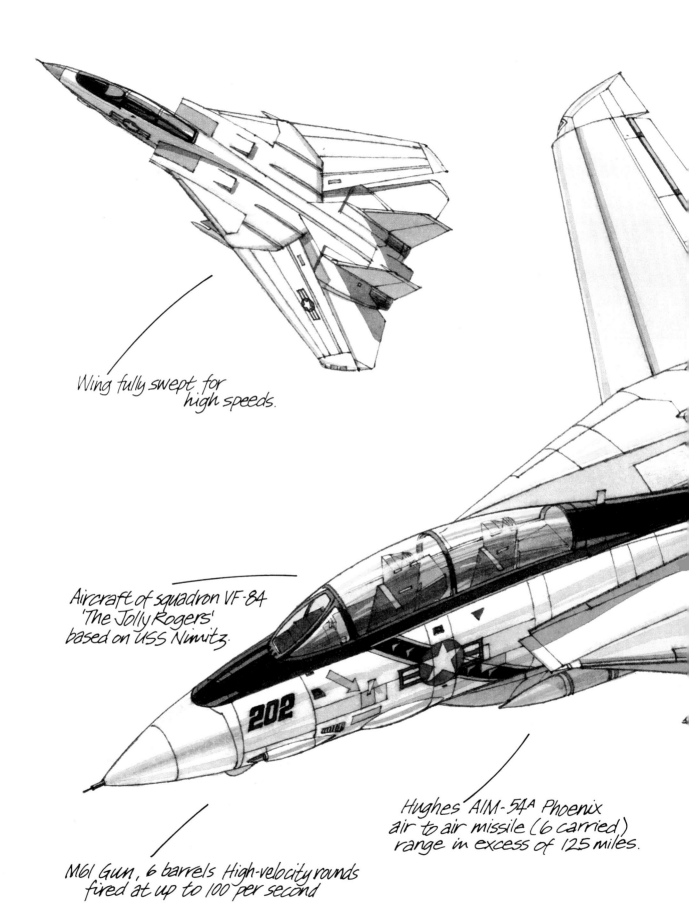

Wing fully swept for
high speeds.

Aircraft of squadron VF-84
'The Jolly Rogers'
based on USS Nimitz.

Hughes AIM-54ᴬ Phoenix
air to air missile (6 carried)
range in excess of 125 miles.

M61 Gun, 6 barrels High-velocity rounds
fired at up to 100 per second

GRUMMAN F-14
TOMCAT

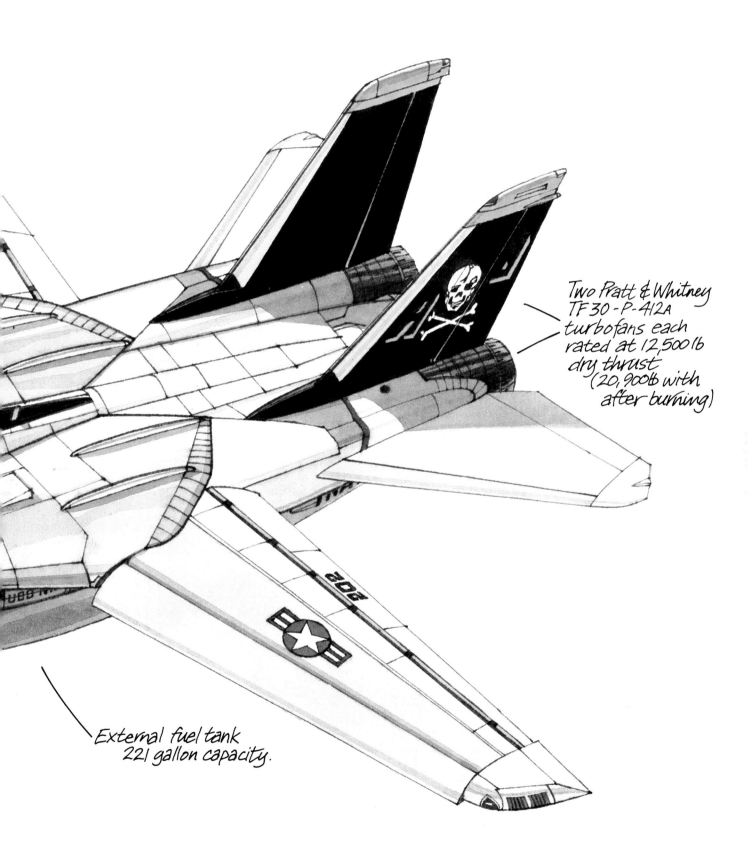

Two Pratt & Whitney
TF30 - P-412A
turbofans each
rated at 12,500 lb
dry thrust
(20,900 lb with
after burning)

External fuel tank
221 gallon capacity.

GRUMMAN F-14 TOMCAT

In 1970 the Tomcat was by far the most advanced fighter flying with the Western powers; today, in some respects, it still is. Yet, like so many successful aeroplanes, it owes its success to a series of chance happenings.

The Tomcat project saw life as an urgent response to the cancellation by the US Congress in 1968 of the much-vaunted F-111B, planned as the US Navy's next fighter. Grumman, the associate contractor on the F-111B, pushed forward a design for a superior carrier-based fighter that the company already had on the stocks.

Early in 1969, Grumman received the go-ahead and the prototype F-14A Tomcat first flew on 21 December 1970. Unfortunately the second flight ended in sudden and total hydraulic failure, caused by pipe fractures, and the aircraft was lost.

Testing continued with the other eleven development aircraft and these proved to be an outstanding success. In fact, Grumman had planned that later versions with much more powerful engines, the F-14B and F-14C, would replace the original. However, rising costs kept the F-14A in production, and at the end of the first production batch threatened the whole programme because Grumman said that they could not afford to continue.

The Tomcat was designed from the outset to fulfil a variety of specialist roles in addition to its primary duty of DLI (deck launched intercept). These include various forms of CAP (combat air patrol): Forcap (interceptor cover for the fleet); Barcap (barrier air defence); and Tarcap (target cover for friendly aircraft). A quite separate design role has been attack on ground targets with heavy bomb and missile loads, though this is not used by the US Navy.

The Tomcat owes its mission versatility to its basic configuration using variable-sweep wings and two crew, together with incredibly powerful and versatile on-board avionics. The wing sweep is constantly adjusted to suit both speed and manoeuvres by the use of a computer-based Mach sweep programmer. In addition, small foreplanes or glove vanes can be extended to give extra control at very high speeds.

The Tomcat was designed to fight with a gross weight, including missiles, of no more than 50,000lb. It is a tribute to its performance that it carries out its various roles with an extra weight penalty up to 25,000lb despite the fact that its internal fuel load has been slightly reduced.

The impressive AWG-9 radar fire-control system and AIM-54 Phoenix missiles were designed as a unit by Hughes eight years before the Tomcat itself. That said, they are still proving superior as a weapon system in the mid-eighties. Even today no other fighter can pick out so many targets at so great a distance and shoot them down.

One of the problems of flying the Tomcat in peacetime, where real combat situations are very few and far between, is that it is very difficult to make full use of the weapon system's outstanding range. In a limited war situation, as so often prevails today, it is important to let potentially hostile aircraft come well within visual range, in order to make absolutely certain of their hostile intentions. This, of course, throws away much of the Tomcat's ability to kill at extreme range.

Recent variants have now been fitted with the Northrop TCS (TV camera set) under the nose. This seeks, locks onto and actually shows the target to both pilot and crewman at extreme ranges, long before a visual sighting could be contemplated. Finding your quarry is one thing. Destroying it is another. And the Tomcat's armament is awesome by any standards, with one 20mm multi-barrel cannon and up to eight missiles. In fact, the Tomcat is the only aircraft in service that can deliver the AIM-54 Phoenix missile which has a formidable range of over 125 miles. Six of these large air-to-air missiles can be carried, along with two AIM-9 Sidewinders for close-range use. It is largely the heavy missile and fuel load that makes the Tomcat one of the biggest modern fighters.

This configuration is often varied by including AIM-7 Sparrows or extra Sidewinders at the expense of the very costly Phoenix missiles. In addition, extra fuel can be carried without reducing the missile complement in under-engine drop tanks, each of 222 gallons capacity. The internal fuel capacity is so large that these are seldom seen.

To date, over 500 F-14A Tomcats have been built, almost all for the US Navy. These have seen various engine improvements, because the initial Pratt & Whitney TF30s of 20,900lb thrust have caused extremely severe problems throughout the service life of the aircraft. Today the TF30-414A is doing much better, but the Navy has switched future production to the General Electric F110,

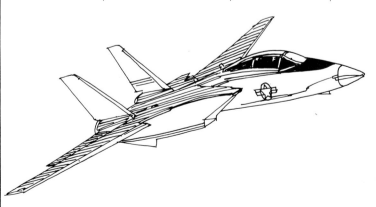

SPECIFICATION

F-14A

Country of origin: USA

Manufacturer: Grumman Aerospace Corporation.

Type: Two-seat carrier-based multi-role fighter.

Year: 1972.

Engine: Two 9480kg (20,900lb) Pratt & Whitney TF30-412A turbofans with afterburning.

Wingspan: 19.54m (64ft 1in) (wings unswept).

Length: 19.10m (62ft 8in).

Height: 4.88m (16ft).

Weight: 33,724kg (74,348lb).

Maximum speed: 2517km/h (1564mph).

Ceiling: In excess of 15,240m (50,000ft).

Range: Approx 3200km (2000 miles).

Armament: One 20mm (M61A-1 cannon, four AIM-7 Sparrow and four AIM-9 Sidewinder air-to-air missiles. Alternatively up to six AIM-54 Phoenix and two AIM-9. Maximum external weapon load in ground-attack role: 6577kg (14,500lb).

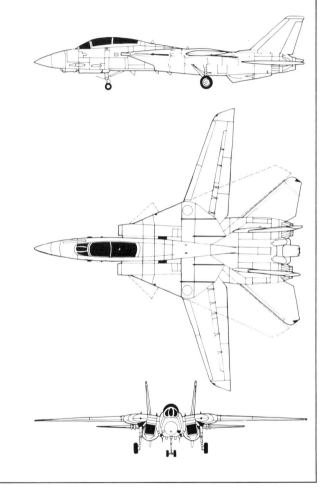

of 29,000lb, for the F-14D, due for delivery from 1987. All Tomcats, and especially the F-14D, are having major improvements to their avionics.

Only one other country, apart from the United States, has taken delivery of the Tomcat. Grumman sold 80 simplified F-14As to Iran just before the Islamic revolution in that country. Lack of operating resources has kept them from a major combat role in the Gulf war with Iraq, although one squadron has kept operational throughout, in some cases being used as airborne radar controllers for other fighters.

Born out of the need to replace the unsuccessful F-111B nearly 18 years ago, the updated Grumman F-14 Tomcat remains a state-of-the-art aircraft in Western fighter technology.

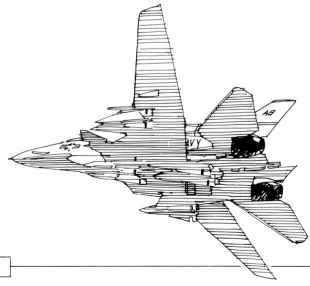

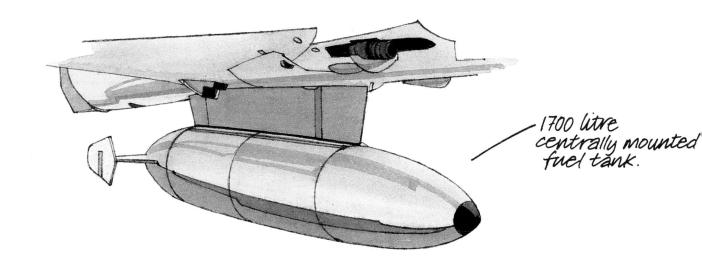

1700 litre centrally mounted fuel tank.

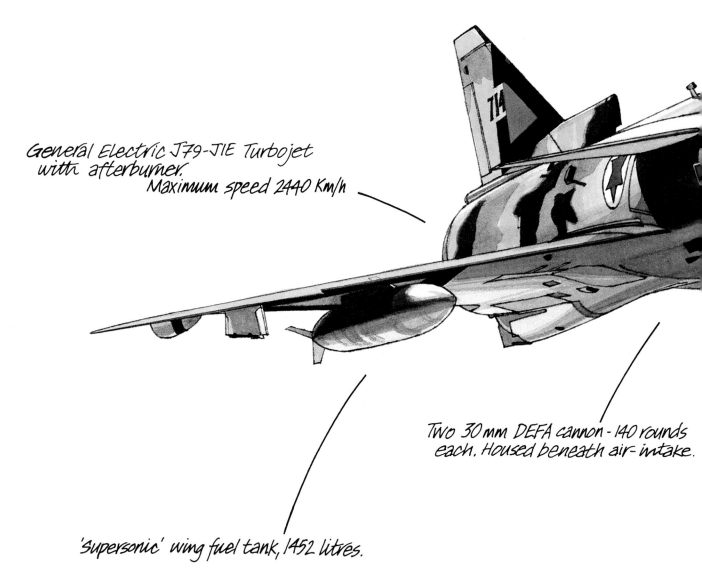

General Electric J79-JIE Turbojet with afterburner.
Maximum speed 2440 Km/h

Two 30 mm DEFA cannon - 140 rounds each. Housed beneath air-intake.

'Supersonic' wing fuel tank, 1452 litres.

IAI KFIR

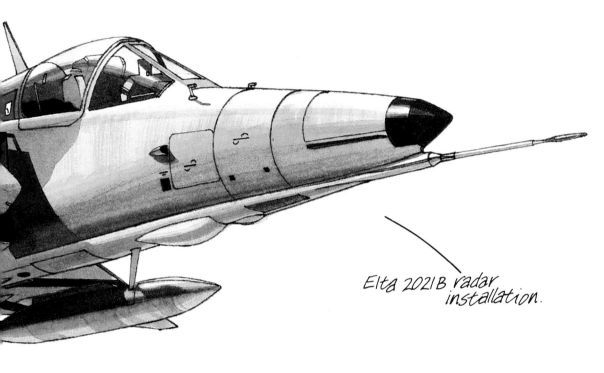

Elta 2021B radar
installation.

Shafrir 2 close-range AAM, two carried.

IAI KFIR

The IAI Kfir was certainly designed and developed at Lod Airport by Israel Aircraft Industries; but curiously, the man most responsible for the entire project was the President of France, General Charles de Gaulle. Had the General not refused to allow delivery in 1967 of the Mirage 5s already developed specifically for Israel, ordered and paid for, Israel would have had no pressing need to make replacements of its own. In the event, IAI first developed an almost direct copy of the Mirage called the Nesher, but Israel did not wish to be tied to the Atar engine. IAI embarked on its biggest ever challenge, converting the Mirage to the General Electric J79 engine.

The American engine is shorter than the afterburning Atar but slightly larger in diameter, and it handles a greater airflow. This demanded total redesign from the inlets to the nozzle, and to cool the engine bay a ram air inlet was added at the front of the dorsal fin. The first installation was tested in a two-seat Mirage IIIB, which, after complete reconstruction, was flown in September 1971. Whilst the production lines were turning out Neshers, which after service with the Israeli air force were sold to Argentina to see extensive combat (as the Dagger) in the Falklands war in 1982, IAI designed a completely new fighter derived from the Mirage and powered by the J79.

IAI went on to make so many far-reaching improvements, reportedly close on 300, that a further two years elapsed before the new prototype was flown and approved for service production. But even then, the aircraft which finally began to roll off the assembly line in 1972 was still not the Kfir. There were reports of an impressive new Israeli delta-wing fighter active in the 1973 Yom Kippur war, but it was usually referred to as the Barak (Lightning). Israeli security was naturally very tight at that highly-fraught time, but it was later learned that the so-called Barak was in fact a J79-engined Mirage 5.

And so out of Nesher via Barak came the first true Kfir, which entered production in 1974, as a multi-role

ground-attack fighter. The first deliveries entered service in June 1975. Apart from the inevitable shorter but enlarged rear fuselage this introduced a new forward fuselage with greater length, a flattened undersurface and almost triangular cross-section; a larger dorsal inlet and four secondary cooling inlets above the fuselage; strengthened landing gears with long-stroke oleo legs; further strengthened structure for higher gross weights and heavier and more varied weapon loads; revised internal tankage, and above all totally new avionics and a redesigned cockpit. Among new weapon options was the Shafrir 2 missile, backing up Israeli-made DEFA 552 guns in the air-to-air role.

Rapid evolution led to the definitive Kfir C2, which was put on show by the Israelis in 1976. This was a singularly impressive war machine, quite the best fighting aircraft produced by IAI thus far, and flown by Israeli pilots, undoubtedly one of the best in the world. It introduced fixed sweptback canard foreplanes mounted high on the inlet ducts, extended outer-wing leading edges with sharp dogtooth discontinuities at their inboard ends, and long strakes on each side of the nose. These aerodynamic improvements had a major effect in improving field length and slow-flying qualities, and in enabling tighter turns to be flown at all airspeeds. The gust response, vital to effective attack at full throttle at low level, has been significantly reduced, and altogether the best compliment that can be paid to this major production version is that Dassault-Breguet copied it in the Mirage III NG. Many C2s have an Elta 2021B ranging radar, and a few have the powerful Elta 2001B long-range interception radar, both of these increasing overall length still further.

In 1983 production switched to the Kfir C7, with a J79-J1E engine giving higher afterburning thrust, a new Hotas (hands on throttle and stick) cockpit, increased weapon load of up to 5775kg and further augmented avionics. Many of the 180-odd earlier Kfirs are being updated to C7 standard (though canards cannot be added to any model prior to the C2, C standing for canard), and in fact IAI is even assisting the air force of Colombia, a Kfir C2 customer, to convert Mirage 5s as nearly as possible to Kfir standard (without canards).

Since 1981 IAI has been delivering small numbers of tandem two-seat Kfirs, the TC2 and now the TC7. These can have dual control, and an even longer nose is sloped down sharply to give both occupants a good view. Most in Israeli service have operational (recon/Elint/electronic warfare) roles, the backseater being the manager of the extra systems.

The later Kfirs are certainly superior to all Mirage IIIs and

SPECIFICATION

C2

Country of origin: Israel.

Manufacturer: Israel Aircraft Industries.

Type: Single-seat fighter bomber.

Year: 1974.

Engine: 8120kg (17,900lb) IAI-built General Electric J79-JIE turbojet with afterburning.

Wingspan: 8.22m (26ft 11in).

Length: 15.65m (51ft 4in).

Height: 4.55m (14ft 11in).

Weight: 16,200kg (35,715lb).

Maximum speed: 2440km/h (1516mph).

Ceiling: 17,680m (58,000ft).

Range: 1125km (700 miles).

Armament: Two IAI-built 30mm DEFA cannon, two Shafrir 2 air-to-air missiles. Five external hardpoints contribute to overall total of 5775kg (12,730lb) of all weapons.

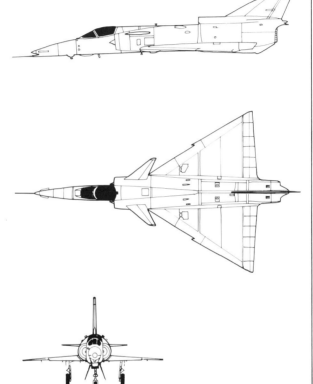

5s and probably equal to the Mirage 2000. Amazingly however, Israel has been able to offer an export version for a mere US$ 5m, a staggering *one-tenth* of the price ($50m) typically being asked for the Mirage 2000. Many export sales have been blocked by the US State Department, but this barrier is now in principle overcome. IAI via the Israeli government has lent the US Navy 12 Kfirs (pre-canard) which serve as F-21s in adversary training.

This adoption by the US Navy has at last set the seal of approval on an outstanding fighter which has had an uphill fight in the past caused by US political problems. Before selecting it the Kfirs — well-used ex-Israeli aircraft — were given a very thorough inspection and flight evaluation, and they emerged clearly as the 'best buy'. It is not yet known if they will eventually be returned to Israel after the US Navy receives its F-16N Fighter Falcons for future air-combat training.

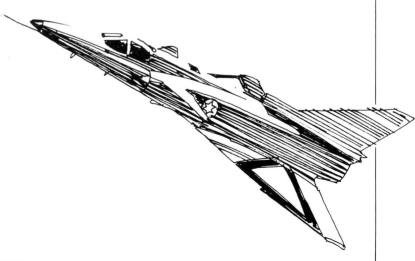

Hydraulically operated airbrake
This very effective brake can be opened at any speed up to the aircraft's limit.

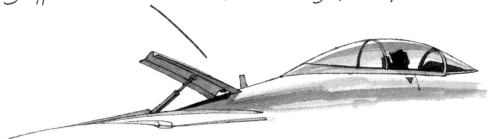

02-8801

Twin fuselage mounted Pratt & Whitney turbofan afterburning engines produce 25,000 lb of thrust each and deliver speeds in excess of Mach 2, with supersonic speeds above 65,000 ft.

McDONNELL DOUGLAS F-15 EAGLE

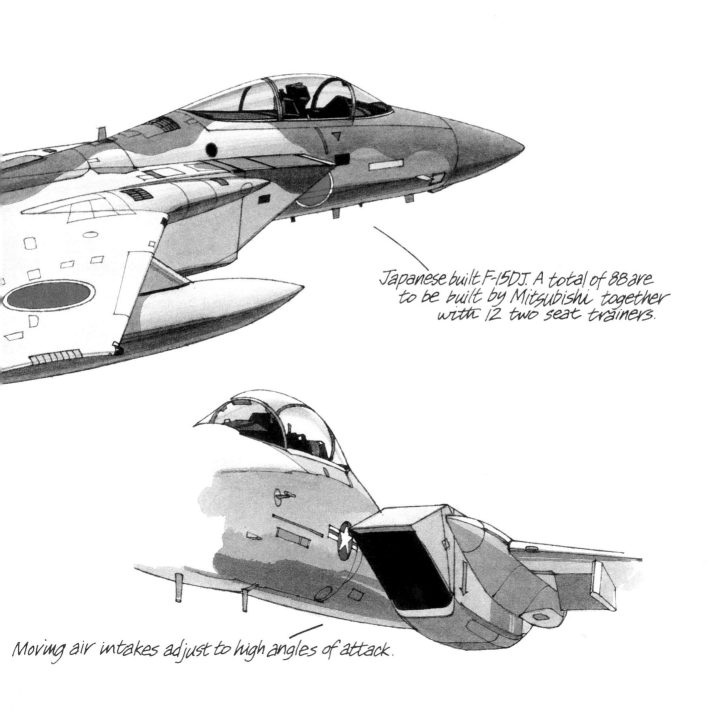

Japanese built F-15DJ. A total of 88 are to be built by Mitsubishi together with 12 two seat trainers.

Moving air intakes adjust to high angles of attack.

McDONNELL DOUGLAS F-15 EAGLE

Many Western observers consider the F-15 probably the best fighter in the world. In 1967 the arrival of the Russian MiG-23 and the MiG-25 led the US Air Force to reconsider the belief that had held sway for a decade: that fighters should be designed to fulfil a variety of different roles. 'What we now need' they said 'is a true air-superiority fighter.'

After the usual intense competition, McDonnell was chosen in 1969 to produce the fighter that would bring true dogfight superiority back to the West.

Nothing is ever simple in aviation and the F-15 Eagle, despite its acclaim as a superb air-to-air fighter, performs excellently in a variety of other roles, as demonstrated by its ability to deliver no less than 23,600lb of offensive weapons. Because the F-15 was designed for one role only, it has an enormous fixed wing. At relatively low speeds, rolling manoeuvres are effected by aileron; as the F-15 reaches supersonic speed these manoeuvres are initiated by a combination of differential taileron and twin-rudder controls.

The two big turbofans are fed by inlets which are not only fully variable according to Mach number but which also tilt downwards in nose-high flight at low speeds. The massive power output is at sea level considerably more than the F-15's clean gross weight, and is a major factor in the F-15s amazing rate of climb and outstanding performance in the vertical plane. The Pratt & Whitney F100 was designed especially for the Eagle, and colossal funding was provided by the US Air Force. The engine was not without its problems, however, and for many years has suffered from 'stall stagnation' and other problems. Competition from General Electric has spurred the new F100-220 version which is designed to fly 4000 combat missions without overhaul.

An important element of the design was to be the inclusion of a special 25mm Gatling-type gun which would use caseless ammunition. However, this was abandoned at an early stage in the project, and replaced by the well-proven 20mm General Electric M61, housed in the right wing root, with ammunition in a tank inboard of the engine duct. When the gun is fired, the rudders are automatically applied just enough to counteract the off-centre recoil.

Visibility is excellent with full 360° view through the bubble canopy. The Hughes APG-63 (now upgraded to APG-70) radar gives the pilot plenty of warning and is capable of detecting airborne and surface targets at long range with marvellous clarity. Initially this information is supplied on a head-down display mounted on the instrument panel. At closer ranges the radar picture is

presented on the HUD (head-up display), with all radar controls on the stick and throttles, which enable the pilot to control the radar and all weapons while manoeuvring. He can select the weaponry using a throttle-mounted switch; as he does this, the radar automatically switches to the correct mode.

Normal missile armament is four AIM-7 Sparrows plus four AIM-9 Sidewinder missiles. The Sidewinder is, of course, well-proven, but the medium-range Sparrow was shown to be somewhat unreliable during the Vietnam war. That earlier AIM-7E version has now been replaced by a longer-range AIM-7L, with the monopulse-guided AIM-7M version also entering service. This will be even more resistant to electronic countermeasures. The Sparrow's greatest 'scalp' to date came when an Israeli F-15 shot down a Syrian MiG-25 on 29 July 1980.

The current production F-15C has an internal fuel capacity of no less than 13,455lb. This can of course, be augmented by external tanks and air-to-air refuelling. The F-15C can also carry two FAST (fuel and sensor, tactical) conformal tanks along the sides of the fuselage which house an extra 9725lb of fuel, and the total fuel capacity for ferry purposes is an amazing 35,075lb – as heavy as three fully loaded P-51s!

The initial order for the Eagle was 729, but this number has risen to 1488, of which over 1000 have been delivered. The first versions were the F-15A and tandem dual-control F-15B, but in 1979 these gave way to the F-15C and F-15D with many improvements. The USAF now plans also to buy 392 F-15E dual-role fighters, with APG-70 high resolution radar, a new computer and programmable armament control system, with avionics managed from the rear seat, and colossal capability in the attack mission. The F-15E will be able to operate at weights up to 81,000lb, about twice as much as the wartime B-17 Fortress!

When one looks at the new F-15E it seems unbelievable that such a modest-sized conventional aircraft can have such capability. The main landing gears each have a single

SPECIFICATION

F-15C

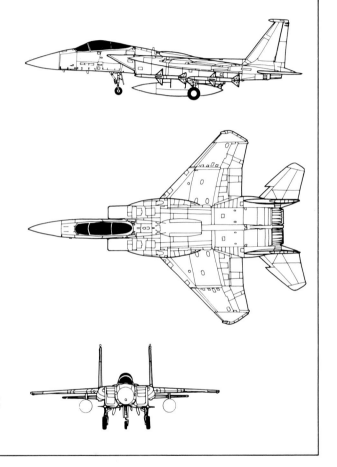

Country of origin: USA.

Manufacturer: McDonnell Aircraft Company.

Type: Single-seat all-weather fighter.

Year: 1974.

Engine: Two 10,637kg (23,450lb) Pratt & Whitney F100-220 turbofans.

Wingspan: 13.05m (42ft 10in).

Length: 19.45m (63ft 10in).

Height: 5.68m (18ft 7in).

Weight: 30,845kg (68,000lb).

Maximum speed: 2660km/h (1650mph).

Ceiling: 18,300m (60,000ft).

Range: 5745km (3570 miles) (with Fast packs).

Armament: One 20mm M61 cannon, four AIM-7 Sparrows and four AIM-9 Sidewinder air-to-air missiles, plus centreline pylon stressed for 2313kg (5100lb); total capacity with Fast pack conformal tanks 10,705kg (23,600lb) of weapons.

leg and a single wheel with a small-section tyre inflated to very high pressure. To take off at a speed exceeding 200mph at a weight in excess of 80,000lb seems incredible, until one realises that this rests squarely on great engine power, superb structural materials and a great length of the best and smoothest concrete. On the other side of the Iron Curtain they have never stopped building aircraft which, on paper, are less impressive, with less weight and giant low-pressure tyres which often cause bulges in the aircraft when they are retracted. The difference lies in the fact that the Soviet warplanes do not need airfields, and in wartime this could be the difference between survival and destruction.

To date, no other aircraft in the Western world has been able to match the F-15's all-round performance. Its combination of excellent high power-to-weight ratio, light wing-loading and massive precision strike capability make it a difficult act to follow. Its only problem is very high cost, both to buy and to operate.

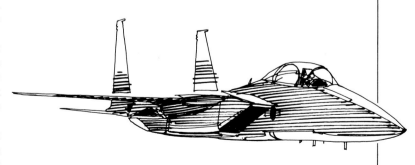

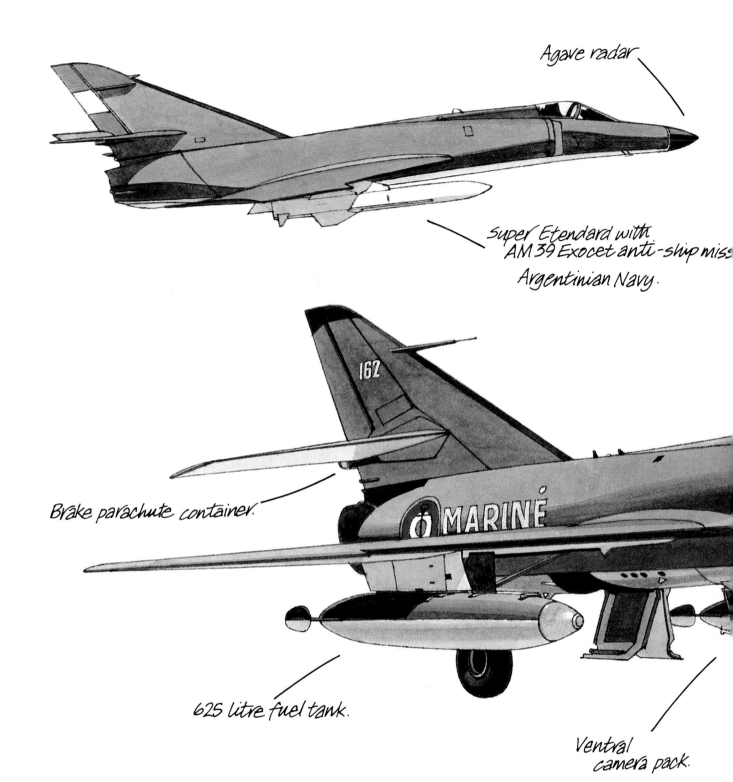

Agave radar

Super Etendard with
AM 39 Exocet anti-ship miss

Argentinian Navy.

162

MARINÉ

Brake parachute container.

625 litre fuel tank.

Ventral
camera pack.

DASSAULT-BREGUET ETENDARD

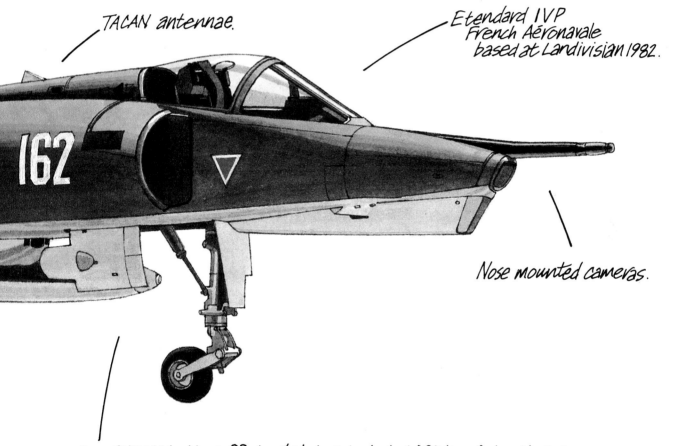

TACAN antennae.

Etendard IVP
French Aéronavale
based at Landivisiau 1982.

Nose mounted cameras.

One SNECMA Atar 8B turbojet rated at 4400 kg of dry thrust.
Maximum speed approximately Mach 1.

DASSAULT-BREGUET SUPER ETENDARD

Ask anybody in the street to count the number of modern combat aircraft he knows by name and he will probably need no more than the fingers of one hand. But the chances are the Super Etendard will be on his list. This is all the more remarkable when you consider that the aircraft is not a fighter but an attack aircraft, and an old subsonic aircraft (flown in 1956) brought a little nearer to the 1980s by fitting improved avionics.

The Super Etendard (French for national flag) is hardly an outstanding modern aeroplane. When it was introduced in 1977 its performance in speed and weapon load were inferior to most of its contemporaries. That the design was adopted by the Aéronavale at all was due to an understandable piece of chauvinism. In the mid 1960s the two French carriers, *Clemenceau* and *Foch*, were equipped with Etendards derived from the 1956 prototype. It was expected that these would be replaced in due course by a special version of the Anglo-French Jaguar. This variant, the Jaguar M, was duly built with full carrier equipment and completed its test programme most satisfactorily.

It came as a considerable surprise, then, that the Jaguar was rejected in favour of Dassault's proposal to produce an improved Etendard, with local airframe modifications, a newer version of the Atar engine (by a wide margin the oldest jet engine still in production) and with much-enhanced avionics.

So how has the Super Etendard become so famous? The answer lies of course, in the South Atlantic. Overnight, the Super Etendard achieved lasting fame by being the aircraft supplied to the Argentine navy, together with the Aérospatiale AM.39 Exocet missiles, that in 1982 destroyed a major ship of the British South Atlantic Task Force, the Type 42 destroyer HMS *Sheffield*. Later another Exocet destroyed the container ship *Atlantic Conveyor*. That it was the Exocet missile that reduced both the *Sheffield* and the *Atlantic Conveyor* to blazing wrecks has done little to harm the Super Etendard's reputation. It avails nothing to argue that results would

have been very different against ships fitted with any modern air-defence weapons. What is still unexplained is how *Sheffield* – unlike the other victim, a warship – apparently failed to detect her illumination by either the radar of the Super Etendard or the radar of the missile, either of which would have caused an instant call to action stations!

What was at least as significant as the apparent sleepiness of the *Sheffield* was the ability of the Argentine navy to assemble Exocet missiles without the benefit of handbooks or instructors. On 1 May 1982 the first missiles had, it was thought, been put together. Super Etendards were readied for a 'knock-out blow' against the British task force, and this was mounted on 2 May (before the sinking of the Argentine cruiser *Belgrano*) only to be frustrated by inflight refuelling failures. The same missiles were used on 4 May when two Super Entendards took off and scored one hit (with a missile that almost certainly failed to explode, but nevertheless destroyed the ship). This did more than thousands of brochures for the French missile (failure to explode or not) and for its carrier aircraft; but by this time Dassault-Breguet had stopped making Super Etendards.

The Super Etendard has the same 45° swept wing as its predecessor, the Etendard, but with drooped dogtooth leading edges and double-slotted flaps. Its SNECMA Atar 8K-50 turbojet delivers slightly greater thrust: Dassault say that fuel consumption is lower, although the engine manufacturer's figures do not appear to lend support to this claim.

Avionics are certainly a great improvement over the earlier Etendard. That said, the Thomson-CSF Agave radar has limited power and versatility compared with alternative systems. A Thomson-CSF VE120 HUD (head-up display) and an inertial navigational system are fitted. A passive radar warning receiver is also standard equipment, as it is in all French tactical aircraft, and there is a choice of ECM jammer and dispenser pods though these occupy at least one of the five pylons. Armament consists of two 30mm DEFA 553 fuselage-mounted cannon, along with five pylons. Maximum external load is extremely low at 2100kg; this is most commonly utilised by one Exocet and one large drop tank with capacity 1100 litres, giving a radius of up to 650km.

Of the 100 Super Etendards originally ordered for the French Aéronavale, only 71 were built because of price inflation. Apart from the Argentine Navy, Libya and Iraq have shown great interest in the Super Etendard. Iraq, particularly, is anxious to purchase the type to use against oil installations in the war being waged against Iran.

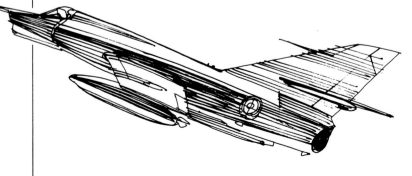

SPECIFICATION

Country of origin: France.

Manufacturer: Avions Marcel Dassault-Breguet Aviation.

Type: Carrier-based single-seat anti-ship strike aircraft.

Year: 1977.

Engine: 5110kg (11,265lb) thrust SNECMA Atar 8K-50 turbojet.

Wingspan: 9.6m (31ft 6in).

Length: 14.3m (46ft 11in).

Height: 3.85 (12ft 8in).

Weight: 11,500kg (25,353lb).

Maximum speed: 1200km/h (745mph).

Ceiling: 13,700m (45,500ft).

Range: 2000km (1243 miles).

Armament: Two 30mm DEFA cannon, five pylons for maximum weapon load of 2100kg (4630lb); in anti-ship role one AM.39 Exocet and one drop tank.

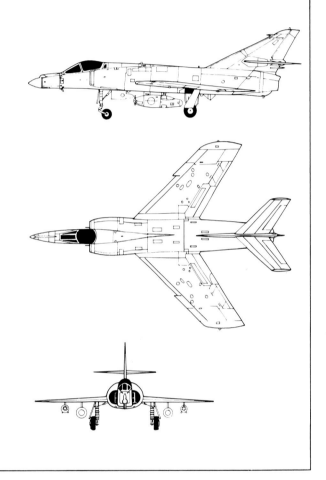

So far, France has resisted this pressure, not so much as a response to international opinion as for purely economic reasons; it would be very costly to reopen the production line. But ignoring possible political problems the Aéro-navale has five Super Etendards on loan to the Iraqis, and these have seen a great deal of action, launching Exocets and bombs against tankers of many nations in the Arabian Gulf, so far with results much less dramatic than in the South Atlantic. Indeed, far from embarrassing France, this sharp-edged support for Iraq is hoped to influence Saudi Arabia to buy the Mirage 2000 rather than the generally more capable Tornado.

It is unlikely the French Navy will replace its carrier-based Super Etendards before the turn of the century, since the *Clemenceau* and *Foch* are due for replacement by two 33,000 tonne nuclear carriers.

In the meantime, the Super Etendard will continue to be talked about as the aircraft that caused the Task Force such serious problems during Britain's mission to regain control of the Falkland Islands after they had been invaded by Argentina.

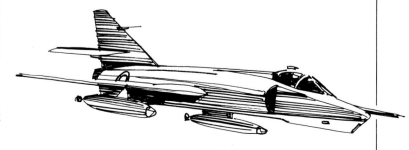

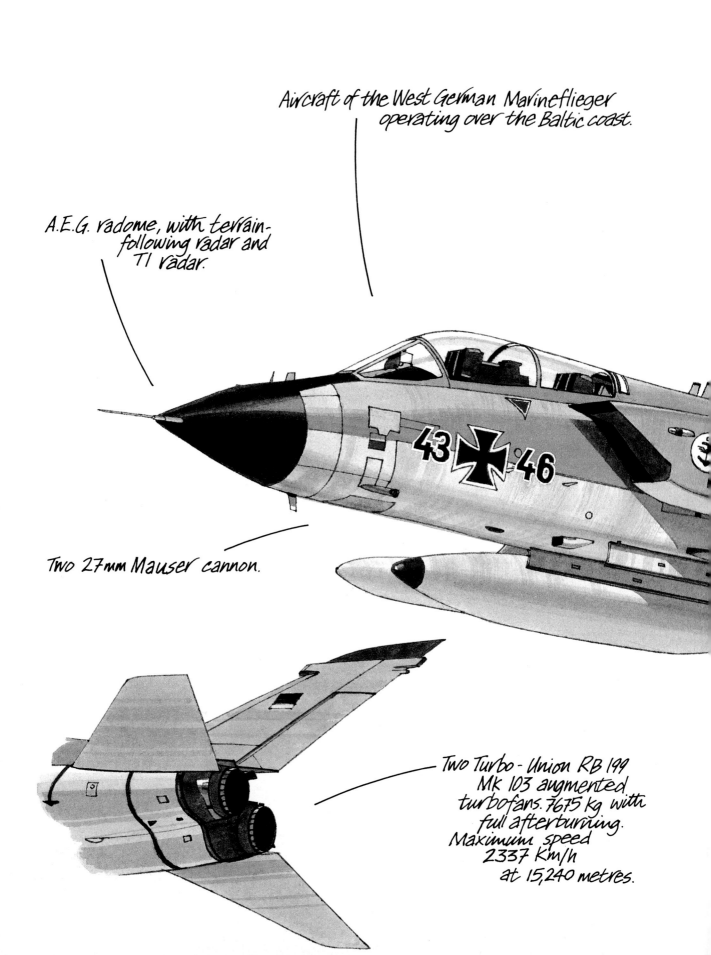

Aircraft of the West German Marineflieger operating over the Baltic coast.

A.E.G. radome, with terrain-following radar and TI radar.

Two 27mm Mauser cannon.

Two Turbo-Union RB 199 Mk 103 augmented turbofans. 7675 kg with full afterburning. Maximum speed 2337 Km/h at 15,240 metres.

PANAVIA TORNADO IDS

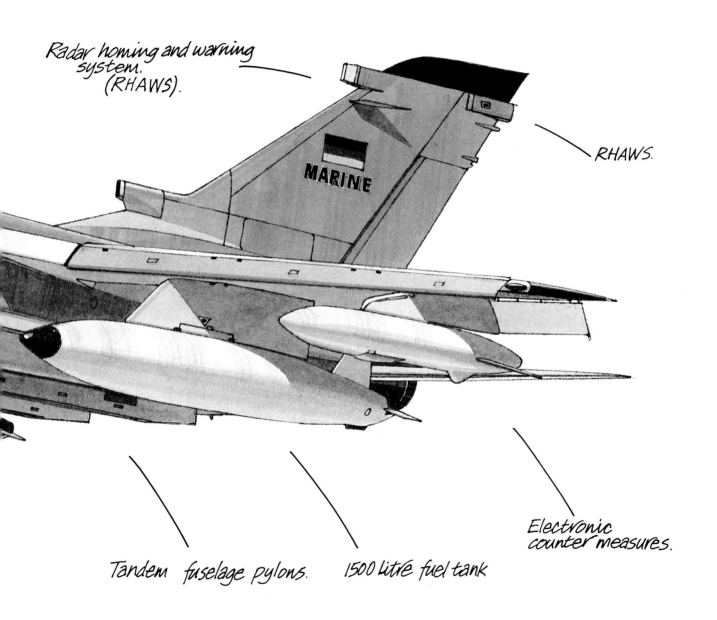

Radar homing and warning
system.
(RHAWS).

RHAWS.

MARINE

Tandem fuselage pylons.

1500 litre fuel tank

Electronic
counter measures.

PANAVIA TORNADO IDS

Is the Tornado the exception that proves the rule? Or does it pave the way for aircraft development in the future?

When the Federal Republic of Germany, Italy and Great Britain joined forces to design and build a multi-role-combat aircraft, few observers believed that it could be anything but a disaster. It is, after all, not uncommon for large aircraft corporations in one country to have problems in pursuing a single strategy.

So how could not one, but *three* different nations combine to produce the total harmony necessary for such a complex project? That they succeeded is amply demonstrated by the result of their collaboration: the Panavia Tornado IDS is certainly the best low-level strike aircraft ever built. Like all modern aircraft, the Tornado is the response to a need. In this case four separate needs from three countries: the British Royal Air Force, the Italian Air Force, the German Luftwaffe and the German Marineflieger (naval air arm). The builders of the Tornado had to clear a vast range of weapons for these four initial customers, probably a greater variety of weapons than any other aircraft in history.

In 1965 the three countries began a series of discussions to determine whether they could collaborate to build a single aircraft that would deliver these weapons in the most cost effective way possible. Critics will point out that it took four years to produce a baseline requirement, but from then on events moved swiftly.

The original specification, agreed in March 1969, called for an MRCA (Multi-Role Combat Aircraft) that would deliver for the RAF a two-seat all-weather attack aircraft; for the Luftwaffe, a multi-role single-seater; for the Marineflieger, an anti-ship aircraft; and for the Aeronautica Militare Italiano, a single-seat fighter. There were many other variations, but without the slightest pressure being brought to bear by any of the partners, all were resolved and a standard aircraft agreed by all customers, with two seats and integral-tank wings.

Panavia was established to build the new aircraft, with British Aerospace and West Germany's MBB taking an equal 42.5 per cent stake and with Italy's Aeritalia holding 15 per cent. At the same time a separate engine company, Turbo-Union, was set up to produce the engine, Rolls-Royce and MTU holding 40 per cent each, with Fiat taking the remaining 20 per cent.

On 14 August 1974, the first Tornado prototype made its first flight at Manching in Germany. From the very start it had used the swing-wing configuration, to match the aircraft to very contrasting conditions. Otherwise the aeroplane was conventional in appearance, with twin engines of amazing compactness.

February 1978 saw the first production Tornado delivered for service tests. Within 18 months, nine prototypes and six production aircraft were all flying for the participating countries. In July 1980 two aircraft were delivered to a special Tri-national Tornado Training Establishment which was set up at RAF Cottesmore in England. At Cottesmore, pilots and navigators receive basic conversion training on the 50 Tornados stationed there and supplied by the three participating nations. Pilots and navigators of all participating nations are mixed up and fly together.

The Tornado is a true multi-role aircraft. Indeed its flexibility of mission is its chief claim to be the most outstanding aircraft of the decade. But it scores heavily in two other areas as well. In its all-weather long-range low-level attack role, the Tornado is without question, supreme. No other aircraft can be flown hands-off at supersonic speed at low altitude, hugging the contours of the ground at 200ft or less, sensing and avoiding all obstacles including pylons and radio masts over long ranges, and then reach and destroy a heavily defended target and return to safety.

All this can be done with minimal attention from the pilot. In fact, one pilot was heard to say soon after his conversion at Cottesmore, 'The navigator flies the ruddy thing, I have nothing to do with it'. Not quite true, but an accurate reflection of the Tornado's astounding low-level performance nonetheless.

All its life Tornado has been the butt of critics not only from rivals in France, and especially, the USA, but also in the home media who eagerly sought supposed faults or shortcomings. Critics were at last silenced when two RAF aircraft entered the USAF Giant Voice navigation and bombing contest in 1984. Against the crack crews of USAF B-52s and FB-111s and RAAF F-111s they took two of the three main trophies and came second in the third. Suddenly air forces realised that the Tornado is a world-beater.

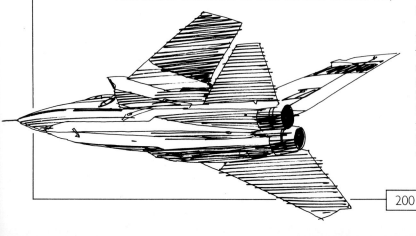

SPECIFICATION

Country of origin: West Germany, Italy and Great Britain.

Manufacturer: Panavia GmbH.

Type: Multi-role combat aircraft.

Year: 1974.

Engine: Two 7675kg (16,920lb) Turbo-Union RB.199 Mk 103 augmented turbofans.

Wingspan: 13.9m (45ft 7in) (wings unswept).

Length: 16.7m (54ft 9in).

Height: 5.7m (18ft 8in).

Weight: 27,220kg (60,000lb).

Maximum speed: 2337km/h (1452mph).

Ceiling: over 15,240m (50,000ft).

Range: 3890km (2415 miles).

Armament: Two 27mm Mauser cannon, three fixed tandem fuselage pylons and four swivelling wing pylons carrying up to more than 8165kg (18,000lb) external load including missiles and bombs.

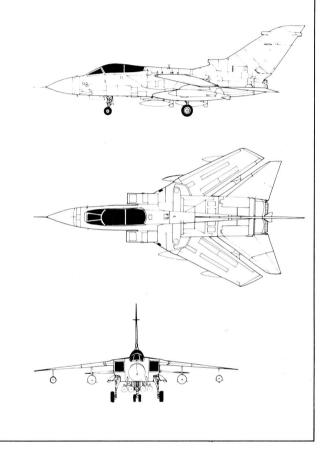

In these days of post Yom Kippur war oil prices, the Tornado's fuel efficiency is extremely valuable. Despite the fact that it is the world's fastest aircraft at sea level, and one of the fastest at any altitude, it uses 40 per cent less fuel on a typical mission than the much older F-4 Phantom, and half the fuel of the F-15 Eagle or Su-24.

Avionics are, of course, the key to the Tornado's success. They include a Texas Instruments multi-mode forward-looking radar with fully programmable software, terrain-following radar (of course!), fly-by-wire flight controls and plenty of capacity for special mission avionics. Options include a neat bolt-on retractable inflight-refuelling probe mounted just below the canopy at the right side, so far used only by the RAF, and extremely comprehensive radar warning systems and electronic countermeasures. All the initial users fit jammer and chaff pods on the outer wing pylons, several types being available.

Internal armament comprises two German Mauser 27mm cannon, housed low in the nose. Seven pylons, with multiple triple ejector racks, can carry an external load of more than 18000lb. Unlike the F-111, which has to carry all its bombs under the wings, the Tornado can carry over five tons of bombs whilst leaving its wings completely free for drop tanks, jammer/chaff pods and other stores.

Missile loads can include Sea Eagle, Kormoran, Maverick, Alarm, GBU-15, Paveway, AS. 30, and BL. 755 cluster bombs, and the giant JP. 233 and MW. 1 dispenser systems, and Sidewinder self-defence missiles.

To date, well over 450 aircraft have been delivered of the 809 ordered. There can be no question that the Panavia Tornado will continue to be Europe's main home-built attack aircraft well into the next century. Meanwhile the RAF is equipping seven squadrons with the even faster, longer and more powerful Tornado F.2 long-range all-weather interceptor, a beautiful aircraft streets ahead of any of the competition.

'Bubble' canopy gives outstanding all-round visibility.

APG-66 Radar in nose cone.

AIM-9J Sidewinder Air to Air missile.

Radar warning
receiver.

GENERAL DYNAMICS F-16
FIGHTING FALCON

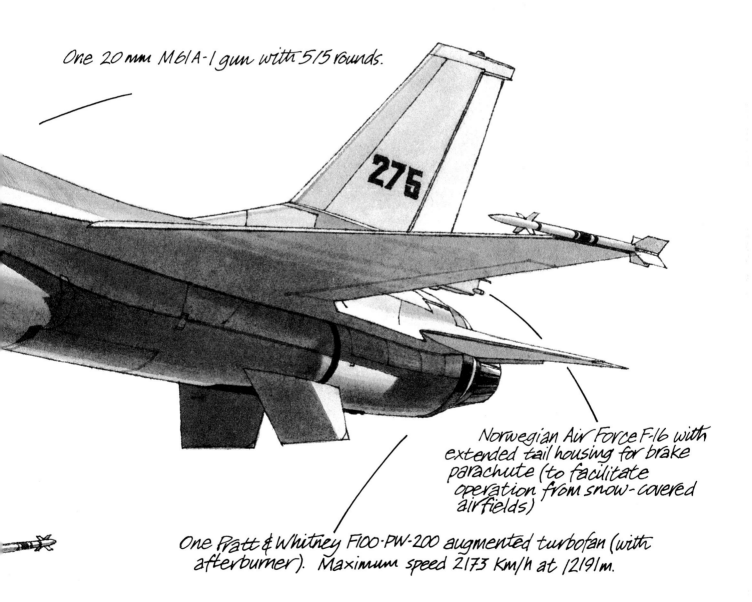

One 20 mm M61A-1 gun with 515 rounds.

Norwegian Air Force F-16 with extended tail housing for brake parachute (to facilitate operation from snow-covered airfields)

One Pratt & Whitney F100-PW-200 augmented turbofan (with afterburner). Maximum speed 2173 Km/h at 12191m.

GENERAL DYNAMICS F-16 FIGHTING FALCON

The F-16 Fighting Falcon was by far the greatest fighter success story of the 1970s. Yet its only reason for existence is the enormous expense of the F-15 programme. In 1972 the US Air Force decided that there might be value in discovering the potential (if any) for an LWF (lightweight fighter) that would be smaller and cheaper than the F-15 Eagle. This was a purely academic exercise; there was not the slightest intention of buying such as LWF for service.

Following an initial design competition, two companies were asked to produce two prototypes each. The result was the Northrop YF-17 with twin vertical tails and two General Electric YJ101 turbojets and the General Dynamics Model 401, which cleverly used one F100 engine as fitted to the F-15. The GD401 flew for the first time on 2 February 1974. Even at that time there was no thought of producing the aircraft in quantity, but foreign interest helped the Americans to realise that a relatively low cost LWF could bring substantial overseas orders without hurting the F-15. And so, following General Dynamics' development of the 401 into a slightly larger aircraft with far more comprehensive avionics, full-scale development was ordered on 13 January 1975. Within five months, four European countries – Belgium, Denmark, Holland and Norway – had entered into a joint development contract, sharing production with General Dynamics.

The F-16 is conventional in configuration, with cropped delta wing and a rear tailplane, but its design is extremely advanced. Flying surfaces are all electronically (fly-by-wire) controlled, including leading-edge flaps and trailing-edge flaperons (combined flaps and ailerons). This combination of leading-and-trailing-edge flaps allows the wing camber to be changed at will, if necessary under automatic control.

In sharp contrast to fighter design from World War I onward, the F-16 has virtually no inherent stability, and it is thus kept under computer control. The pilot is seated under a completely transparent canopy in an almost fully reclining position. This is not in order to accommodate him within the slim fuselage lines, but to resist violent acceleration loads: the F-16 can pull a sustained 9g in turns, more than any other Western aircraft. The control column is not placed centrally, but is a short handgrip on the right-hand side, with a special arm-rest; the 'stick' senses the pilot's input forces and transmits to the control system signals that cause the exact rate of manoeuvre demanded.

Most F-16s so far have been powered by the same advanced Pratt & Whitney F100 turbofan as the much bigger twin-engined F-15 Eagle. The engine is fed by a chin inlet of simple fixed type, because no attempt was made

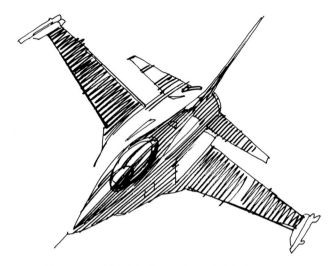

to achieve very high Mach numbers. With thrust greater than clean gross weight Mach 2 can be attained without such complication.

Armament is impressive for a lightweight fighter and comprises a single 20mm General Electric M61A-1 cannon, a central under-fuselage pylon capable of carrying almost 2200lb and three pylons under each wing able to support a total of 17,399lb, together with another 425lb on the wing tips. These limit loads are not used, and maximum external load is 12,000lb of assorted bombs rockets, cluster dispensers, Maverick, Durandal and other attack missiles, with Sidewinders for defence. This load has to be slightly reduced when the aircraft is to carry out manoeuvres resulting in forces of up to 9g.

In addition to the countries who are participating in the F-16's manufacture (European customer aircraft are assembled in Belgium and the Netherlands), it has also been ordered by Egypt, Israel, Pakistan, Singapore, South Korea, Turkey and Venezuela.

Continuing a procedure that is standard for most modern fighters, a proportion of all production aircraft are ordered as two-seat trainers.

The initial production F-16A and two-seat F-16B were succeeded in 1983 by the F-16C and two-seat F-16D, with new radar, totally upgraded avionics, a new cockpit and many extra items including two Lantirn pods filled with infra-red, laser and other types of sensor which assist in night attack.

General Dynamics also developed a totally new F-16XL with a giant 'cranked arrow' wing and no tailplane. Immediate further development of this into a two-seat multi-role combat aircraft was lost to the two-seat McDonnell Douglas F-15, but its performance is so

SPECIFICATION

F-16C

Country of origin: USA.

Manufacturer: General Dynamics Corporation.

Type: Single-seat fighter-bomber.

Year: 1978.

Engine: 10,814kg (23,840lb) thrust Pratt & Whitney F100-200 augmented turbofan.

Wingspan: 9.45m (31ft) over empty missile launchers.

Length: 14.52m (47ft 7in).

Height: 5.09m (16ft 8in).

Weight: 17,010kg (37,500lb).

Maximum speed: 2173km/h (1350mph).

Ceiling: Over 15,240m (50,000ft).

Range: Over 3890km (2415 miles).

Armament: One M61A-1 20mm cannon, one centreline pylon and eight wing pylons able to carry up to 5420kg (11,950lb) at loads up to 9g. This figure rises to 5443kg (12,000lb) at lower g forces.

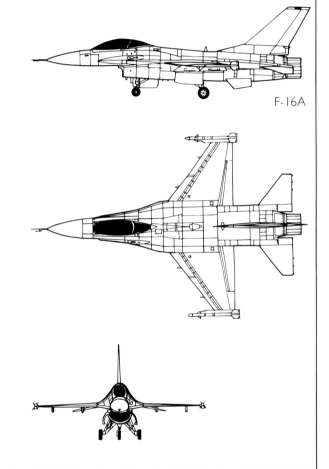

F-16A

incredible that there is a good chance that the USAF will buy a production version, probably the F-16F, in due course. A proposed simplified variant powered by the J79 turbojet of 18,000lb thrust did not find buyers, but General Electric's far bigger and newer F110 engine in the 30,000lb thrust class has already been adopted for future production, and has also been selected by Turkey and for the third batch for Israel.

In its own way the Fighting Falcon is already a legend. It is certainly respected by pilots of older MiGs who may have to dogfight it. But one thing is certain. The amount of research and development that is continuing with this relatively young LWF means that we shall continue to see new and even more advanced versions of the F-16 in the years to come.

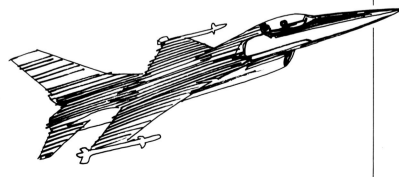

INDEX

ACKNOWLEDGEMENTS

The authors and publisher are especially grateful to Kenneth Giggal for his considerable contribution to the text of the book, and to Bill Gunston who gave so much help, advice and support in the production and editing of the text and in authenticating illustrations and facts.

Thanks are also due to Jim Gifford and Tom Copeland who were responsible for the three-view drawings.